THE GUARDIAN
OF MEMORY

By

Joseph Janusz Poznanski

Table of Contents

Dedication

For my father - Henryk (Chaim) Poznański.

For his parents – Leila Golda and Yosif Aleyzer.

For his brothers - Abram, Leon, Shmul, and Moyshie.

About the Author

Joseph Janusz Poznanski was born in post-war Poland and raised by his father, a Holocaust survivor haunted by the war and the devastating loss of his entire family. Joseph's mother passed away at the age of 25 when he was three years old. Growing up, Joseph witnessed his father's struggles with emotional trauma amid a society that, though outwardly quiet, harboured underlying tensions. Over time, these tensions surfaced in waves of antisemitic scapegoating directed at Poland's tiny Jewish remnant community. Leaving Poland became an exodus experience, profoundly challenging Joseph's identity and his sense of belonging. Joseph primarily dedicates this book to his father's life and mission to protect sites of war crimes where millions of innocent Jewish people perished, including his parents and brothers. Joseph holds a PhD in Counselling Psychology and has dedicated his career as a psychologist to helping others affected by trauma. Joseph is happily married and a proud father of three children.

PART – I

VISION AND HOPE

1. My father and his family

In moments of tranquility, my father sought solace in sipping his black tea with lemon, a practice steeped in generations of familial lore. Seated in the heart of our Warsaw apartment, the faint aroma of citrus mingled with his tales of a boyhood shrouded in mystery and melancholy. His narratives, imbued with sadness and entwined with a yearning for the family he lost, cast a spell upon the very walls of our kitchen, where we usually spent our time together. Throughout my youth and well into my adulthood, he would revisit and narrate the same familial saga with a consistency that imprinted these histories onto my very essence.

"I was a mere wisp of a child, scarcely four or five years old, with a mane of thick blond curls, already a polyglot in the making," he'd recount, a glint of reverence in his voice. "Returning home each evening from Hayder, I effortlessly traversed the realms of language, seamlessly translating a Talmudic prayer from the ancient sacred Hebrew, then to Yiddish, and then to the cadences of Aramaic and mystical Targum, and finally to the mundane echoes of Polish, much to my mother's delight." "She would sprinkle a pinch of salt upon me, telling me softly, this is your talisman, a shield against the envious gazes that seek to shroud your brilliance in shadows".

In the stillness of those evenings, as my father's voice wove the embroidery of his lost family, I felt the weight of generations upon me. His stories were not just recollections but living entities, breathing through the walls of our modest home in the apartment block on Nowiniarska Street, number 8. Each word he spoke was a thread in the fabric of our identity, a link to a lineage that seemed almost mythical in its blend of tragedy, culture, and survival. His eyes

1

would often drift to the window, where he captured the light of the Warsaw sky hanging above the mundane buildings rising from the ruins of the destroyed city. In that light was a reflection of hope and desolation, a silent testament to the resilience of a city that had risen from its ashes, much like my family.

As he spoke, the golden hue of dusk would cast a gentle glow upon his face, highlighting the lines etched by time, the turmoil of victory and sorrow. His stories seemed to draw strength from the very cityscape outside, as if Warsaw itself lent him the courage to revisit the past. "In those days," he'd continue, "our home was a sanctuary amidst chaos, a place where the warmth of my mother's embrace could shield me and my brothers from the world's harsh realities."

My father spoke of his mother, my grandmother, with a reverence that bordered on the sacred. "She was a woman of great strength and greater sorrow," he'd say, his voice tinged with a melancholy that seemed to echo through the ages. "She carried the weight of our history in her heart, and every grain of salt she sprinkled upon me was a fragment of her love, her protection."

As he sipped his tea, I could almost see the ghostly figures of our ancestors standing beside him, their faces a mosaic of joy and sorrow, hope and despair. They were with us in the steam from his cup, the lemon's tang, and the air we breathed.

Curiosity about my father's lineage, a family I never had the chance to know beyond his vivid recollections, sparked within me easily during my childhood. These individuals, enshrouded in mystery, came alive only within the contours of my father's memories. His mother, Leya Golda, stood at the forefront of these reminisces, exalted in his narrative as a paragon of maternal grace unlike any other. Golda, akin to the fantasized image of my mother Barbara, emerged as a figure of unreachable beauty and boundless love in the wall-hanging of my father's mind.

"My mother was beautiful," he would often say, his voice warm with adoration. "Her presence alone commanded admiration from everyone in our street." Golda's essence was a complex blend of passion and domesticity; a multilingual artist, fluent in Russian, Polish, and Yiddish, who once graced the stage as an amateur actress in her hometown's theatre in Biala Podlaska.

"She possessed an ethereal beauty, with cascading black hair, deep, soulful dark eyes, and a voice that could only be described as melodic." My father's tone would soften in these moments, and a soulful reverence took hold as he revealed what persuaded his mother to marry his father: "Her heart chose Yosif Layzer, my father, a man of humble means from Złoczew, over her many wealthy suitors. It was his love that captured her heart and soul."

The room seemed to fade away as he spoke, replaced by vivid imagery of his past. I could see Golda standing on a small stage, her voice filling the room and capturing the hearts of all who listened. Her beauty was not just in her physical appearance but also in her strength and warmth, qualities that my father cherished deeply.

In these stories, my father's eyes would light up with a mixture of joy and sorrow, the memories both comfort and a reminder of what had been lost. Golda's life, though touched by tragedy, was also filled with moments of profound love and happiness. Her choice of Yosif, a man whose love was pure and unwavering, spoke volumes about the values she held dear, values that my father passed on to me through his stories.

My father's tales of love, loss, beauty, and resilience shaped my understanding of our family's history. They were more than just stories; they were the threads that connected me to a past I could never physically touch but could always feel deeply within my heart. I was a child whose mother died three years after I was born. She vanished from my life experience; all I had was my father. His stories were "my inheritance." They were the lens through which I viewed the world, the compass that guided me through life's labyrinth. As my father's voice wove the tapestry of our lineage, I knew it was my duty to carry these stories forward, to ensure that the legacy of Golda, Yosif, and all my uncles and members of my paternal extended family would live on in the hearts of future generations, and that the whispers of the past would never fall into silence.

Yosif, born into the Poznański family in 1881 in Złoczew, embarked on a tumultuous journey, from serving an extended 15-year-long conscription in the Tsarist army to ultimately settling in the industrious city of Kalisz. Amidst the backdrop of World War II, only Yosif's adoptive sister, Regina and her husband, Arek, along with their son, Mula, emerged as the solitary links to my father's past. Their fate led them to American shores in 1948, and from there onwards, my father lost contact with the only remnants of his extended family.

Golda was born in 1888, the fourth child of Hirsch and Elka Hinda Beckerman, in the quaint countryside town of Biala Podlaska. Hirsch and Hinda nurtured a vibrant family of three, Lev, Shimon, and Sara, when Golda arrived. The family experienced a sorrowful turn with Hirsch's untimely death. Eventually, Hinda found love in the arms of Abram Goldsztajn, with whom she had her fifth child, a daughter

4

named Esther. Years went by, and Hinda's five children became adults.

The fabric of my father's 'family narrative' weaved through moments of joy and sadness, with Hinda's marriage to Abram Goldsztajn blossoming into the birth of their daughter Esther, with Golda cherishing her half-sister dearly. Then, sadly, the shadow of grief once again enveloped the family with Abram's death in 1923, marking a poignant milestone in my father's early years. His recollection of his step-grandfather's funeral centered on the procession led by a horse-drawn hearse provided by the 'Havre Kadisha' (Jewish Funeral Service). The horse, it seems, remained etched in my father's early memory. At the tender age of four, he saw his mother's tears, but the solemnity of the occasion did not diminish his childlike wonderment. "I was excited by all the fuss; I was too young to realise the significance and the sadness of the occasion," he claimed.

As he recounted these stories, the cadence of his words reflected the bittersweet nostalgia. The light from the Warsaw sky, filtering through the window, seemed to lend a gentle glow to his face, as if the past were reaching out to touch the present.

In those moments, I felt the weight of our lineage, the legacy of strength and survival passed down through generations. The stories of Lev, Shimon, Sara, and Golda were not just echoes of a bygone era but living threads in the fabric of my identity. They were the foundation upon which my understanding of family and heritage was built.

There was Lev, who embraced the spirit of adventure and hope and set sail for the United States in the early 1900s, finding a new home in the bustling city of San Francisco. His brother, Shimon, however, carved a different path, a path of fierce dedication to the underground communist movement, eventually claiming Russia as his sanctuary, where he zealously continued his activism. However, the heavy hand of fate caught up with Shimon, culminating in a tragic end just before the outbreak of the Russian Revolution. He was publicly hanged due to his audacious involvement in a daring plot to assassinate the Lord Mayor of Odessa. Meanwhile, their sister Sara found love with the Gotbaum family and, like Lev, sought the promise of a new beginning in the United States, making her abode in the Jewish enclave of Brooklyn, New York, in 1918. Aunt Sara's support from across the Atlantic buoyed the family through Poland's interwar hardships. Her generosity offered hope amidst adversity, ensuring that the Poznański family could transcend their financial strife and clothe themselves with the promise of a brighter future.

In the shadow of the early 1930s, as the chill winds of economic depression swept across Europe, Sara persistently implored Golda and Yosif to seek refuge in the USA. Despite her urgings, Golda remained firm and unwilling to forsake her ailing mother. The stringent policies of US authorities barred individuals like Hinda from securing permanent residence anyway. Golda remained by her mother's side until Hinda passed away in 1934. Her final resting place was marked within the hallowed grounds of Kalisz Jewish Cemetery, far... far away from her daughter Sara, in New York.

∞∞∞∞∞∞

The genesis of my awakening to my deep Jewish heritage remains veiled in the misty recollections of my childhood. At the tender age of six or seven, my father, a sage wrapped in the cloak of bygone eras, unveiled a hidden facet of his past. He said he was once known as

Chaim, a name imbued with profound significance in Hebrew: "May Israel Live Long." Through his words, he painted a tapestry of his family's faith, distinct from the echoes of the Warsaw churches that resonated in my young ears. His narrative wove a tale of an ancestral belief steeped in age-old traditions, and the central spiritual figure that formed the bulk of these recollections was his father, Yosif.

Amidst his reminiscences, my father spoke fondly of his family's humble abode on the ground floor of the building at 2 Poznańska Street in Kalisz. I was captivated by the synchronicity between our family name and the street that cradled my father's formative years. However, it wasn't until 1947 when archival documents from Polish annals unearthed a pivotal juncture in my father's journey, a formal shift from Chaim to Henryk. This symbolic act marked a period of profound metamorphosis, underscoring the intricate sway between heritage and identity and the enduring influence of one's roots on the fabric of selfhood.

These recollections, shared by my father in the quiet moments of our lives, became the bedrock of my connection to the past. They were the lanterns that illuminated the path of my ancestry, guiding me through the labyrinth of history with the wisdom and warmth of those who came before. Over time, his tales became the solitary channels through which the very essence of his lineage, stretching across epochs, seeped into the recesses of my mind. Yet, with no photos to gaze upon, no physical relics or papers to witness their existence, my father's memories of his loved ones were nearly imperceptible, dissolved by the ravages of World War II. The voids left in the wake of these tragedies were partly assuaged not by concrete tokens of remembrance but by the oral narratives my father intricately crafted. These passionate narratives, interwoven with the scant threads I could glean from the archives in Poland and the broader strokes painted by historians chronicling that tumultuous period, have culminated in a mosaic of my familial past. Though textured with fragments, this mosaic served as a guiding light that helped illuminate the shadowy contours of my forebears' lives.

Through this amalgamation of sources, oral traditions, archival snippets of paper, and historical accounts, a semblance of their joys, struggles, and triumphs began to take shape, bridging the chasm between the tangible and the ephemeral, the known and the lost. In piecing together these fragmented glimpses, I unearthed a treasure trove of resilience, love, and legacy that transcended the confines of time and memory, anchoring me to a lineage woven with threads of strength and endurance.

Though incomplete and scattered, these stories provided a sense of continuity, connecting me to a distant and immediate past. They were the foundation upon which I built my understanding of who I was and where I came from. As I delved deeper into my family's history, I found a profound sense of belonging, a connection to a lineage that had weathered countless storms but remained unbroken. This legacy, passed down through generations, became a source of strength and inspiration, a reminder of the enduring power of memory and the indomitable spirit of my paternal ancestors.

The family history on my mother's side remains distant to me. Had my mother lived, I would passionately wish to know the crevices of her family fold. But mercilessly, fate cut her life short, and for all of my life, she has been a mystery to me. I often felt her subliminal presence; I often spoke to her on my silent nights. I fondly remember my maternal grandmother, Lucyna, and my only aunt, Wiesia. Yet, I rarely had the opportunity to listen to their accounts of life experiences that were vital for me to understand.

Curiosity about my father's siblings often tugged at my thoughts, beckoning me with questions about their personalities and fates. "What were they like?" I would ask, envisioning figures shaped by hardship and hope, each carrying their unique narrative within the larger family saga. Through the bits and pieces shared, framed by the silences and the shadows where no stories could reach, I tried to reconstruct the images of my uncles, to imagine the laughter that might have filled their home, the challenges they faced, and the dreams they harboured within a world that was rapidly changing around them. Each story, each fragmentary piece of information, felt like a precious puzzle piece in the quest to understand where I came from and, by extension, who I am.

Abram, the eldest brother, carried the passionate hope of witnessing Spain's transformation into the Socialist Republic amid its Civil War, a dream left unfulfilled by the march of time and the onset of global conflict. Abram's idealism and commitment portrayed him as a figure of both strength and vulnerability, a dreamer caught in the crosswinds of history. I easily sensed that my father's vision for a better world lingered within him as a testament to his brother's unyielding spirit.

Leon (in Yiddish: Leib), the embodiment of street smarts, etched a path veiled in mystery, eventually merging with the vast, inscrutable expanses of the Soviet Union from which he never emerged post-war. In stark contrast to Leon's enigmatic fate, Samuel (Yiddish: Shmul), the family's beacon of talent and intellect, wove enchantment through his singing and academic brilliance. My father's Aunt Regina, recognising the luminescence of Shmul's potential, opted to nurture

9

it through the corridors of a prestigious private secondary college, a testament to her belief in the power of education. However, as if guided by a tragic script, the advent of WWII shattered these aspirations. The German armies' relentless advance across Poland's border, just as the echoes of a long summer holiday faded, marked a grim prologue to the ensuing global turmoil, extinguishing the light of hope that had flickered for Shmul's future.

Finally, there was Moyshie, the youngest of them all. The outbreak of WWII on September 1, 1939, a mere week shy of his ninth birthday celebration, marked a tragic interruption of his childhood's joy and the abrupt end of an era for him and his family. Moyshie's innocence and the promise of a future unburdened by conflict were cruelly snatched away, leaving a haunting void.

My father painted each brother's story as a vivid tableau of hopes dashed and destinies altered by the cruel tides of history. Amid the warmth and affection that permeated every memory my father shared about his family, a sad undertone lingered, the tragic reality that their lives were mercilessly cut short. This blunt contrast between my father's cherished remembrances and the grievous truth of loss, in my perception, seemed to paint a complex portrait of my father's family, navigating their precarious existence with love and resilience at its core.

In these retellings, the ghosts of my uncles seemed to come alive, their voices whispering through the annals of time, carried on the winds of my father's words. Abram's impassioned speeches about a fairer world, Leon's mysterious disappearances, Shmul's melodic voice filling the room, and Moyshie's innocent laughter, all these fragments coalesced into a haunting symphony of what once was and what could have been.

As my father spoke, his eyes often glazed over, caught between the past and the present. His voice was a fragile bridge connecting me to a lineage marked by brilliance and tragedy. In his stories, I found not just a recounting of history but a profound meditation on the nature of memory, loss, and the enduring strength of the human spirit. Further, I found my roots, deeply entwined with the past, guiding me as I navigated the complexities of my identity and my place in the world.

Apart from expressed memory fragments depicting aspects of love, beauty, brilliance, and tragedy, my father also frequently spoke about the challenges of poverty. "Ojciec (English: Father) struggled to find work," he recounted, evoking the grim spectre of financial hardship that haunted his family's daily lives. Yet, in the face of scarcity, the spirit of unity and understanding within his family remained unbroken. A few times, my father painted a dramatic picture of his mother's distress. Her concerns about lack of money and food dissipated into the void as they were met with Yosif's silent actions, a re-tying of shoelaces serving as a metaphor for the weight of unspoken worries, mixed with hidden feelings of guilt and helplessness in the face of adversity.

And yet, amid the relentless grip of economic depression during the mid-1930s, the Poznański family carved out moments of sustenance and warmth against the stark backdrop of their hardship. Golda, with her alchemy of frugality and culinary skill, transformed simple ingredients into nourishing meals. A solitary tomato, an egg, or a whisper-thin slice of cheese became the heart of her delectable sandwiches. Each element carefully layered atop bread generously spread with schmaltz (Polish: szmalec); such was Golda's ability to conjure comfort from scarcity.

11

Every Friday, as twilight heralded the arrival of Shabbat, Golda's kitchen became a sanctuary of tradition and togetherness. The ritual of preparing fish for the sacred meal was infused with more than just the act of cooking, it was a thread connecting the family to their faith, cultural heritage, and each other. My father's memories were vivid, including the recollection of their Shabbat table, an inspiration of hospitality and warmth in their humble single-room home. It was here that a familiar figure found solace and companionship, a homeless Jewish elder who had made a dwelling in the cellar of their building. During these sacred moments, he was no longer just a man fragmented from society but a valued guest, sharing their meal's communal embrace. This simple act of inclusion and kindness illuminated the depths of humanity and resilience that flourished within my father's family home. In a world that often turned its back on those in need, Golda and Yosif extended their hands in kindness, embodying the true essence of tzedakah (charity). "In those moments, we were all equal, sharing the same food and the same blessings," my father would say, his voice filled with emotion.

As he recounted his past family home life, my father's voice would soften, his eyes reflecting a mixture of reverence and sorrow. "It was a hard life," he'd say, "but we had each other, and that was enough." The vivid tableau he painted of those times was a celebration of the enduring spirit of his family amidst times of hardship. The warmth of Shabbat candles, the aroma of freshly baked challah, and the laughter that filled their modest apartment were the threads that he wove together into what seemed to be a vivid tapestry of love and resilience.

Though tinged with the sorrow of loss and hardship, these memories were also imbued with a profound sense of gratitude and love. They were a reminder that even in the darkest of times, the light of human kindness and the strength of familial bonds could shine brightly. Through my father's stories, I could almost see the flickering Shabbat candles, hear the melodic prayers, and feel the warmth of his family's embrace.

My father's entire family - registered in the historical records of the Kalisz Council

∞∞∞∞∞∞

The connection between my father and his father, Yosif, traced a quieter path than my father's vibrant bond with his mother, Golda.

Yosif's world was cloaked in silence and steeped in religious devotion. It was a spiritual and historical landscape that was vast yet unspoken, creating a certain distance, both physically and emotionally, from the embrace of his family. Unlike Golda, whose nurturing presence served as the family's steadfast anchor, Yosif was a man of profound faith, finding solace and completeness in the intricate accents of Talmudic prayer, the purifying rituals of the mikvah, and the offerings of 'mitzvahs' ('good deeds'). All these integral aspects of his faith were woven into Yosif's pursuit of the greater good.

Yosif's professional life began entwined with the delicate art of cotton craftsmanship, dedicating his hands to creating handmade lace curtains. This trade placed him within Kalisz's vibrant lacework and embroidery industry, an industry that esteemed the town as the lacework capital of the Russian Empire. Here, amidst threads and patterns, many Jews found their livelihood, whether as industrialists, intermediaries, or diligent factory workers. From 1920 to 1921, Yosif proudly stood at the helm of his shop, a brief chapter of prosperity swiftly closed by the relentless march of technological advancement and the suffocating grip of economic depression. But, undeterred, Yosif adapted, channelling his innate knowledge into making homemade herbal potions. This new venture transformed him into a healer who felt no compulsion to demand payment from those trapped in poverty's clutch. His was a philosophy of selflessness, a belief that divine reward for his deeds rested in the improved health of his community rather than in material gain. "Hashem will reward me for my troubles, and your health is important," he would proclaim, embodying an altruism that, while noble, ensured only a modest and erratic income for his family.

In these recollections, my father's voice would often take on a reflective tone, a blend of admiration and sorrow. "Ojciec was a man of deep faith," he would say. "But he was also a man of few words. His actions spoke for him." Despite the emotional distance, my father held a deep respect for Yosif. The quiet acts of kindness, the selfless dedication to helping others, and the steadfast commitment to his beliefs left an indelible mark on my father. "He was a good man," my father would say, his eyes reflecting pride and longing. "He lived his life with integrity and taught me the importance of doing the right thing, no matter the cost." I understood the profound impact that Yosif had on my father's life, shaping his values and guiding him through the complexities of his journey.

Indeed, I felt a deep connection to Yosif, a man I had never met but whose legacy lived on through my father's words. His life, filled with acts of kindness and unwavering faith, was a source of inspiration and a reminder of the enduring power of love and the importance of staying true to one's beliefs. Through my father's stories, I could piece together the mosaic of Yosif's life.

The material world was of secondary importance to Yosif, who diligently orchestrated his daily activities around the far more critical events—his scheduled *Davening times* (i.e., Prayer times). The cornerstone of his daily life was his commitment to prayer. With meticulous precision, each evening, Yosif plotted out the forthcoming day's endeavours with accuracy regarding the time each earthly commitment or task would demand. This wasn't merely a practice in time management but a practice in profound devotion. Every other responsibility he bore was carefully threaded around the unchallengeable schedule of his prayer times. All his daily activities had to be planned around these sacrosanct intervals. The rhythm of

Yosif's prayer set the tempo for every aspect of his existence. The dawn would break to the murmured rhythm of his morning prayers, and as the day unfolded, the calls to worship punctuated his hours, guiding him like the hands of a divine clock. Work, family, and social obligations all bowed to the sanctity of these moments, underscoring his deep reverence for his spiritual duties.

This unwavering dedication to prayer was a ritualistic adherence and a profound expression of Yosif's inner world. His prayers were conversations with the divine, moments of solace and reflection that gave him strength and clarity. The precision with which he managed his time reflected his desire to honour these sacred dialogues, ensuring that nothing mundane would encroach upon the sanctity of his spiritual communion.

For Yosif, even the simple act of walking to a nearby village to deliver his healing potions took on a dimension of careful calculation. Depending on the distance he needed to travel, he would meticulously determine the precise moment of departure necessary to ensure his timely return home, safeguarding his ability to partake in his daily rituals without faltering.

Most important were the predawn hours when the world around him slumbered in the darkness of their single-room abode. Adorned in his traditional Tallit (the Jewish Prayer Shawl), his sacred garment, Yosif connected not only to his faith but to a lineage of believers who had come before him, turning each whispered prayer and each silent meditative moment into a bridge spanning the chasm between the temporal and the divine. While Golda and his sons were still asleep, in these serene moments, Yosif, illuminated by the soft glow of a kerosene lamp, would immerse himself in the sacred texts of his thick prayer book. The gentle flicker of the light cast dancing shadows on the walls, creating an atmosphere of solemn introspection. These were the hours when Yosif felt closest to the divine, the stillness of the early morning providing a perfect backdrop for his spiritual communion. In those hushed moments, Yosif's prayers were not just words but lifelines, binding him to a higher purpose. His thick prayer book, worn from years of devotion, was a repository of wisdom and solace. With each page turned, he continued the journey deeper into his faith, reaffirming his beliefs and commitments. The rhythmic murmurs of his prayers filled the room with quiet, sacred energy, a stark contrast to the bustling activity that would follow as the day began.

This daily ritual of predawn prayer was the cornerstone of Yosif's existence. It was a time of solitude and reflection, where he could gather his thoughts and fortify his spirit for the challenges ahead. These moments of quiet devotion were a sanctuary for him, a time when the cares of the material world fell away, leaving only the purity of his connection with Hashem (Hebrew: God).

My father often marvelled at this aspect of Yosif's life. "Ojciec (*Polish:* Father) was a man of remarkable discipline," he would say, his voice tinged with admiration. "His devotion to prayer was absolute. It was the axis around which his entire life revolved." My father chose not to focus on the fact that the rest of the family, while respectful of Yosif's faith, often found it challenging to navigate the rigidity of his schedule. Nevertheless, Yosif's dedication was a profound example of faith's power and the discipline required to uphold it. I often wondered if Yosif's meticulous devotion had shaped my father's understanding of what it meant to live a life of integrity and commitment.

With the arrival of each Saturday, Yosif would lead his sons in a ritual as predictable as the dawn, first to the mikvah for spiritual cleansing, followed by a visit to the barber for a haircut. These acts were more than mere routines; they were sacred traditions that anchored their lives in the rhythms of faith and community.

The insistence that his sons join him in these rituals, from prayer at the local Shul, colloquially embraced within the community as slang for a synagogue, to the purifying waters of the mikvah, was Yosif's way of passing down a heritage steeped in reverence and tradition. Yet, for my father, this mandated participation in ritualistic observance was met with internal resistance. My father's sentiments toward these acts were marked with indifference. He felt uncomfortably obligated to participate in something that he secretly rejected.

He always mimicked the motions of prayer merely as a facade, a tender deception aimed at sparing his father's feelings. His *sotto voce* murmurings, feigned prayers beneath his breath, clumsily camouflaging his half-hearted attempt to bridge the chasm between Yosif's expectations and his truth: Atheism. The rituals that brought Yosif solace and fulfilment left my father feeling confined, a prisoner of his father's expectations, which he could not embrace.

In the stillness of the synagogue, my father would glance at Yosif, observing the passion and intensity with which he prayed. The sight was both awe-inspiring and alienating. Yosif's face, serene and uplifted, seemed to be in communion with a higher power, while my father's heart remained untouched by the sacred words he recited. The gap between them, bridged by love but widened by divergent beliefs, became more pronounced with each passing ritual.

With its cold, cleansing waters, the mikvah was another point of contention. While Yosif approached it as a sacred act of purification, my father saw it as an unwelcome activity. The chill of the water and the solemnity of the act felt like a performance he was compelled to participate in rather than a spiritual renewal. He would shiver from the cold and the internal conflict that these rituals stirred within him.

As Yosif sat silently meditating at the barber, my father's mind would wander. He respected the discipline and order that Yosif's faith instilled, yet he couldn't shake the feeling that these acts were empty motions for him. The haircuts, the prayers, the *mikvah*, all felt like parts of a play in which he was an unwilling actor, performing his role to avoid disappointing a father he deeply loved but could not fully understand.

Despite his inner turmoil, my father continued participating in these rituals, driven by a complex mix of love, duty, and the desire to maintain peace. He mastered the art of deception, his lips forming prayers that his heart did not echo, his hands mimicking the motions that held no real significance for him. It was a delicate dance of appearances, a tender lie crafted to shield Yosif from the painful truth.

Yosif, in his contemplative silence, may have sensed some of this dissonance, but he never spoke of it. Perhaps he hoped that my father would eventually find his connection to the divine through continued exposure. Or maybe he understood that faith and devotion could not be compelled, only nurtured; a journey which each person would have to undertake in their own time and in their way; and each person's path to faith and fulfilment would have to be uniquely their own.

Yosif's silence on my father's lack of genuine engagement in religious practices was perhaps his way of showing love and understanding. His silence created a space where my father could wrestle with his beliefs without worrying about being challenged.

19

This quiet acknowledgment of his son's struggle was a form of nurturing that spoke to the depth of Yosif's love and wisdom.

∞∞∞∞∞∞

My father spoke about the stark contrast between himself and his father and himself and his eldest brother, Abram. "Abram was different. He was an intellectual; he never raised his voice," my father would recall, his tone suffused with warmth and admiration. He regarded Abram with unmistakable reverence, positioning him not just as an elder sibling but as a role model whose footsteps he aspired to follow, albeit from a distance.

While Yosif's presence was marked by solemnity and spiritual rigour, Abram brought a quiet, reflective intelligence that resonated deeply with my father. Abram's approach to life was grounded in reason and contemplation, offering a plain contrast to the rigid ritualism that Yosif embodied. My father saw in Abram a kindred spirit, someone who navigated the complexities of the world with a gentle wisdom that he himself yearned to emulate.

Abram's intellectual pursuits were also a source of inspiration for my father. "He read voraciously," my father would say, his eyes lighting up with pride. "Books were his sanctuary, his escape from the confines of our reality." Abram's calm, measured voice, thoughtful insights, and ability to engage with ideas beyond the immediate circumstances of their lives created an aura of quiet strength that my father deeply respected.

In those moments of reflection, my father often contrasted Abram's demeanor with his struggles. He spoke of his brother's unshakeable calm and the sense of purpose that seemed to guide him effortlessly through life. "Abram had a way of seeing the world that

20

was both compassionate and wise," he would say, his voice tinged with longing. "He could discuss the works of great philosophers and relate them to our everyday experiences, making sense of the chaos around us."

In recounting these stories, my father painted a picture of a household rich with contrasts and complexities. Yosif's fervent faith, Abram's intellectual serenity, and my father's journey of questioning and seeking answers all coexisted within the fabric of their family life. These differences did not create rifts but instead wove a tapestry of diverse perspectives, each contributing to the family's collective strength and resilience.

Through my father's narratives, I understood the profound impact of these relationships on his development. The silent strength of Yosif, the intellectual guidance of Abram, and my father's freedom to explore his own beliefs all played a crucial role in shaping his identity. These familial bonds, marked by tension and tenderness, taught my father the value of understanding, acceptance, and the importance of forging one's path with integrity.

"Abram was the embodiment of quietude and respect, a man who navigated the world with a gentle demeanour, earning esteem from those around him. Mother never harboured or voiced a grievance against him." From my father's many recollections, Abram, like Yosif, was an avid reader, not of Torah or Talmud, but of books to do with the emerging communist movement across the European continent. My father recalled how night after night, in the soft glow of the kerosene lamp, Abram penned letters to his distant acquaintances. It seems both Abram and Yosif had to find their private time to do things that were important to each of them:- Yosif's prayer before the break of dawn and Abram's letter writing to communist comrades in the late hours of the night.

"I found myself perpetually fascinated by Abram's correspondence." My father would reflect on his teenage amazement. "He had established a network across Europe, connecting with communists far and wide." This specific detail of Abram's life, as recounted by my father, seemed to carry the allure in my father's imagination. Presumably, from his early teens, my father viewed Abram as a figure who, amidst the quiet of the night, engaged with ideas and movements that transcended the confines of his immediate world, his single-room family abode in the small town called Kalisz. In my father's perception, Abram was a man whose intellectual pursuits and principled communications with comrades across borders illuminated a path of thought and action, casting him not only as an admired elder sibling but as a symbol of a broader, more profound engagement with the world's tumultuous currents.

Golda remained a silent bystander to Abram's clandestine endeavours; her maternal instincts perhaps urged prudence over inquisition. Yosif, meanwhile, had little awareness of his eldest son's urgent pursuits. He found his refuge in devotion, away from the gravitational pull of any socio-political perspective. At the same time, he did not assume that his burning need to practice his faith was more important than his elder son's nightly activities. He never complained about any disruptions to his sleep and seemed to respect Abram's motivations and aspirations without knowing what they entailed.

The relentless grip of the Great Depression wrought havoc indiscriminately. Yet, the cruel bias against Jews, who found themselves trapped in the crosshairs of economic boycotts and marginalisation, exacerbated the struggle for survival in families like my father's.

Not surprisingly, my father harboured a deep-seated scepticism towards religious observance. In his mind, religion was an impotent response to the Jews' plight in Poland. His voice would often drip with bitterness when he spoke of the local clergy, who, in his eyes, stoked the embers of hate amongst the impoverished and uneducated through their venomous anti-Jewish rhetoric. "They preached from the pulpit their hateful ideas about Jews being Christ's killers," he recounted with palpable disdain, his words painting a vivid picture of a society steeped in prejudices and scapegoating. "Polish Churches adorned their walls with paintings vilifying Jews as malefactors, leeching off the divine and coveting the blood of innocent Polish children." My father's lament etched the glaring, grotesque imagery of antisemitism, raised into the consciousness of those who listened with conviction to the subtly hateful tenets of the 'authoritative clergy.'

And so, like Abram, my father saw this swirling societal antipathy and found solace and hope in the promise of Communism. "In such a suppressive social environment, for me and many other young Polish Jews, communist ideology was the enlightenment and liberation for struggling souls. It presented itself as a panacea to the manifold maladies afflicting our society: poverty, racism, backwardness, religious zealotry, human greed, and rampant inequality. Communism emerged as the sole bulwark against the tide of anti-Semitism," he would assert with conviction. For my father and those like him, drawn to the promise of egalitarianism and brotherhood, Communism did not just offer a political manifesto, but a world shorn of its prejudices and injustices.

As a teenager, my father found himself deeply engrossed in the medley of challenges facing Poland, notably the profound hardships and pervasive poverty afflicting the Jewish community, alongside the allure of a more equitable and tolerant future, as envisioned by Karl Marx. By the time he was 16, he had delved into the depths of Marx's Capital and was already conversant with the philosophies of Frederic Hegel, spanning Materialism, Socialism, Rationalism, and Pantheism. It was a time when the air in Poland was thick with the zeal of Endecja, the right-wing National Democratic Front Movement, its presence an ominous backdrop to the pressing social discourse.

In the dimly lit corners of his modest family home, my father would pore over the dense pages of Marx and Hegel, his mind a fertile ground for the revolutionary ideas that promised a new dawn. The harsh realities of life in the western Jewish quarter of Kalisz, where poverty and the surrounding anti-Semitism were everyday companions, fuelled his yearning for change. The intellectual rigour of Marxist theory offered him not just an escape but a vision of a world where justice and equality might prevail over the suffering he witnessed daily.

My father, with a group of like-minded youths, would gather in clandestine meetings to discuss the potential for a society reformed by socialist principles. These gatherings were not merely intellectual exercises but acts of defiance against the oppressive status quo. The young men, faces illuminated by the flickering light of candles, shared a bond forged in their shared hopes and struggles.

The presence of Endecja, with its nationalist rhetoric and vehement anti-Semitism, loomed large. The Endecja's influence was a constant; it was an oppressive force, casting long shadows over the aspirations of those who dared to dream of a different Poland. The tension between the burgeoning socialist ideals and the reactionary politics of Endecja created an atmosphere thick with anxiety and anticipation. Each whispered conversation in the secrecy of trusted communist cell members was a small act of rebellion against the tide of hatred and intolerance.

Despite the oppressive environment, my father's resolve only strengthened. He found solace in the idea that the downtrodden could rise against their oppressors through collective effort and solidarity. The works of Marx and Hegel were his guideposts; the philosophy of Materialism taught him to see the world as it was, with all its inequities, while Rationalism offered the tools to envision what it could become. Socialism and Pantheism spoke to the unity of all people, transcending the divisions sown by ignorance and bigotry.

In these years, my father's identity was forged in the crucible of ideological struggle. The intellectual battles he waged were as real and significant as his physical hardships. His mind, sharpened by study and debate, became a weapon against the injustice he saw around him. The promise of a fair and just society was a theoretical ideal and a tangible goal that drove him forward.

The harsh realities of the world tempered the zeal and determination of his youth, but they never wavered. My father's journey through the labyrinth of philosophy and politics was a testament to his enduring belief in the power of ideas to shape and transform the world. It was a belief that would guide him through the tumultuous years ahead, with indestructible hope that would carry him through the darkest times.

My father's foray into activism, fuelled by his quiet rebellion, was marked by the audacious act of plastering communist posters across

25

the bare walls of street-corner buildings. The clandestine activity, conducted under the cover of night, was his way of giving voice to the oppressed, of fighting back against the systemic injustices that plagued people's lives, especially in the Jewish community. However, the path he chose was fraught with danger. In one such moment of defiance, he was caught in the act by an 'Endek', a member of the right-wing National Democratic Movement. The confrontation was swift and brutal; he found himself on the receiving end of a walking stick, the assault leaving him bloodied but unbowed.

Rather than deterring him, this encounter only galvanised my father's resolve, bolstering his determination to stand against the tide. The raw injustice of the attack deepened his commitment to the moral and economic principles espoused in the Communist Manifesto. It was as though the very ideals he stood by were forged anew in the crucible of adversity. For my father, the painful strike of the walking stick reinforced his belief in a cause greater than himself, dismantling the oppressive structures of his time and striving toward the vision of a society anchored in equality and camaraderie.

His clandestine activities continued, and each act of rebellion was a defiant stand against the forces of oppression. The posters he plastered on the walls were more than mere symbols; they were calls to action, rallying cries for the downtrodden and disenfranchised. In the dead of night, with the world shrouded in darkness, my father's quiet rebellion aimed at lighting a spark of hope in the hearts of those who longed for change.

∞∞∞∞∞∞

Amid the tumultuous 1930s, widespread poverty, spurred by the Great Depression, brought severe economic hardships to Poland. July of 1936 brought Abram's incarceration at Bereza Kartuska because of his underground political activities. After serving three months at this torturous detention centre, in the second week of October that year, Abram was released home in a grossly diminished state of health. This left my father as the central pillar of support for his family. Leon, Shmul, and Moishe were still children. Luckily, my father secured a job at a factory owned by Mr Flakowicz, a man whose uncle was a prominent Jewish Zionist. Flakowicz, who knew the plight of the Poznański family, extended an offer to my father to work as a 'tradesman', crafting curtains on a spinning wheel.

This gesture of goodwill was remarkable as it diverged from the norm among Jewish business owners of the time. In Kalisz, a city where factories under Jewish ownership were commonplace, it was virtually unheard of for Jewish proprietors to hire fellow Jews. The prevailing wisdom suggested that Jewish workers observed Shabbat and, therefore, did not work on Saturdays; they could not be exploited; furthermore, favouring Jewish employees over gentile Poles risked inciting animosity, potentially leading to acts of violence against the Jewish community.

Flakowicz's offer was a lifeline. For my father, it was more than just a job; it was an opportunity to uphold his family's dignity amidst the grinding poverty. With its rows of spinning wheels and the steady hum of industry, the factory became a place where he could channel his resolve and resilience to support his ailing brother, his parents, and his younger siblings.

The work was demanding, but my father embraced it with an enthusiasm born of necessity and hope. The rhythmic motions of the spinning wheel, the careful threading of fabric, and the intricate designs that emerged under his skilled hands became a meditation of

27

sorts, a way to find order and purpose amidst the chaos of his family lives.

In reflecting on this period, my father often expressed his gratitude to Flakowicz. He was grateful not just for the job but also for the respect and dignity it afforded him. This gratitude was a reminder that even in the darkest times, some chose to act with compassion and integrity, lighting a path forward for others to follow.

Upon securing employment at the Flakowicz factory, my father gradually acquainted himself with gentile Poles. Intriguingly, some were persuaded to contemplate joining the Communist Union of Polish Youth (KZMP) after he shared his ardent convictions. At Flakowicz's factory, my father received an Employee Union Membership Card, which Jews generally did not have the privilege to receive. Nevertheless, most members of my father's communist underground KZMP cell were Jewish.

In an unexpected turn of events, to my father's surprise, Leon, a mere sixteen-year-old, confided in him that he knew a group of youngsters burning with the aspiration to align themselves with the KZMP. They were Itzkowicz, Szer, and Warski. This revelation broadened my father's circle and intertwined their destinies, forging a deep camaraderie among them, sewn from shared ideals and youthful resolve.

००००००

On the chilly evening of October 20, 1936, my father worked a night shift at Flakowicz's factory. The air inside was thick with the scent of oil and metal, the rhythmic hum of machinery creating a sombre symphony against the backdrop of his thoughts. As the clock neared 2:00 a.m., unexpectedly, Leon appeared on the factory floor.

His face was shadowed by worry, and his eyes were wide with an urgency that pierced through the mechanical noise.

Leon navigated the industrial maze, weaving between the hulking machines to find his brother. His voice, laden with urgency, barely rose above the hum of machinery as he delivered the heart-wrenching message, "Quickly, mum wants you home…Abram passed away." The heavy and irrevocable words hung in the air, each syllable a blow to the heart.

Without a moment's hesitation, they both vacated the premises in a rush, the factory's cold, metallic environment giving way to the night's chill. The weight of the news settled heavily between them as they hastened home, their breath visible in the frigid air, mingling with the unshed tears. The streets, usually bustling with evening activity, seemed eerily quiet, as if the world itself mourned alongside them.

As they hurried through the darkened streets, memories of Abram flooded my father's mind. He recalled Abram's gentle voice, calm demeanour, and how he seemed to bring a sense of peace and wisdom to their tumultuous lives. The realisation that Abram's light had been extinguished began to deepen an aching void in my father's soul.

When they finally reached home, the sight that greeted them was one of profound sorrow. The family gathered in the dimly lit room, their faces etched with grief. Golda, their mother, sat near Abram's still form, her shoulders shaking with silent sobs. The room was filled with the muted sounds of mourning, a profound grief that resonated deeply within the walls.

My father approached his mother, placing a gentle hand on her shoulder. The weight of his presence seemed to offer some small comfort, a reminder that despite their loss, they still had each other. Golda looked up, her eyes red-rimmed and filled with lament and sadness that words could not capture.

Abram's passing marked the end of an era for the family. He had been a pillar of strength and wisdom, a guiding light in their darkness. His absence left a void that could never truly be filled, a stark reminder of the fragility of life and the relentless march of time.

At the tender age of 20, Abram's untimely passing marked the culmination of a life fraught with turmoil and sacrifice. Ravaged by Uraemia (i.e., Kidney Failure), his condition was a disturbing reminder of the harrowing time he spent on a frigid cement floor in the confines of Bereza Kartuska's prison cell. Abram's health had deteriorated irreversibly, each breath a struggle, his body a battleground against an insidious disease.

His imprisonment, a consequence of his unwavering dedication to communist ideals, was marked by unspeakable torment. The prison walls echoed with the silent screams of his suffering, the cold cement floor a merciless companion that sapped his strength day by day. Abram emerged from captivity a mere shadow of his former self, his spirit unbroken, but his body profoundly impacted and frail. The idealism that once burned brightly within him was now tempered by the stark reality of his physical decline.

In the dim light of their single-room abode, the family watched helplessly as Abram's condition worsened over the eight days since his return home. His once vibrant eyes, dulled by pain, still held a spark of the intellect and passion that defined him. Even in the face of adversity, the gentle strength he had always shown became a poignant reminder of the depth of his calm and tender soul.

Despite the best efforts to care for him, the relentless progression of Uraemia could not be halted. Each day was a testament to his enduring will and his quiet determination to remain a source of hope and inspiration for his loved ones. Yet, the disease showed no mercy, and the weight of his past struggles bore down on his weakened body.

In his final moments, Abram's thoughts lingered on the distant horizon of Spain, a passionate desire woven into his parting words, "How I wish I could witness the victory of the Spanish Republicans." Such was his inspirational commitment and decency. Even in the throes of his mortality, his voice carried the weight of his dreams and the zeal of his convictions.

My father later discovered from Leon that Abram's last act of love and selflessness was a touching gesture directed towards his mother. In a loving request for her to seek respite, to retire to rest rather than endure the vigil by his bedside, Abram quietly whispered, "Mama, please rest. " His eyes, soft with tenderness, accompanied the plea. "You have done so much. It is time for you to take care of yourself."

Golda, her heart breaking, honoured his wish. She leaned over and kissed his forehead, a motion laden with the weight of a thousand unspoken words. Her tears fell softly, a silent promise that she would always carry his memory with her. With a final, lingering glance, she withdrew to her rest, leaving Abram to find solace in the night's quiet.

In this moment of selfless release and serene acceptance, Abram found his peace. His breathing slowed, and a calm settled over him as if the burdens of his earthly tribulations were finally lifting. The dimly lit room, filled with the soft murmur of distant prayers, became a sanctuary of tranquillity. Abram's thoughts, no longer tethered to the pain and struggles of his mortal existence, turned to the horizon of eternity.

As he lay there, his mind drifted to the memories of his short yet impactful life. The faces of his loved ones, the ideals he had fought for, and the unfulfilled dreams that had fuelled his spirit mingled in a tapestry of his fading reflections. The struggles, the sacrifices, and the moments of profound connection with his family and comrades gave him a sense of fulfilment. In those final moments, he understood that his life, though fraught with challenges, had been one of purpose and meaning. Gently, his loving spirit slipped away, like a whisper in the wind, across the night sky.

As Golda anxiously returned to his bedside at about 1:00 am, she found him at rest, his face serene and free from the agony that had plagued him. She clasped his hand; her tears fell like silent drops of love, pain, and a strange, bittersweet relief. She knew that Abram had found the peace he so desperately sought. His final act of love, his words granting her the gift of rest, still echoed in her mind.

That night, as they sat together in their grief, my father felt the weight of responsibility settling more heavily on his shoulders. The loss of Abram was a devastating blow, but it also steeled his resolve to honour his brother's memory and his legacy so it would resonate through the generations to come. Through this profound loss, my father's spirit was tempered by the fire of adversity. As Abram's body lay still, the room slowly filled with the soft glow of morning light. Abram's legacy lived on in the hearts of those who loved him, a tribute to the unbreakable bonds of family and the eternal light of hope and compassion.

In the Jewish tradition, the eldest son's death requires the father to stay away from the funeral. Instead, the second-oldest son takes on the duty of bidding farewell to his brother. Out of love and remembrance, my father personally arranged Abram's funeral meticulously. Avoiding the Havre Kadisha, the sacred Jewish Funeral Directors, he made sure Abram's final rites did not follow traditional religious customs. Instead, the ceremony was a tribute to Abram's beliefs as a freethinker, reflecting his spirit of independence and non-conformity.

The funeral day broke with a heavy sky, as if the heavens themselves mourned Abram's untimely passing. At the peaceful clearing atop a gentle hill within the Old Jewish Kalisz Cemetery grounds, friends and family gathered, their faces marked with sorrow and respect. Present at the graveside were not only mourners such as immediate family members and friends but also comrades and activists from the secret KZMP. All came to honour Abram's steadfast commitment to the cause of freedom and equality.

As the crowd stood in reverence amidst crimson flags gently flowing upon the soft autumn wind, my 17-year-old father stood in front of the gathered mourners, his voice steady with emotion as he began addressing the assembly. He spoke of Abram's resolute commitment to justice, intellectual curiosity, and deep compassion for those around him. With adult-like confidence, he painted a vivid picture of a young man who lived with passion and purpose and whose spirit could not be confined by traditional boundaries. As he spoke, the wind rustled through the trees, a gentle reminder of the natural world that Abram had loved so deeply. In a poignant tribute to his fallen brother, my father proclaimed, "The struggle of the Republicans in Spain was Abram's struggle for freedom and

33

equality," encapsulating the profound connection between Abram's hope for a better world and the noble crusade of the Spanish Republicans. My father's courage, defiance, and "unity narrative" immortalised Abram's legacy as an emblem of his unwavering resolve in the face of poverty and oppression.

The ceremony was simple yet profoundly moving. There were no chants or prayers, no formal rituals to mark the passage from life to death. Instead, there were moments of quiet reflection where each person present could connect with their memories of Abram and find their own way to say goodbye.

The gathered crowd solemnly sang the anthem of solidarity: the 'Internationale' (in Polish: 'Międzynarodówka'). With voices gaining in passion and conviction, reverberating through the sombre autumn air, the crowd paid homage to Abram, reflecting his devotion to the ideals he held dear.

And then, in a final farewell, my father asked a close friend of Abram's to step forward and play a piece of music on a violin, a haunting melody that spoke to the depths of their grief and the beauty of Abram's spirit.

As the final notes of the music faded into stillness, the crowd began to disperse slowly, each person carrying a piece of Abram's legacy with them. My father lingered a while longer, his heart heavy yet filled with a sense of fulfilment. He had honoured his brother in a way that truly reflected who Abram was —a freethinker, a man of integrity, someone who had lived and died on his own terms.

Through this experience, my father learned that accurate remembrance comes from the heart. Rituals or conventions do not bind it, but it is a living, breathing tribute to the person who has passed. With its simplicity and sincerity, Abram's funeral became a lasting symbol of the love and respect that bound them together as a family.

On the 7th of March 1948, a monument was erected on the grounds of the Jewish Cemetery to commemorate seven communist activists listed as "fighters against fascism, for free democratic Poland." This monument no longer exists as the cemetery had been badly vandalized.

2. Abram's last wish

Shortly after Abram's passing, a profound sense of purpose took hold of my father, igniting a fierce determination to honour his brother's final wish: the triumph of the Spanish Revolution. Compelled by a deep-seated conviction, he resolved to join the International Brigades and to stand shoulder-to-shoulder with the Republicans in their valiant struggle against General Franco's oppressive Fascist regime. The echo of political change resounded in 1936, as Léon Blum ascended to the role of France's Prime Minister, marking a historic moment as both the first Socialist and the first Jewish leader to do so. As the Spanish Civil War news reached Poland, my father's thoughts frequently wandered to Abram. He imagined sharing with him the tumult and hope of these turbulent times. With every passing day, my father's commitment to his socio-political and communist ideals deepened, fuelled by a passionate zeal and his enduring love for his brother's memory.

For my father, Kalisz had swiftly transformed into a constraining stage, his aspirations reaching far beyond its boundaries, energised by a yearning to emerge as an ideological catalyst. As 1936 drew to a close, whispers of his name began to stir within the shadows of the secret police, branding him a radical revolutionary, a threat to the established order. Golda, his steadfast confidante, recounted ominous visits that pierced the tranquillity of their home. On two separate instances, enigmatic figures loomed at their doorstep. Assertive knocks marked their second arrival, a threatening certainty in their actions, suggesting the intruders' unnerving awareness that someone was home. Confronted with no alternative, Golda yielded to the inevitable, revealing her doorway to the two strangers cloaked in the mundanity of office attire. Presenting themselves as law officers, they inquired after her son, their intentions veiled beneath the guise of formal inquiry.

My father was acutely aware that the shadows cast by the undercover operatives were drawing ever closer. He felt the weight of their scrutiny, not just on him but potentially extending to comrades within his KZMP cell. As 1937 dawned, he embraced a routine dictated by caution and his instinct to evade. Each day, he rose with the stars, greeting the day before the sun dared to unveil its face, a strategy born from the necessity to sidestep the unwelcome advances of those who sought to silence his voice and quell his purpose and vision.

The atmosphere grew increasingly oppressive, each day unfurling with more incredible difficulty than the last. Close allies, including his dear and loyal friend Leon Szer, had vanished into the clutches of the secret police and, possibly, been spirited away to the dreaded confines of Bereza Kartuska. This place, notorious for its absence of judicial process and negating the right of appeal, became a hellish reality for those unfortunate enough to be ensnared. Within its walls, further interrogations were implemented with the torment of torture.

My father stood at a difficult crossroads, fully cognizant of Bereza Kartuska's looming shadow over him and the risk of sharing the same grim fate as his brother and colleagues if he were to linger in Kalisz any longer. The weight of this understanding pressed upon him, a daunting reminder of the stakes in his fight for ideological freedom and justice.

The narrative of Bereza Kartuska paints a grim picture of the systemic cruelties inflicted under the pretext of safeguarding public security, peace, and order within Poland. However, the stark reality was that its prisoners were overwhelmingly those whose political beliefs positioned them as adversaries to the Polish National Front Regime (Endecja). From 1936 to 1939, this forbidding institution predominantly housed members of the Polish Communist Party (KPP), the Peasant Party (SL), and the Polish Socialist Party (PPS), along with Jews, who were unjustly branded as financial speculators.

Their incarceration, typically lasting from three to six months, was marked by harrowing abuses under the guise of 'interrogation'. Prisoners endured excruciating physical and psychological torments: beatings with boards, humiliation, and tortures, often culminating in death. The morning ritual alone, where inmates were forced to lie face down for the guards to walk over their bodies and beat them with truncheons, underscored the dehumanising brutality that pervaded Bereza Kartuska.

In addition to physical assaults, the detainees were subjected to cruel and unusual punishments designed to break their spirits. They were compelled to adopt a painful, duck-like gait and given mere seconds for bathroom use under threat of further punishment. Many were made to sleep on cold concrete, and outside the torment of 'interrogations', they faced backbreaking hard labour or the agonising isolation of the "Karcer" – a cell for prolonged solitary confinement. The aftermath of their time in Bereza Kartuska was often as lethal as the detention itself, with many prisoners succumbing to kidney failure (Uraemia) shortly after their release. [1] This speaks volumes about the lasting impact of the inhumane treatment they were subjected to, marking a dark chapter in the history of Poland's political repression.

Bereza Kartuska known as "Isolation Detention" (Polish: Miejsce Odosobnienia) [2]

In the dim, hushed hours of an early July morning in 1937, the stillness of the household was gently fragmented by Golda's whisper to my 18-year-old father, "Chaim, your taxi will be here soon... get up." Her voice was cautious, threading through the silence to avoid disturbing the others. The weight of unspoken worries and unvoiced hopes lingered in the air, making each word she uttered seem like a fragile thread binding them to the moment.

Within twenty minutes, they both emerged into the brisk embrace of Poznańska Street, its sleepiness mirroring the cold that hung in the air. The street, usually bustling with life and activity, now lay under a shroud of quiet as if it, too, held its breath in anticipation. The cobblestones, slick with a thin layer of moisture, glistened under the weak light of the streetlamps, casting long, eerie shadows that danced in the periphery.

Golda's breath formed small, fleeting clouds in the frigid air, her eyes reflecting determination and sadness. She pulled her shawl tighter around her shoulders, a silent gesture of comfort against the chill and the unknown future. My father's young face, set with resolve, glanced at her with gratitude and trepidation. This journey, this step into the wider world, was as much about leaving behind the safety of his home as it was about venturing into the vast unknown.

The taxi arrived slowly, its headlights piercing through the early morning fog like the eyes of some ancient creature. The driver, an old man with a kind yet weary face, nodded in silent acknowledgment as they approached him. Golda hugged her son, her hands lingering on his shoulders for a moment longer than necessary. It was as if she was trying to imprint this last touch, this final connection, onto her memory.

Golda leaned in through the open window as my father settled into the back seat. Her eyes, filled with unspoken words, met his. "Take care of yourself, my son," she whispered, her voice trembling with emotion. "I will write to Ms Gliksmann and tell her you might need a place to stay when you get to Brussels." Her words were a bridge, connecting my father to the future promise of sanctuary. As the taxi engine started, she imparted a final plea, "Be careful, Chaim ... please write ... let us know how you are." Her words lingered in the air, a mingling of hope and concern.

He nodded, unable to trust his voice, and reached out to grasp her hand one last time. The bond between them, forged in love and hardship, seemed to stretch and strain with the distance that was about to grow between them. Golda straightened up, her eyes never leaving his face, even as the taxi began to pull away.

My father offered a brief wave through the open window, a silent goodbye fused with the potential of keeping in touch. The taxi dissolved into the hopeful morning, carrying him towards an uncertain future, away from the familiarity of home and into the unfolding story of his journey.

As the taxi moved down the street, the familiar sights of Poznańska faded into the early morning gloom. The houses seemed to whisper farewells with their sleepy, perspiration-covered windows and silent walls. My father looked back through the rear window, his heart heavy with sadness, fear, hope and anticipation. The world he was leaving behind was all he had ever known, yet the world ahead, unknown and vast, called to him with a promise of new beginnings.

For Golda, standing alone on the cold street, the departure was a moment of profound solitude. She watched until the taxi's taillights disappeared around the corner, then slowly turned back towards her home. Each step she took felt heavy, burdened with the weight of letting go. The house she returned to was the same, yet irrevocably changed, the echoes of her son's departure reverberating through its walls. An unconscious thought was in her mind, "Will she lose Chaim like she lost Abram?"

A chapter closed in that quiet early morning hour, and another began. Golda's whispered words, her gentle touch, and the steadfast love that had guided her son thus far would continue to be his anchor and guiding star, no matter where the world's roads would take him.

The taxi traversed 25 kilometres southwest along the Kaliska Road towards the township of Ostrów Wielkopolski. From there, the taxi travelled west and finally turned south on an old, cobblestone path. In the middle of nowhere, alighting in seclusion, my father ventured further on foot through the untouched expanse of grasslands, making a cautious descent into the depth of the ravine known as "Zduna." He rested until nightfall. Under the cloak of night, his passage continued, crossing the narrow creek that delineated the Polish border from Germany. This boundary, a silent witness to the confluence of Greater Poland and Silesia, now bore testimony to my father's resolve.

With each careful step, he navigated the murky waters, his skimpy belongings and jacket hoisted above to ensure they remained dry. The cold and unforgiving water seemed to grasp at his legs, each step a struggle against the current and the weight of his uncertainty. Emerging from the muddy creek onto the other side, a farmhouse silhouette broke the horizon, with a stable looming nearby. The dark and silent structure stood in the vast, empty landscape, offering a glimmer of hope in the enveloping darkness.

As if guided by the unseen hand of fate, he approached the stable subdued under the veil of darkness, its doors parting to welcome him into an unexpected aroma of freshly cut hay, a reminder of the harvest at the season's end. The smell, earthy and familiar, evoked a sense of temporary reprieve from the world outside. Here, amidst the shadows, he sought refuge, suspending his wet clothing to reclaim some warmth.

The stable, filled with the quiet rustle of straw and the occasional soft snort of a resting animal, became a sanctuary. The hay, piled high and still retaining the day's warmth, provided a makeshift bed where he could finally rest his weary body. My father stretched out, his mind racing with thoughts of the journey ahead, the unknown dangers, mixed with feelings of hope that had driven him this far.

The night pressed close in the stillness, wrapping him in a blanket of solitude. The distant cold stars watched over him as he lay there, each one a silent witness to his passage. The stable's wooden beams, sturdy and weathered, offered a sense of security, a brief respite from the relentless pursuit of safety and freedom.

My father's thoughts drifted to the family he had left behind. Their faces etched in his memory, their voices a distant echo in the quiet night. The decision to leave had been painful but necessary, a choice born out of love and the desperate need to survive. In silence, my father surrendered to exhaustion. As sleep claimed him, it was not just a body that rested but a spirit that momentarily found solace in the heart of the unknown. For the next four or five hours, his journey paused, his dreams perhaps filled with visions of what lay ahead or memories of what he had left behind.

The night slowly gave way to the first light of dawn, the sky shifting from inky black to the soft hues of morning. The crow of the rooster opened my father's eyelids. Once a shadowy refuge, the stable began to reveal its details in the growing light. My father stirred in his realisation of the new day, bringing a renewed sense of purpose.

As he prepared to move on, he took one last look around the stable, a silent farewell to the temporary haven that had sheltered him. The path ahead seemed fraught with danger but also filled with hope. Each step he took from this point was a step towards a new beginning, a journey that would test his resolve and fortitude, and hopefully fulfil the promise of a brighter future. His steps carried him towards Milicz, the first German town beyond the border. There, he secured a bus ride to Breslau, and from Breslau, he seamlessly transitioned onto a train bound for Berlin.

In his youth, my father sharpened his ability to speak Hoch Deutsch, a High German dialect closely resembling Yiddish. By the age of 17, he had immersed himself in the works of prominent German writers and poets such as Heinrich Heine, Rosa Luxemburg, Goethe, and Schiller. He possessed a deep understanding of German history and culture, fostering a sense of confidence in his almost imperceptible accent. With his dark blond hair and piercing blue eyes, he bore a striking resemblance to any other Aryan individual.

As the sun began to dip in the late afternoon, around five o'clock, the train drearily navigated through the bustling outskirts of Berlin. Despite the advancing hour, the day retained a pleasant warmth. Peering out from his window seat, my father observed the organised chaos of life in the German capital unfolding beneath him. The streets were a hive of activity, a blend of the mundane and the extraordinary, each scene a vignette of urban life under the looming shadow of the swastika.

Upon arrival at the Central Berlin Station, the designated stop beckoned him to disembark. Among the lingering few passengers trickling out of the carriage, he stepped down onto the platform and proceeded towards the main exit gate. The station was a cavernous space filled with the echoing footsteps of travellers, the murmurs of hurried conversations, and the distant clatter of departing trains.

While traversing the platform, a palpable sense of scrutiny weighed upon him as he sensed a man's eyes fixed upon him from some distance. The observer's features gradually sharpened into focus, a figure clad in a nondescript suit adorned with a conspicuous swastika emblem on his lapel. The man's gaze was piercing, a silent accusation that carried the weight of authority and suspicion.

Undeterred by the unsettling gaze, my father affected an air of nonchalance, feigning ignorance of the scrutiny shaping its narrative. His heart pounded with the intensity of a drum; each beat was a reminder of the precariousness of his situation. As he strode past, the stranger's voice cut through the air with an accusatory edge, questioning my father's origins with brazen certainty, "Du! Du hast die Grenze überquert, nicht wahr?" (English: You! You crossed the border, didn't you?!).

Startled but composed, he paused briefly, his attire betraying traces of hay and mud. The remnants of his illegal journey clung to him like silent witnesses. He met the man's unwavering gaze and, asserting himself in clear Hoch Deutsch, interjected, "Ein Moment!" before swiftly launching into a sprint. The sudden burst of motion ignited a frenzied pursuit behind him, the distant sound of a shrill whistle echoing amidst the racket as my father deftly navigated through the congested crowd.

"Entschuldigung, bitte, entschuldigung!" he uttered hasty pleas in between heartbeats, weaving through the throng of unsuspecting commuters. The platform transformed into a chaotic blur, his path a desperate zigzag through the urban labyrinth. Each turn and dodge was a calculated gamble, a dangerous dance that demanded precision and nerve.

He sought refuge aboard a leisurely tram homeward bound with weary commuters. The tram, a moving shelter of anonymity, offered a fleeting respite. Seizing a discarded newspaper, he shielded himself behind its flimsy veil, momentarily cloaking his narrow escape in the shadow of imminent danger. The rhythmic clatter of the tram's journey supported his racing thoughts; the ordinary sounds contrasted with the adrenaline-fuelled chase.

Relief mingled with tension as his thoughts echoed the silent sentiment: 'Oh… that was close.' The newspaper rustled softly in his hands, its mundane headlines a surreal juxtaposition to the life-and-death drama that had just unfolded. Hidden behind the printed words, he stole glances at the passing scenery, each familiar landmark reassuring that he had evaded capture, if only for the moment.

As the tram trundled along, my father allowed himself a brief moment of introspection. The near miss had been a blunt reminder of the hazardous nature of his journey, the thin line between freedom and captivity. In that fleeting moment of safety, my father felt the weight of his resilience. The world outside the tram continued at its relentless pace, oblivious to the silent battle fought within him. As he sat there, hidden in plain sight, he knew that the journey was far from over, but his spirit was undeterred, ready to face whatever challenges lay ahead.

To my father, Berlin was alive, thrumming with the presence of the secret police who monitored public spaces and scrutinised behaviour they deemed suspicious. The city appeared vastly more expansive and definitely more dangerous than Kalisz. The sprawling urban landscape, with its ceaseless movement and oppressive vigilance, created a backdrop of constant tension and unease.

He disembarked from the tram in the heart of Berlin, his steps brisk as he navigated a busy, wide boulevard adorned with the red, black, and white Nazi swastika flags. The flags fluttered ominously in the breeze, casting long shadows over the crowds of people moving purposefully along the street. Every glance seemed to carry an implicit threat.

Spotting a taxi rank, he approached confidently, masking his inner turmoil with a façade of calm. "Jüdischen Gemeinde Judenrat, bitte," (English: Jewish Community Support Service, please), he told the taxi driver, who nodded and set off. Inside the taxi, he shook most of the hay from his clothes, the remnants of his harrowing journey falling away like the vestiges of a past life.

The driver, a stoic figure with a hardened expression, navigated the bustling streets with practised ease. My father peered out the window, absorbing the city's atmosphere. Berlin was a place of unambiguous contrasts, its grand architecture and vibrant streets juxtaposed against the pervasive fear and oppression that lurked beneath the surface. The weight of the swastikas, the ever-watchful eyes of the Gestapo, and the relentless propaganda created an environment where every step felt fraught with danger.

As the taxi wove through the labyrinthine streets, my father's mind raced with thoughts of his next steps. The Jewish Community Support Service was a potential lifeline amidst the suffocating atmosphere of the city. It was where he might find assistance and a way to continue his journey. The need to remain vigilant to avoid arousing suspicion was paramount. Each action, each word, had to be measured with care.

The taxi halted before a large edifice titled 'Waisenhause Der Jüdischen Gemeinde.' The façade blended seamlessly with the surrounding structures. My father paid the driver, thanked him, and stepped out, his eyes scanning the area for any sign of menace.

He took a deep breath as he approached the entrance, marked by steps. He ascended quickly to reach the front ornamental door and pressed the buzzer. An elderly man opened the ornate, heavy doors. "I am a Polish Jew seeking refuge and assistance in Berlin," my father explained in pressured Yiddish. The man surveyed the street outside, then met my father's gaze before inviting him in. He was led through a corridor to a nearby office. The elderly man gestured for him to wait at the doorway while he conversed quietly with a slightly younger official seated behind a desk. After a brief exchange, the younger man rose and addressed my father directly.

"What is your name?" he inquired.

"Heinrich... from Blumenshtad, Poland... I have no papers. I crossed the border, and I'm seeking a temporary refuge," he implored.

"I understand," the official replied, his tone threaded with doubt. "We are troubled, Heinrich, that you come to us during such times," he added, disappointment shadowing his words. "Regrettably, you cannot stay here," he conveyed gently. "We must avoid any provocations with the authorities. Should they discover we are sheltering an illegal Polish Jewish refugee, we will have Sturmtruppen (English: Stormtroopers) at our door," he explained, his voice tinged with anxiety.

"Please, Heinrich, you must leave," he insisted.

Opening a small metal cash box, the man took out 600 Deutschmarks. "This should aid you in getting by and might cover a few nights at the Interlaken Hotel, a modest place not far from the Reichstag," he suggested reassuringly. "Please make sure you speak to no one of your visit here."

"Bitter Shein; Danke Schoen," My father expressed his gratitude. The elder ushered him back down the corridor. "Good luck, young man," he voiced as he opened the doors to the bustling world outside.

In the twilight hours of that first day in Berlin, my father encountered the formidable bastion of Nazi public policy. Since their ascension to power in 1933, Hitler's National Socialist regime had been resolutely committed to enacting a plethora of restrictive and discriminatory laws targeting German Jews. This surge of legislative malice aimed not only to isolate and publicly demean Jewish German citizens but also to intrude upon the most private aspects of their lives. The expectation for decisive support of this anti-Jewish legislation permeated every stratum of government, demanding compliance from employees across both public service and sectoral boundaries.

This odious legal framework swiftly cast its shadow over public spaces, manifesting in signs that declared Aryan exclusivity over community areas, shops, and other civic amenities, effectively ostracising Jews. The cityscape, once a tapestry of diverse interactions and vibrant culture, had transformed into a stark montage of segregation and hate.

My father, navigating the streets of Berlin, saw firsthand the extent of the regime's reach. Signs emblazoned with "Nur für Arier" (Aryans Only) were plastered across cafes, parks, and libraries, turning public spaces into minefields of exclusion. The starkness of the message was a brutal reminder of his outsider status, a mark of the pervasive hostility that had seeped into every corner of society.

The impact of these laws was more than just physical exclusion; it was an assault on the very dignity of Jewish existence. Jews were no longer citizens of their own country; they were pariahs, stripped of their rights and humanity by the relentless machinery of Nazi ideology. The regime's propaganda successfully transformed public opinion, turning neighbours into enemies and sowing distrust and fear.

The isolation was palpable, a heavy cloak that draped over the Jewish community, smothering the connections that once wove them into the fabric of German life. Families were torn apart as Jewish children were expelled from schools and Jewish professionals were barred from practising their trades. The economic strangulation was severe, but the psychological toll was even more significant. The sense of belonging and the feeling of safety within one's homeland were systematically dismantled.

For my father, each step through Berlin's streets reminded him of his precarious situation. The city, with its grand boulevards and bustling markets, had become a labyrinth of danger. Every glance, every casual interaction, was fraught with the potential for betrayal.

He had to navigate this new reality cautiously, constantly aware of the eyes that watched and judged.

The pervasive sense of surveillance extended beyond the physical realm. The regime's policies intruded into the private lives of Jews, dictating whom they could marry, where they could live, and even what they could own. The Nuremberg Laws, with their pseudoscientific definitions of racial purity, codified this intrusion, reducing human relationships to a sterile calculus of bloodlines and ancestry.

Amidst this chilling backdrop, my father observed signs that brazenly stated "Jews Unwelcome" at park entrances, public baths, train stations, and restrooms. The windows of most restaurants, grocery stores, and fashion boutiques bore the exclusionary proclamation "Jews Not Permitted." Legal firms and medical clinics were not spared, as they brandished plaques announcing, "Aryan Legal Practice" and "Aryan Medical Practice." By 1937, the regime had escalated its oppressive measures, barring Jewish doctors from treating non-Jewish patients and revoking the practice licenses of Jewish lawyers. The streets of Berlin, once bustling with a diverse tapestry of lives and cultures, had been transformed into a hostile landscape where every signpost, every plaque, was a dagger aimed at the heart of the Jewish community.

My father's journey through Berlin was not just a physical passage but a profound confrontation with the stark realities of Nazi oppression. Each sign, each exclusionary proclamation, was a challenge to his resolve, a test of his courage and identity. As the shadows lengthened and night enveloped the city, my father found a brief moment of consolation. He reaffirmed within himself that he carried the strength of his ancestors and the rock-solid belief in the sanctity of his identity. In all its hostility, Berlin could not strip him of his essence. In the heart of darkness, he held onto the light of his heritage and his family's love that would guide him through various storms, including his experience of this repressive city.

During his stay in Berlin, which lasted about a week, my father sought refuge in the modest yet welcoming confines of the Interlaken Hotel, where he registered himself under the guise of an Austrian Kaufmann (Sales Representative). The hotel proprietor, a man of few words, exuded a warmth and friendliness that contrasted sharply with the prevailing outside climate of fear. The Interlaken was a place of quiet civility amidst the turbulence, its unassuming façade belying the sanctuary it offered to weary travellers.

My father felt secure talking to the proprietor, who manifested openness and a helpful, friendly demeanour. The man relished sharing personal anecdotes and concerns without reservation, creating an atmosphere of fragile normalcy. On a particularly revealing occasion, he confided in my father about his son's affiliation with the Hitler Youth movement. With a heavy heart, he admitted, "You know, Heinrich, I make it a point never to inquire about a guest's religion or Jewish identity. However, should my son ever discover that one of my guests was of Jewish heritage, he would not hesitate to inform the Gestapo. Such an event would undoubtedly seal the fate of both the guest and me, dooming us to the horrors of a Konzentrationslager."

The proprietor's words hung in the air like a chilling reminder of my father's precarious situation. The hotel, with its warm fireplace and a genial host, was a fragile safety bubble in a city rife with danger. Each day spent there was a delicate balancing act, a tightrope walk between maintaining the guise of normalcy and the ever-present threat of exposure.

The man's genuine kindness was shadowed by an underlying fear, a recognition that the regime's ideologies had taken root even within his own family. The Hitler Youth, with its insidious indoctrination, had created a chasm between father and son, turning kin into potential adversaries. For my father, this internal conflict mirrored the broader societal rift, where trust was scarce, and betrayal could come from the most unexpected quarters.

The Interlaken Hotel, modest as it was, became a microcosm of the larger world outside. It was a place where the threads of 'personal' and 'political' intertwined, constantly shifting the boundaries between safety and peril. My father's assumed identity as an Austrian Kaufmann was his shield, but the proprietor's discretion provided the actual protection.

At the hotel, my father encountered guests whose behaviour hinted that they were in a situation akin to his own. His instincts were right. The trio of Berliners he befriended were plotting to depart Germany for France, aiming to join the efforts in the Spanish Civil War. As their camaraderie deepened, my father revealed that his aim was also to reach Paris and join the Republican Socialist Movement, to fight against Franco. Unlike him, however, the three men possessed valid travel documentation. One of them offered my father a piece of helpful advice, "Heinrich…your best bet is to head south, towards Aachen. It's the simplest border crossing point. You'll need about 300 Deutschmarks. Make your stay at the Franz Strasse Hotel. There, someone will instruct you on your next contact and meeting location. And heed this advice: when you cross the border into Belgium and then into France, make sure to inform any enquiring official along the way that you are coming straight from Poland, without layovers. By stating that, you will dispel any doubt of espionage."

∞∞∞∞∞∞

After enduring a lengthy train journey across Germany, my father arrived at Aachen. He easily found the Franz Strasse Hotel, nestled within the charming Old Town of Aachen, a mere two to three kilometres from the Belgian border. With its nondescript exterior, the hotel offered no hint of clandestine activities. He checked in, maintaining the persona of Heinrich, the Austrian Sales Representative. The historic hotel, brimming with character, was situated in a scenic location. From the windows of his room, my father gazed down upon a tranquil, tree-lined street, touched by the crisp night's air. Just a month prior, Aachen had been the epicentre of a remarkable event, a massive gathering of nearly a million Catholics from across the nation, united in protest against Hitler's National Socialist regime. However, the city was eerily quiet on the night of his arrival. Several small groups of guests were present in the buffet's dining room. My father sat at the table alone, attempting to read a newspaper he found on the train. Whispered conversations and surreptitious glances disrupted his concentration. He kept to himself, thinking each guest could be a potential ally or adversary. The hotel's buffet offered a warm welcome with steaming coffee, sandwiches, biscuits, and fruit. Fortified by this spread, my father pondered his next steps in seeking guidance. He left the dining room and went to the reception desk, discovering it was deserted, bathed in the glow of a solitary lamp. Just as he reasoned that the morning would bring opportunities for inquiries, someone called out to him.

"Can I help you?" A voice disrupted his contemplation, emanating from the distant end of the elongated, softly illuminated corridor. Turning towards the voice, my father recognised the middle-aged man who had checked him in. As the man approached him, he hesitated for a moment but then, in a hushed tone, ventured, "Sir, do you know of a passage to Belgium?"

"There are several routes one might consider," the man replied, his gaze piercing as he studied the enquirer, "Will you be travelling by public means, or do you have your own mode of transport?"

"I plan to go on foot, Sir," my father responded.

"Come into my office," the man directed with a blend of authority and warmth. Within his private confines, he furnished my father with contacts and detailed instructions for meeting an individual who could facilitate the border crossing into Belgium, albeit for a steep fee of 400 Deutschmarks.

The following day, my father made his way to the agreed-upon 'point of contact.' Guided by a man in his 60s, he navigated through dense brush and a hilly terrain. Roughly 600 meters past the border into Belgium, their paths diverged. Alone, he ventured onward. After several hours, he arrived at the quaint village of Eupen. A brief pause allowed him to gather his strength with a modest meal of bread and a few sips of milk, fuelling him for the next 30 kilometres along a well-trodden country road. Eventually, he reached a highway and boarded a bus headed for Liege. In the streets of Liege, while seeking directions, he encountered a middle-aged Jewish woman named Byra, who, astonishingly, was from Kalisz. She offered him a place to stay with her family. That Saturday, a young man from the Jewish community accompanied my father to a local synagogue for supper. They returned to Byra's apartment at 9 pm. Before he departed by train for Brussels, my father spent three days there, carrying Byra's family kindness and her unexpected connection.

The train glided smoothly across fields blanketed in the rich colours of autumn. As if on cue, rain began to fall, captivating my father's attention. He watched the raindrops shatter upon impact, spilling and skittering in unpredictable patterns along the windswept glass pane. Outside the window, the world morphed into a blur of rain-streaked hues, but inside, his mind was clear, replaying a vivid memory. The image of his mother persisted, an afterimage that refused to fade. Golda's resolute yet tender figure stood against the backdrop of their Poznańska Street home. Her voice, a blend of concern and love, echoed in his thoughts: "I will write to Ms Gliksmann... Be careful, Chaim... Let us know how you are."

He saw her eyes brimming with unspoken fears and loving concern, watching him as he stepped into the unknown. The rain seemed to mirror her suppressed tears. As the train pressed on, the rhythmic clatter of the wheels provided a soothing counterpoint to his inner turmoil. The landscape outside, with its muted palette of autumn shades, seemed to echo the complexity of his emotions, beauty tinged with melancholy, change shadowed by uncertainty. The relentless yet purifying rain washed over the fields and trees, a cleansing curtain between past and future.

Inside the carriage, my father clutched his few belongings, each item a tangible link to his former life. The warmth of his mother's last embrace lingered, a ghostly comfort against the chill of the unknown. Her words, "Be careful, Chaim," reverberated with a timeless resonance, his guardian's whisper guiding him through the fog of doubt.

In the reflective surface of the rain-streaked window, my father caught glimpses of his face, youthful yet etched with lines of worried curiosity and resolve. The reflection seemed to merge with the landscape outside, a symbolic union of his inner and outer worlds. The rain began to ease, the downpour softening to a gentle drizzle. The landscape outside slowly emerged from the watery blur, revealing hints of the journey ahead. My father's thoughts turned to the future, to the unknown paths he would tread, guided by the love and words of his mother. Her voice, "Let us know how you are," resonated with a promise of connection that transcended the miles and uncertainties ahead.

In the stillness of the carriage, amidst the soft murmur of fellow passengers and the fading rhythm of the rain, my father felt a surge of quiet strength. The memory of his mother, her voice, and her tenacious love was a source of solace and courage, a constant companion along his adventurous path.

Upon reaching Brussels, he found the residence of Ms Gliksmann, the daughter of Mr Gliksmann, an old Hasidic Jew who had once lived in Kalisz. Ms Gliksmann was a generous, middle-aged, and welcoming soul. She invited my father to stay in her residence at Place du Jeu de Balle. He stayed there for about four weeks, free of charge. It was a time for him to regather his strength, surrounded by the kindness of connections rooted in his family's past.

After a month's stay, he embarked on his next journey, taking a train to Quiévrain, a quaint municipality in the Belgian province of Hainaut. There, he crossed from Belgium into France. About half a kilometre from the border, a French gendarme on a bicycle asked my father for his passport. As he did not have it, he was asked to return to Belgium. My father persevered; he redirected his path and decided to walk on foot to a little French town called Valenciennes. From there, he caught the train to Paris. Straight from Paris' Gare d'Orsay Central Station, he took the taxi to a designated address, the residence of his cousin Tovia.

Tovia's father and my father's paternal grandfather, Samuel Nathan, were brothers. Tovia greeted him warmly, with a touch of surprise. His apartment was small, and the prospect of my father staying there was awkward and unlikely. Fortunately, to his relief, Tovia came up with an alternative. He suggested his sister's place. Without hesitation, my father accepted the option. Dora, a lady in her late fifties, was kind, and her residence was spacious. To his surprise, a Polish visitor was already staying in Dora's welcoming apartment. He happened to be my father's distant cousin, Bernard Poznański, who, like him, did not have a passport or a temporary visa for his stay in France. Dora suggested that my father share the room with Bernard, who seemed friendly and about a decade older.

In the evening, my father initiated a conversation with Bernard. "I see that, unlike Berlin, Paris is much more a cosmopolitan city, filled with artists and political activists from the rest of troubled Europe," he said casually. The air in their small room was thick with the residue of the day's events. Bernard's response was mildly reserved. "Well, I guess this is true. If you visited Hitler's Germany, you can see the contrast, given that France is a liberal, tolerant, and inclusive society," he stated, conveying a hint of ambivalence.

My father, undeterred, leaned forward, his eyes alight with the passion of his thoughts. "And what is more amazing is that the French Prime Minister, Léon Blum, is a Jewish Socialist leader," he expressed, his words laden with amazement. Bernard shrugged slightly; his expression was one of cautious detachment. "Sure, Chaim, but just because he is a Jew does not necessarily make him a great leader," he stated resolutely, his tone firm but not unkind.

My father persisted with his line of thinking, the spark of his idealism refusing to be dimmed. "Blum faces a lot of opposition from right-wing conservatives, and it is damn disappointing that his government is not able to support the Republicans in their Spanish Civil War effort." His words hung in the air, a reflection of his inner turmoil and the complexities of the political landscape he found himself navigating.

Bernard looked at my father, slightly bewildered by his intensity. "Well, I hope you can sleep well tonight after a long day of travelling," he said, his voice gently suggesting a retreat from the charged topic.

My father, sensing the need to relent, nodded. "Yes, enough politics. Goodnight," he responded, a wry smile playing on his lips as he settled back into bed.

The two men retreated into their thoughts as the room fell into a contemplative silence. The conversation, though brief, had touched upon the heart of their differing perspectives. My father's idealism and Bernard's pragmatism were like two sides of the same coin, each necessary to understand the full picture of their turbulent times.

The flickering street lamplight cast long shadows on the walls, creating a dance of light and dark that mirrored the complexities of their discussion. My father's mind wandered back to the streets of Paris, to the vibrancy and the struggles that defined the city. He thought of the artists and activists, the ideals that drew people to this haven of freedom, and the battles yet to be fought.

Bernard, meanwhile, reflected on his own pragmatic views. He respected my father's passion, even if he did not fully share it. In his heart, he hoped that their different outlooks would somehow complement each other in the days to come.

As the night deepened, the two men drifted off to sleep. Now quiet and still, the room held the echoes of their somewhat short conversation, a dialogue with a brief quest for understanding.

In the heart of Paris, amidst the uncertainty and the promise of change, with all its shadows and flickering lights, the night became a canvas for my father's dreams, a space where the past and future intertwined in the quiet embrace of sleep. The following morning, after breakfast, my father went to Place de Belleville, where volunteer recruits enlisted for service in the International Brigades that fought alongside the Spanish Republican military forces. The air was crisp, filled with the sounds of a city awakening to the promise of a new day. As he approached the gathering place, his heart pounded with a mixture of anticipation and resolve.

He recalled the situation vividly. "After my long journey, I thought my dream of joining the fight for a free Socialist Republican Spain was finally going to crystallise."

He stood patiently in a line of men, stripped of their clothes, awaiting the military doctors' preliminary medical assessment. The room was filled with the low murmur of conversations, each sound amplifying the gravity of the moment. My father's mind was a whirl of thoughts and emotions as he waited for his turn.

As he stood there, the morning air's chill mingled with the warmth of his hopes. He thought, "If only Abram knew how far I got." The memory of his brother filled him with both pride and sorrow. Abram's spirit seemed to hover nearby, like a silent witness to my father's perseverance and courage.

The line moved slowly, each step bringing him closer to realising his dream. The men around him, each with their own stories and motivations, shared a collective sense of purpose. The military doctors, their faces stern and professional, conducted the assessments methodically with minimal dialogue. My father watched as each man was examined, their physical readiness scrutinised with an unyielding eye. As he waited, my father's thoughts drifted to the journey that had brought him here. The miles travelled, the obstacles overcome, each moment had tested his resolve. He remembered the faces of those who had helped him along the way, the brief moments of kindness that had made all the difference.

Finally, his turn came. He stepped forward, his body and mind ready for the awaited scrutiny. The two doctors who sat at the examination desk eyeballed his relatively healthy and robust body. One of them stood up and began palpating my father's neck behind his left ear. The doctor's hands were firm but gentle, their touch a reminder of humanity that persisted even in the midst of war.

The doctor was visibly intrigued by the swelling, which was quite sensitive to touch. The medic muttered words in French to his colleague. Both conversed while focusing their attention disconcertingly on the discovered node. A few moments later, they ended their conversation. The examining doctor gestured to my father to stand aside and wait.

At that moment, my father felt perplexed and singled out. Unlike others stepping forward to the next stage of the medical examination, he was made to stand aside for nearly 20 minutes, feeling quite humiliated. The minutes dragged on, each one stretching his patience and gnawing at his resolve. The sense of exclusion weighed heavily on him; the sting of standing apart from the others contrasted sharply with his earlier experience of hope and unity.

Then, a man dressed formally in a suit approached my father and spoke to him in German. "Junger Mann, Sie hatten den medizinischen Test aufgrund eines großen unbehandelten Abszesses an Ihrem Hals nicht bestanden" (English: "Young man, you had failed the medical test due to a large untreated abscess on your neck"). His words were harsh and not what my father wanted to hear. "Übrigens, es gibt nicht genug Waffen, um sie an die erwachsenen Soldaten zu verteilen, geschweige denn an kranke Teenager" (English: "By the way, there are not enough guns to distribute to the adult soldiers, let alone sick teenagers"), the man added sarcastically. His last words struck my father like a blow. The sting of rejection mingled with the pain of humiliation. The man's sarcastic tone only deepened the wound, his dismissive attitude starkly contrasting the idealism that had driven my father this far.

As the man walked away, my father stood there, grappling with the crushing disappointment. The dream that had sustained him through his journey now seemed distant and unattainable. The reality of his situation settled heavily upon his shoulders, the weight of unfulfilled aspirations pressing down on him.

As he left the examination area, his head held high despite his heavy heart, his spirit remained unbroken. The rejection at Place de Belleville was a setback, but he refused to be broken. As he wandered the streets of Paris, his thoughts were a turbulent mix of frustration and sorrow. The bustling city, with its lively cafes and vibrant boulevards, seemed indifferent to his inner turmoil. He felt like a shadow moving through the crowd, his aspirations momentarily eclipsed by the weight of his disappointment.

Yet, amidst the despair, there was a flicker of resilience. The same spirit that had carried him through his journey thus far refused to be extinguished. My father knew his struggle was part of a larger battle requiring persistence and commitment. The rejection he faced was a setback, but it was not the end of his story. As he walked, he remembered the faces of those who had helped him along the way, the moments of kindness and solidarity that had sustained him. Again, he thought of his mother's words, her voice a gentle anchor in his memory: "Be careful, Chaim... Let us know how you are." He thought of Abram, whose spirit had been his guiding star and whose memory continued to inspire him.

∞∞∞∞∞

"Ouch! Oh, it hurts!" Chaim exclaimed, hunched over the washbasin, his head bowed as his fellow Kalisian, Zelman Samuel, expertly wielded a razor to slice open the cyst on the back of Chaim's neck. "You've got some wicked stuff seeping out of your neck, my friend," Zelman remarked with a wry grin as he pressed the cyst with both hands. "How much longer?" my father asked, his voice laden with concern and palpable tension. Zelman didn't respond; he continued his work, focused and unyielding. "Ah... Oh... Oy!" Chaim groaned. "We're almost there, Chaim... not much longer now." "I think you'll need a glass of vodka after this, to replace the lost fluids," Zelman chuckled. "Sure," my father replied, his tone supportive. "Okay... I think that's it. Now, you need to dress it with an antiseptic," Zelman said, exhaling in relief. My father lifted his head and turned sharply to the right to view the wound in the mirror. The cut was deep, but the swelling had subsided.

My father met Zelman at a meeting of the Popular Front's local branch, nestled near Pigalle, the vibrant red-light district of Paris. Zelman, a few years my father's senior, had opted not to enlist in the Civil War in Spain. Instead, he journeyed to Paris to engage with the Communist Popular Front movement. Zelman introduced my father

60

to Professor Kreckler, a former German academic who had become a dissident and an active member of the French Communist Party in Paris. Aside from his political endeavours, Kreckler also operated an antique furniture business in Paris.

Kreckler took my father under his wing, teaching him the art of restoring antique tables and chairs, replacing broken wooden components, mastering the use of a lathe, and applying French polish. My father thrived under Kreckler's tutelage, who paid his illegal immigrant employees generously in cash. Despite Kreckler's intellectual background, he was a hands-on worker and demonstrated genuine care for his staff. During lunch breaks, he would sit with his employees, sharing sandwiches he bought for the group.

Having fled Nazi Germany following Kristallnacht, Kreckler found refuge in Paris, a city known for embracing individuals of diverse political and philosophical beliefs. Affectionately, he nicknamed my father "our Polnishé Heinrich." Thanks to the fair wages from Krekler, my father and Bernard were able to afford a stay in a modest hotel, sharing a single room for about nine months

My father felt a quiet astonishment at how Léon Blum, a Jewish radical socialist, had ascended to power in France. At the same time, he was equally disheartened by Blum's dual dismissals. To him, Blum epitomised his promising vision for the communist movement across Europe. French democracy, in my father's view, shone brightly against the dark, oppressive, and racially charged backdrop of Adolf Hitler's Nazi Germany.

As he navigated the lively streets of Paris, each corner teeming with a blend of art and culture, my father's thoughts often wandered back to Kalisz, to the familiar image of his parents huddling around the kitchen stove. Despite the vibrancy surrounding him, a pang of guilt tugged at his heart; it had been too long since he last wrote to them. Reflecting on this, he resolved that he should write. Tonight.

My father often initiated discussions with Bernard, who was less politically invested and not as inclined to engage in debates at late hours of the night. As they rested in their beds in their hotel room overlooking the dim lantern lights of Bellville, my father looked at the shadows on the ceiling to gather his thoughts. He felt restless and conflicted about his socio-political vision.

"Bernard, if Blum was able to come to power in France, then there is a chance that the same could happen in Poland", my father stated provocatively to elicit a response. "What's Blum in Poland?" Bernard replied, half dozing off. "No! I meant to say that the communist movement in Poland needs to rise against the forces of Endecja first," my father clarified. "An improbable scenario", Bernard responded unenthusiastically. "The majority of Poles dislike the Reds and the whole idea of Marxist ideology. There are just not enough Jews to drive such a movement," Bernard expanded lethargically. "Well, I predict that Franco's regime will fall by the end of the year, and the French Communist Party will win the next election. I mean, people cannot ignore the fact that Blum made momentous changes. The guy has brought a new social welfare system to France, better conditions for the workers, legitimised trade unions, and new laws protecting workers' rights. That is such progress. Admittedly, he was slow in supporting the Republicans." Pausing to gauge Bernard's interest, my father continued, "I suppose there will always be a right-wing political party that prioritises trade for the benefit of profiteers over the masses. What do you think, Bernard?"

There was silence. My father listened to his companion's steady, rhythmic breathing, realising that Bernard had drifted into sleep.

As the summer of 1938 drew to a close, the French government intensified its efforts to crack down on illegal migrants and dissidents. My father and Bernard, lacking visas, were acutely aware that their time in France was drawing to a close. In December of that year, a foreboding letter arrived for my father from the French authorities, demanding that he present his passport details to the French Immigration Department. The letter warned that a refusal to comply would result in his arrest and deportation.

Despite the ominous warning, my father and Bernard disregarded the authorities' demands, keeping themselves undeterred for the next four months. However, their respite finally ended when French Gendarmes knocked on their hotel apartment door. The officers presented them with a stern ultimatum: leave France within three days or face imprisonment and an extended detention before being forcibly deported back to Poland.

With the help of the Jewish Welfare Organisation (JOINT), my father and Bernard paid for their Polish Passports at the Polish Consulate in Paris, and in May 1939, they returned to Poland. In Poznań, they parted company as my father changed for the train destined for Kalisz. This was the last time he saw Bernard.

My father walked away from the bustling Kalisz train station, making his way through the streets that led to his old neighbourhood. The lush expanse of Kalisz Park cast a welcoming embrace with its ornate green landscapes, a vivid contrast to the memories housed in every corner. As he approached the familiar "Rooster Pond," the sight of willows gracefully arching over the tranquil water momentarily stirred within him a deep nostalgia. This serene haunt had been a playground in his youth, where he and his friends would chase the fleeting shadows of tadpoles in the shimmering pool.

The unchanged façade of Poznańska Street greeted him as he neared home. It was dinner time; the air was thick with domesticity. He paused at his front door, savouring the muffled inflections of everyday life emanating from inside. Through the wood, his mother's voice carried the weight of habitual concerns, her words weaving around the subject of monthly expenses with his father.

With a surge of resolve, my father finally knocked. The door swung open to reveal Golda, her face awash in the dim hallway light. Recognition flickered, then flamed into sheer astonishment. For a moment, she stood frozen, a sculpted figure of disbelief, before her features crumbled into an expression marred by joyful tears. With a sob, she managed to raise her arms, embracing her son as if trying to confirm he wasn't just a phantom borne from her daily thoughts or prayers.

"Chaim...my Chaim...oh my God...you're home...oh my God...son, you are home!" Her voice broke, each word a crescendo of relief and elation. In the background, Yosif lingered by the dinner table, his expression a tableau of shock and wonder, the sudden disruption rendering him nearly statuesque. This homecoming was not merely a return, but a rejuvenation of the bonds that time had stretched but never broken.

Notes

1. Piętka Bohdan (2014). Bereza Kartuska – czarna karta historii II RP. Myśl Polska, nr 39-40

2. https://en.wikipedia.org/wiki/bereza_kartuska_prison

3. Dark clouds of hate

Upon his return to Poland, my father swiftly became aware of the deepening repression aimed at the Jewish community in Kalisz, spearheaded by the nationalist right-wing Endecja (pron: Endetzya) movement. Economic boycotts were rampant, devastating many small Jewish businesses as local Poles were openly discouraged from patronising Jewish commercial ventures. Even the marketplace, like Dekert's Market in Kalisz, was starkly segregated into Christian and Jewish sections, reinforcing the division.

Amidst these escalating tensions, the Jewish communist movement gained momentum, its strength and influence burgeoning. In Kalisz, the Jewish community was politically diverse, with three significant movements.

First, there was 'Aguda Jisroel,' a party primarily composed of Orthodox Jews. For members of 'Aguda,' religion was not just a private matter but a cornerstone that shaped all socio-political discussions. This party championed the freedom of religious practice and expressed unwavering loyalty to the State and Government of Poland.

Second, many parties within Kalisz were fundamentally Zionist, inspired by Theodor Herzl's vision. These groups advocated for transforming the Jewish community in Poland into a modern, secular, and nationally self-governed entity, ultimately aspiring to the creation of a Jewish State in Palestine.

Third, there was the left-wing 'Bund,' which aimed for solidarity with the Polish Socialist Workers' Union, and there were also various Communist factions, which were heavily comprised of Jewish members. These included the Communist Party of Poland (KPP) and the Polish Union of Communist Youth (KZMP). These parties, operating under the shadow of strict illegality, faced intensified surveillance and repression by Polish authorities, particularly with heightened activities of the secret police in Kalisz from 1936 onwards. [1]

My father was deeply involved in forming the clandestine KZMP cells in Kalisz. He spent his nights canvassing the city, boldly plastering Communist slogans on the walls of buildings, like: 'Join the Marxist Youth Movement in the Struggle for Freedom and Equality' or 'Young Socialists Unite Against Poverty, Racism, and Nazism'. He vividly recounted one harrowing episode: "Once Szpilka (Eng: 'Pinprick', a nickname for a night-shift police officer) caught me red-handed. Normally, Szpilka would confront me sometime after the deed when I had already finished plastering my placards. He would ask to see my hands, hunting for traces of glue. I was usually prepared, having a bottle of turpentine at the ready to wash off any residue swiftly. However, luck was not on my side one night when Szpilka spotted me with his piercing eyes as I posted a Marxist message on the front window of the Kalish Post Office, deep in the quiet of the night. I remember my desperate run through the Miejski Park, my mind racing with anxiety over being spotted by Szpilka in the very act."

My father always vividly recounted his daring deeds amid the tensions and risks of his underground political activism during fraught times in Kalisz. His stories weren't just narratives of rebellion but also lessons in resilience, shrewdness, and the unyielding pursuit of his vision, which he considered just and moral.

A few days later, early in the morning, my father sat at the kitchen table, having his usual black coffee with a slice of dark bread for breakfast. The room was quiet; the only sound was the occasional clink of his cup against the saucer. Suddenly, there was an unexpected firm knock at the door. Golda, already acquainted with the firmness of that knock from several previous occasions, felt a familiar knot tighten in her stomach. She hesitated, her hand lingering on the doorknob before finally opening it.

Two familiar civilian police officers stood before her, their expressions stern and unyielding. "It's okay, Mum… I know what this is about," my father called out to her from across the room as he stood up from the table. His voice was calm, starkly contrasting with the tension that filled the air. He grabbed his coat, its weight a familiar comfort, and walked out onto the chilly, still sleepy Poznańska Street, where the police car was conveniently parked in front of the apartment building.

Golda watched him go; her heart again heavy with worry. She thought, "What has he done now?" as she cleared the half-full warm cup of coffee and the small plate with a half-bitten slice of bread left behind on the kitchen table. Each movement was deliberate as if she could dispel her fears through the simple act of tidying up.

The street outside was cloaked in the quiet of early morning, the usual hustle and bustle yet to awaken. The sky was dull grey, promising another cold day. My father walked with a sense of resignation, each step echoing his determination to face whatever lay ahead. The police officers flanking him seemed indifferent to his resolve, their duty a mechanical routine.

As he approached the police car, my father couldn't help but glance back at the apartment building. The place that had been a sanctuary, filled with the warmth and love of family, now felt like a distant memory. He saw his mother standing at the building's front entrance, her silhouette sharpened by the morning light. Her worry was visible, even from a distance, weighing heavily upon him.

Inside the car, the atmosphere was tense. The officers exchanged brief, perfunctory words, their tones devoid of any warmth or empathy. My father's thoughts were a whirlwind of speculation. He knew the risks he had taken, the lines he had crossed. But the uncertainty of the situation gnawed at him, each moment stretching into an eternity.

As the car pulled away from Poznańska Street, my father's mind drifted to the sacrifices his family had made, the countless times they had stood by him during the storms of political unrest or personal upheaval.

Back in the apartment, Golda whispered a silent prayer, her hands clasped together in a gesture of desperate hope. The apartment, usually filled with the sounds of daily life, now felt oppressively silent, each tick of the clock amplifying her anxiety.

As the car sped through the quiet streets, a sense of calm washed over him. The family bonds, shared dreams, and sacrifices gave him strength. He closed his eyes briefly, letting the memories and hopes to fortify his resolve. Whatever lay ahead, he would face it with the same courage and conviction that had brought him this far.

My father was arrested and found guilty of engaging in subversive activity and defacing public property.

The prison experience was yet another story that had to be told. My father eagerly described this significant life event: "They had this ritual in the prison, where every newcomer had to fight with Juzwiak, the toughest guy in the prison, serving a long sentence for burglary and murder. He was a tall, muscular bully with a very thick neck. I was warned a few times that I would have to fight this guy, that there was no way out of it… it was going to happen." My father paused for a moment and then said: "And it did happen". I remember waiting attentively to hear my father's next segment. "A few days after I was incarcerated, in the afternoon, Juzwiak came out of his cell and stepped into the main prison area. The prisoners formed a circle around the man. There was silence; Juzwiak looked at me and gestured with his hand towards me… encouraging me to step forward" towards the middle."

Kalisz Prison, built in 1840, accommodated almost 200 prisoners at any one-time time

Kalisz Prison – main prison area

"Of course, I knew straight away there was no choice...I had to face Juzwiak; I had to deal with this situation", my father said confidently. "Before he realised, I ran towards him and threw myself at his waist; he lost his balance, and as he tried to regain it, I was already behind him. I jumped on his back, grabbed his head in a headlock and held it tight. He tried to wrestle and punch my legs with his fists, but I just kept on holding on to his neck until I got his head in a gridlock. Once this happened, I started to twist his head to the side. He was struggling – let go, you little bastard – but I just kept on twisting that bulky head until we both fell to the floor. I did not let go; I kept my grip as tight as I could. I asked him: - You had enough? For a few minutes, he would not answer, so I squeezed my grip even tighter, giving all I had to make him suffer in pain. I asked: - What about now? Silence. I thought I was going to break his neck. Finally, he faintly said: - Enough...enough, and I let go of my grip.

∞∞∞∞∞

No matter how often I heard this story, I felt deeply moved and overtaken by its meaning. It was as if I was watching a movie about a brave man who could survive the direst of circumstances. As time passed, I became acutely aware of my father's courageous acts and his vulnerability as a man. A man who could not easily protect himself from the unfriendly, hidden forces of the society he lived in and invested himself into. Despite his charisma and a 'larger than life' demeanour, he was also a man who may have come across as somewhat vulnerable. He was short in stature, overweight for his height, and walked with an energetic, uneven gait, slightly leaning to the right side. His trousers and suit jacket seemed crinkled, and the hair on his balding head was often easily tossed out of place.

Being Jewish and living in Poland during the interwar period was not easy. Gentile Poles perceived Jewish identity as different and unacceptable to the Polish Roman Catholic way of life. The Jews living in such an environment were vulnerable to humiliation and bullying, which was unleashed upon them through physical assaults and harassment. However, the prevailing negative attitudes towards them formed only a part of the problem that Polish Jews had to rise above. They had nowhere to go; they lived in Poland for 800 years, and although Poland was their homeland, they were strangers within it. Strangers in their own home.

My father, with his small stature and unassuming appearance, embodied the struggle of many Jews of his time. His physical presence might have seemed insignificant, but his spirit was formidable. His uneven gait, crinkled attire, and often dishevelled hair were inconsequential compared to the fierce determination and moral strength he carried within.

In a world that judged and marginalised him for his Jewish identity, my father's vulnerability was a testament to his humanity. He faced a society that saw him as an outsider, an unwanted element in the fabric of Polish life. Yet, he persisted, driven by a sense of justice and a commitment to his beliefs. The weight of history pressed heavily upon him, but he stood resilient, a symbol of defiance against the forces that sought to diminish him.

Living as a Pole with a Jewish heritage in Poland meant enduring daily indignities and threats. The hostile stares, the whispers of prejudice, and the tacit acts of rejection were all part of the harsh reality. Like many others, my father had to navigate a world where simply being himself was an act of bravery.

My father refused to be ashamed or fearful. His life was a tapestry of small rebellions, each act of resistance a thread of defiance against the broader narrative of oppression. He understood that the negative attitudes towards Jews were rooted in ignorance and fear, and he rose above them with dignity. His existence was a testament to the endurance of the Jewish people, a reminder that they had survived for centuries and would continue to do so despite the challenges.

The irony of their situation was that Poland was their homeland, a place where Jews had lived for 800 years. Yet, they were treated as strangers, aliens in their own land. This paradox was a source of both pain and strength. The sense of belonging was intertwined with the experience of exclusion, creating a complex identity that was both deeply rooted and perpetually marginalised.

My father's courage was in his actions and his very being. He embodied the resilience of a people who had faced centuries of adversity and yet continued to contribute to the society that often rejected them. His life was a quiet protest against the forces of hatred and intolerance, a living testament to the strength of the human spirit.

As I grew older, I came to understand the full measure of his bravery. He was not just a man who fought for a cause; he was a man who lived his beliefs every day in the face of overwhelming odds. His vulnerability was his strength, his ordinary appearance a mask for the extraordinary resolve within. He taught me that true courage is not always loud and visible; sometimes, it is the quiet determination to stand firm in the face of relentless adversity.

In his crinkled suit and uneven gait, my father walked a path of honour and resilience. He showed me that being different in a world that values conformity is an act of bravery. His life was a vision of hope, a reminder that even in the darkest times, the light of humanity can prevail.

There were three and a half million Jews in Poland before the outbreak of WWII. Most lived in cities and tiny towns, known in Yiddish as the 'shtetls'. In Warsaw, one-third of the city's population was Jewish. And like Warsaw, a third of the Kalisian population was Jewish, congregating mainly in the poorer sections of the town on the western side.

"Kalisz, one of the oldest cities in Poland, known as Blumenstadt in German, a town of flowers," my father would proudly say. He would then delve into the town's rich history, how it served as a border town between Poland and Germany and a central point along the old Amber Track for traders of antiquity. In the 1200s, Prince Boleslav, Duke of Kraków, granted the town's Jewish residents a charter known as the 'Statute of Kalisz'. This charter, a testament to the resilience of the Jewish community, granted them settlement rights and specific religious and financial freedoms. The 'Statute of Kalisz' later formed a legal foundation for Jewish rights in Poland. There is evidence that Jews came to Kalisz in the twelfth century as refugees who fled to Poland, attempting to escape the Crusader massacres, which took place in the Rhineland area of today's Germany. Coins from this era were stamped with names in Hebrew letters, revealing Jewish minters already living in Kalisz during the 1200s. Like in other parts of Europe, in Kalisz, Jews lived as moneylenders, artisans, and import-export merchants, dealing in livestock, horses, agricultural products and textiles. One thing that Polish Jews were not permitted to have was the ownership of rural land.

The Jewish population of Kalisz declined somewhat in the seventeenth and eighteenth centuries. The decline was due to the disruption caused by the Polish-Swedish War (1655-1659) and many fires, including a plague in the 1700s. Even so, by 1793, when Prussia annexed the region, Jews owned about a quarter of the buildings in Kalisz. At that time, Jews constituted 40 per cent of the town's population; they dominated the textile trade and made up half the town's craftsmen.

From 1815 until 1918, Kalisz was under Russian Tzarist rule. In 1881, Russian authorities expelled Jewish residents from Kalisz if they happened to lack Russian citizenship. Once again, the Jewish population in Kalisz dropped dramatically. At the same time, the

74

general population of Kalisz increased considerably because of the city's economic growth. In 1902, a new railway was built to facilitate efficient transport of goods and workforce between the Russian Empire and the German States, linking significant cities such as Warsaw and Lodz (Polish: Łódź). [3]

'Statute of Kalisz' formed a legal foundation for Jewish rights in Poland [2]

Over the centuries, in Poland, many Polish Jews lived separately from the Polish Catholic majority. At home, my father's family spoke Yiddish, and his father, Yosif, attended the local synagogue and practised his davening (i.e. recitations of the prescribed liturgical prayers) at fixed times of the day. In Poland, many Polish Jewish families engaged in a religious practice that was distinctly different from Polish Catholicism. For the most part, Jewish families kept their traditions and aspirations to themselves. The religious Jews in their communities voiced no public comment about politics, Catholicism, or any other sociopolitical currency that was present in their milieu.

Only a year before my father's birth, in 1919, Poland became the Second Polish Republic, marking the end of more than 100 years of foreign rule. The new State of Poland was devastated by the past economic exploitations of its partitioners. By the early 1920s, the country fell into a deep depression like the rest of Europe. Poverty was endemic, and Polish Jews were the least likely group to gain any employment. Endecja, otherwise known as the Polish National Democratic Front (Polish: Narodowa Demokracja), upheld the 'ethnic assimilation' policy and fuelled anti-Semitic propaganda during those early years. Tensions between Polish Catholics and Polish Jews intensified even more when the Russian Jews began to migrate from Ukraine to Poland to escape the pogroms and the massacres that were happening there. The 'ethnic assimilation' policy stipulated that Ukrainian, Lithuanian, German, and Prussian communities were to be subjected to imposed Polonization if they wished to reside within the borders of Poland. Jews were the only ethnic group that was excluded from the Polonization process. The Endecja fundamentally aimed to eliminate the Jewish population in Poland by whatever means that was deemed appropriate. [4]

From the start of Poland's rebirth in 1918, the emerging socio-political forces ranged from feminism and secularism to militant Catholicism and Fascism. Josef Pilsudski's left-wing Sanacja (English: Purification Movement) promoted 'ethnic inclusion' as a counter position to its rival, Roman Dmowski's right-wing Endecja movement, which was fuelling intense radicalism and hate towards the Jewish population in Poland. Dmowski and his Endecja constituents viewed the expulsion of Jews from Poland as the vital solution to Poland's devastating economic problems. "Poland for Poles, Jews to Madagascar" were the popular notions in the collective thinking of frustrated Catholic nationalistic masses. [5]

76

In March 1919, Polish militant Nationalists organised pogroms of Jewish communities across Poland. Roughly five months later, on the 8th of August 1919, my father was born. During the early 1920s, Endecja incited Polish Catholic students to bully and harass Jewish school children. There were many anti-Jewish riots, and universities took increasingly restrictive measures to prevent Jews from entering academic courses. In 1926 Josef Pilsudski came to power for the second time and replaced Endecja's 'ethnic assimilation' policy with the 'state assimilation' policy. The citizens were judged by their loyalty to the State, not by their religious or cultural identity. During Pilsudski's reign, and later during Kazimierz Bartel's administration from 1928 to 1935, life in Poland had improved for many Polish Jews, as they felt relatively safe during those years. Many of them opted for secularism and assimilation. [6]

In May 1935, Pilsudski passed away. The Polish Endecja emerged again, but this time, as a broader and more powerful right-wing Nationalist political force poised to exclude Jews from Polish society. Anti-Semitism once again began to escalate. Discrimination and violence against Jewish communities across the Polish countryside and shtetls rendered many Jews increasingly more destitute and vulnerable. Endecja demanded a singular ethnoreligious (Polish Catholic) framework as the foundation of Polish national identity. Essentially, militant Nationalists supported the Fascist model of fostering the Roman Catholic faith and eradicating all Jewish cultural elements from the Polish socio-political landscape. Obedience to authority, discipline, and intolerance of Jews were crucial elements of the Camp of Great Poland (Polish: Obóz Wielkiej Polski; OWP), an organisation created by Dmowski and his ilk. The OWP appealed to young activists who aspired to become young militants on university campuses. These Nationalist students believed that followers of Pilsudski's Purification Movement (i.e. Sanacja) secretly allied with the Jews for one purpose only: to kill Poles. These entrenched and hateful beliefs underpinned the National Democratic movement's repressive and aggressive attitudes towards Jewish university students and Jewish communities across Poland. For National Democratic right-wing militant followers, Jews were alien, anti-Polish, and an obstacle to the aspirations of the Polish Society. [7]

Dmowski once stated: "Catholicism is not an appendix to Polishness, but its essence". Dmowski believed that anyone who wished for Poland to exist as a separate entity from the Church was deemed an enemy of the Polish nation. This new perspective evolved into a massive wave of young Poles, who were inspired by the Polish Nationalist Right and the notion of Militant Catholicism. Concepts like 'Communism', 'Socialism', 'Sanation', and 'Jews' represented antichrist forces that had to be dealt with and eliminated. 'Catholic Totalitarianism' embraced 'Fascism', and Fascism embraced 'Catholic Totalitarianism'. [8] The militant Endecja strongly upheld the principle of 'Numerus Naullus', which stood for ending enrolments of Jewish students in public schools and universities; ending Jews' participation in administrative governing bodies, military, and in specific professions such as medicine, law, or accountancy. Jewish estates were to be confiscated and transferred for various uses by the Polish authorities and economic reforms [9].

Against this background, young militants of the Camp of Great Poland, OWP, frequently instigated pogroms against Jewish communities and Jewish university students. My father often reflected on these times and would say enthusiastically, "As a young teenager, I was never scared of the Endecja thugs. I was ready. Anyone who would say something racially motivated would give me enough reason to fight them. I was never afraid to grab some racist 'Endek' and beat him to a pulp".

Notes

1. Pakentreger, Aleksander (1988). Żydzi w Kaliszu w latach 1918-1939. Państwowe Wydawnictwo Naukowe. Jewish Historical Institute in Poland. Warsaw 1988

2. Arthur Szyk (1894-1951). Statute of Kalisz, frontispiece (Casimir the Great) (1927), Paris.jpg

3. https://en.wikipedia.org/wiki/history_of_the_jews_in_kalish

4. Kunicki M. S. (2012) Between the Brown and the Red Nationalism, Catholicism, and Communism in Twentieth Century Poland: The Politics of Boleslaw Piasecki Ohio University Press. Athens p. 7

5. Ibid., p. 8

6. Ibid., p. 10

7. Ibid., p. 11

8. Ibid., p. 12

9. Ibid., p. 17.

4. September

A day after WWII began, September 2nd, 1939, my father and his parents, Shmul, Leon, and Moyshie, hastily abandoned their home in a desperate escape to Koźminek, a tiny refuge 18 kilometres east of Kalisz. The air was thick with urgency and fear as countless Jewish families surged eastward, grasping at the tenuous hope of safety.

In Kalisz, the once-familiar streets echoed with an eerie silence as the ominous shadow of the Wehrmacht settled over the city. The realisation that many Jewish families had fled their homes did not go unnoticed by the invaders. By the 3rd and 4th of September, the fragile tranquillity was shattered by the chilling proclamations blaring from German vehicles equipped with loudspeakers: "All Jews must return to their homes." The air vibrated with cruel commands cloaked in authority.

Hope dwindled as reports of German soldiers' relentless advance filtered through. By September 5th, the once-safe haven of Koźminek was no more. Wehrmacht troops, accompanied by the menacing Nazi SS, infiltrated the village. The invading forces' presence was a stark reminder that even the most remote corners of one's world were not beyond their merciless grasp.

Determined to stay one step ahead of the encroaching danger, my father fled Koźminek, heading eastward towards the distant river Warta. As he trudged along the dusty road, a familiar silhouette emerged through the heat waves ahead, stirring a spark of recognition and hope within him. Quickening his pace, he squinted, straining to see more clearly. Could it be? His heart pounded. "Leon!" he shouted, his voice cracking with urgency.

The figure ahead paused, then turned. A heartbeat later, it was confirmed, it was indeed Leon. Relief mingled with fear as the two embraced. "What are you doing here?" my father asked breathlessly, gripping Leon's shoulders as if to anchor himself in this fleeting moment of human connection.

Leon's eyes were shadowed with grief, yet his voice remained steady, almost too calm. "Just like you, Chaim, I'm running away from the Krauts." His gaze flickered, haunted by the images he had witnessed. "They loaded Mum, Dad, Shmul, and Moyshie onto the trucks. I ran away. I reckon the Krauts don't want us dispersing all over. That's why they're taking everyone back to Kalisz," he finished, his voice trailing into a sombre conclusion.

My father's expression hardened with resolve. "We should go to Łódź and see Aunt Regina," he said. The two continued their journey with a silent nod, clinging to the fragile hope that Aunt Regina might offer them the sanctuary they desperately sought.

After a day of walking, exhaustion etched into their weary bodies. They finally stumbled into the small village of Ozorków, some 80 kilometres from Kalisz. The sight that greeted them was a stark reminder that safety was still a distant dream. German soldiers were omnipresent, a suffocating shroud over the tiny township.

As they navigated the unfamiliar streets, their hearts sank at the sight of the Jewish Synagogue on Wyszynski Street, now reduced to rubble and ashes. The sight of the destruction spoke volumes; the ruthless force that was intent on erasing Jewish identity and heritage had arrived.

The new German authorities had renamed Ozorków to Brunnstadt. The rebranded tiny town was soon engulfed in a wave of brutal anti-Semitic terror. Nazi troops, emboldened by their mission of hatred, escalated their attacks, targeting the Jewish community of Ozorków with ferocious intensity.

In the first few weeks of the invasion, the place witnessed unimaginable atrocities. Six thousand Jewish souls, once vibrant members of the Ozorków community, were mercilessly murdered.

A day later, Leon and my father, weary and dishevelled from their arduous journey, finally reached the relative sanctuary of Regina's comfortable apartment in Łódź. The contrast between their ragged appearances and the apartment's warmth was stark. Regina greeted them with open arms, her happiness evident despite the palpable tension of the times. "Come in, come in," she urged, her voice laced with welcome and worry. She quickly made them comfortable, offering steaming cups of coffee and putting together a modest meal. Her simple gesture was a balm to their battered spirits.

Regina, who had studied accountancy at Vienna University, and her husband, Arek Jakubowicz, an economist, were well-acquainted with the apprehensions that now hung over their world like a dark cloud. Arek was not home; he was visiting his family. They settled into an uneasy conversation. With a bitter tone, edged with sadness, my father said, "It does not look like Shmul will be going to his new school this week, Aunt Regina."

Regina's eyes reflected shared sorrow as she nodded, her lips pressed into a thin line of concern. "Yes, everything is closed, and people are frightened. Nobody knows what will happen," she said in a voice almost a whisper, heavy with worry and uncertainty. After a moment, she added with deep, maternal concern, "You both need to get back to your mum and dad. They probably need you." Her words hung in the air, laden with the weight of impending hardship and the enduring strength of family bonds.

Though a temporary haven, the apartment could not shield them from the encroaching darkness. But in that brief respite, surrounded by the cares and comforts of Regina's home, Leon and my father found a fleeting moment of relief and the resolve to continue their journey back home.

Regina's apartment was a modest oasis of warmth and normalcy amidst the chaos and ominous tension hanging in the air outside. The flickering candlelight cast gentle shadows on the walls, and the aroma of freshly brewed coffee mingled with the scent of home-cooked food, evoking memories of safer, happier times. Regina's presence, her quiet strength and unwavering support wrapped around them like a comforting blanket.

As they sipped their coffee, the conversation turned to the uncertainties of their situation. Regina's voice, though steady, betrayed the undercurrent of fear that gripped them all. "We hear rumours daily, but it's hard to know what to believe," she said. "The streets are filled with whispers and worry. People are vanishing without a trace. It's like living under a dark cloud that keeps getting darker."

Leon, usually the more stoic of the two, looked unusually vulnerable. "We've seen so much already, Aunt Regina. The things they're doing... It's hard to keep hope alive," he confessed, his voice thick with emotion.

Regina reached out, placing a reassuring hand on his. "Hope is what we must cling to, even in the darkest times. It's what will see us through this." Her eyes met my father's, and she added, "And as a family, we must stay together and support one another. That's how we'll survive."

The mention of the family brought a fresh wave of determination to my father. He knew his parents needed him now more than ever. The journey home would be fraught with danger, but the thought of reuniting with his family strengthened him. He glanced at Leon, seeing the same resolve reflected in his brother's eyes.

They talked late into the evening, sharing memories and stories, finding comfort in the familiar rhythms of family life. At about nine o'clock, Arek returned home. He appeared somewhat weary, but the unexpected surprise of seeing Leon and Chaim pleased him. His shoulders, usually square and confident, now slumped with the weight of the day's burdens, yet his eyes lit up with genuine warmth upon seeing his family. Leon recounted briefly what had happened in Kalisz and Kozminek, his voice steady but edged with the residual fear and exhaustion of their experiences.

Arek listened intently, his face a mask of concern. When Leon finished, Arek sighed deeply and nodded, his worries mirrored in their shared silence. "It's a troubling time for all of us," he said, his voice low and filled with a quiet resignation. "My mother is aging, and I worry about her constantly. The future... It's uncertain for all of us."

He paused, glancing at Regina, and then continued, "We have to take things one day at a time," trying to infuse his words with a strength he barely felt. "We can't let fear paralyse us. We have to be there for each other, now more than ever."

The room fell into a contemplative silence, each lost in their thoughts. The flickering candlelight cast long shadows on the walls, adding to the sombre mood. Despite the warmth of the apartment, a chill seemed to settle over them. Sensing the need to shift the mood, Regina stood up and began preparing a light supper. The familiar clatter of dishes and the comforting aroma of food provided a small semblance of normalcy.

As they sat down to eat, the conversation turned to lighter topics, a brief respite from the heavy burden of their shared anxieties. They talked again about their memories of good times, the small joys that still punctuated their lives. Each laugh and smile was a small act of defiance against the darkness encroaching upon their world.

Later that night, as they prepared for bed, Arek placed a reassuring hand on my father's shoulder. "We'll get through this," he said firmly, his voice steady and sure. "We have to believe that. For our own sake and for the sake of those we love."

My father nodded, feeling a renewed sense of hope. The warmth of Regina and Arek's home, and the kindness and love they found there, were anchors in the storm of their lives. As they settled into their makeshift beds, my father reflected on the day's events. Despite the fear and uncertainty, there was a glimmer of hope. The love and support of family, the simple acts of kindness and solidarity, were powerful antidotes to the darkness.

The room gradually fell silent, each person drifting into their thoughts and, eventually, into a restful sleep. The flickering candlelight slowly dimmed, but the warmth of their shared connection remained.

The following morning, the sun rose with pale light, filtering through the curtains and casting a soft glow over Regina's apartment. The world outside was still, and the city was not yet fully awakened. Arek, Regina, Leon, and my father gathered around the breakfast table, the air filled with the comforting aroma of freshly brewed coffee and the warmth of family togetherness.

As they ate, the conversation returned to the uncertainties that weighed on their hearts. Arek's face, usually calm and composed, now showed lines of worry as he spoke of his aging mother. "She's not as strong as she used to be," he said, his voice tinged with sorrow. "I fear for her, especially now, with everything that's happening."

Regina placed a reassuring hand on his arm. "We'll do everything we can for her, Arek. She's a fighter, just like you." Leon, his eyes still tired from his broken sleep, turned to my father. "We need to get back to Mum and Dad. They're probably frantic with worry about us." His voice was steady, but the underlying urgency was palpable. My father nodded, feeling the same pull to return home, to be with his parents in these troubling times. "Sure, the sooner we're back, the better," he concurred.

Regina's eyes filled with concern. "Be careful," she urged, her voice soft but earnest. "The roads aren't safe, and there are dangers everywhere. Promise me you'll take care of each other."

"We promise," my father replied, his voice filled with determination. "We'll get home safely. We'll be together again soon."

The weight of their impending journey settled over them as they finished their breakfast. Arek and Regina helped them gather their things and pack food and essentials for the road. The apartment, a haven of warmth and love, seemed to cling to them, a final embrace before they stepped out into the uncertain world.

The goodbyes were filled with unspoken emotions, lingering hugs, and promises that echoed with hope. Regina's eyes shone with unshed tears as she kissed their cheeks. Arek's firm handshake conveyed a silent promise of support, a reminder that they were not alone. Regina packed a small bundle of food for their journey. "Take care of each other," she said, her voice thick with emotion. Then Arek added, "And remember, no matter what happens, you have family here."

As they stepped out into the chilly dawn, the reality of their situation came crashing back. But the memory of Arek and Regina's warmth, hospitality and steadfast support stayed with them, adding to their strength and resolve.

The streets of Łódź were quiet as they began their journey, the city still shrouded in the early morning mist. The sun climbed higher, casting a golden light over the city rooftops. Leon and my father walked side by side, their steps in sync, their hearts united by a shared purpose. The familiar landmarks seemed to echo the uncertainty looming over them. But with each step, their urgency to get closer to their family home grew with every passing moment.

∞∞∞∞∞

After three arduous days of traversing the countryside, Leon and my father finally neared the outskirts of Kalisz, maybe an hour before dawn broke. Their reprieve was short-lived; a German army patrol intercepted them along the main road. My father's voice trembled with astonishment and pride as he recounted what happened next. "Suddenly, Leon vanished into the darkness," he said, still struck by the memory. "Leon was always so sharp and street-wise. He always managed to sneak out of difficult situations," he added, a touch of envy colouring his words.

My father was not so fortunate. Arrested by the Germans, he was led to a fenced yard behind a church, where he and other young men were forced to dig a deep ditch in the early hours of the morning. The air was thick with tension, the sky still cloaked in the dark hues of night. As he toiled, the harsh clink of shovels against the earth offered a grim symphony. Suddenly, at around 9 o'clock, he noticed a group of elderly Jews being rounded up.

Wehrmacht soldiers, with faces twisted in mocking smiles, coerced the old men into posing for group photographs. The soldiers laughed and jeered, their mirth a stark contrast to the fear and humiliation etched on the faces of their victims. These staged photos, a grotesque charade, were meant to deceive the Red Cross and the outside world about the Wehrmacht's treatment of Jews. The soldiers' laughter echoed across the yard, a chilling reminder of the cruelty that had become commonplace.

My father watched, his heart heavy with a mix of anger, sadness and disgust. To him, the elderly men, forced to smile for the camera, represented his community's suffering, their dignity stripped away in an instant. The soldiers' mockery was not just an insult to these men

87

but a pervasive dehumanisation that had taken root. Each camera click was a lie, a falsification of reality meant to hide the brutal truth.

As my father dug, his mind raced with thoughts of resistance and survival. The ditch they were forced to create was not just a physical task but a symbol of the grave they were all being pushed towards. The dirt beneath his feet was heavy, with the weight of countless lives disrupted and destroyed. He could feel the cold sweat on his brow, mingling with the dirt and grime, each shovel full of earth, a bitter reminder of his community's plight.

In the afternoon, any pretence of humane treatment vanished. The same soldiers lined the elderly Jews against the church wall and executed them in cold blood. My father recounted this event that seared into his memory. "While everyone stopped digging to watch this horrifying incident, I slipped into the nearby bushes and waited for the night to come." The darkness of the night cloaked his movements as he made his way to a hiding spot behind the church.

As night enveloped the yard, my father remained motionless, petrified and unsure of when, or if, it would be safe to flee. The Germans, displaying their ruthless efficiency, forced the remaining diggers to bury the executed Jews in the freshly dug mass grave. The grim work continued through the night as my father remained hidden.

The silence of the night was punctuated by the muffled sounds of shovels striking the soil. My father lay hidden, every muscle was tense, and his heart was pounding in his chest like a trapped bird. The cool night air, once a source of comfort, now felt like a shroud, pressing down on him with the weight of his fear and despair. As he lay there, memories of his family flashed before his eyes: his mother's gentle smile, his father's stern yet loving gaze, and the laughter of his siblings. He knew he had to survive, not just for himself but for those who awaited his return.

The hours stretched on, each one an eternity of waiting and listening. The Germans, methodical in their cruelty, ensured that the bodies were buried with no trace of the atrocity left behind. The diggers, without choice, performed their grim task in silence, the weight of the night's horrors etched into their faces.

Eventually, the sounds of shovelling ceased, replaced by the low murmurs of the soldiers as their captors finished their grim task. My father waited, his breath shallow, until the yard fell silent again. The soldiers and their captors finally departed, leaving the yard shrouded in an eerie stillness. He slowly stuck his head out of his hiding spot. Now, a silent eyewitness to the day's atrocities, the yard felt like a haunted space. Every shadow seemed to harbour danger, every rustle of the leaves a potential threat. The weight of what he had seen pressed heavily upon him. The day's events replayed in his mind; each recalled moment was a blunt reminder of the cruelty he had witnessed.

Then, something unexpected happened. Through the veil of darkness, he noticed a shadowy figure moving towards the church's back entrance. My father retreated fully to his hiding spot, his heart pounding in his chest, each beat a deafening roar in the stillness of the night. As he remained almost catatonic, he heard the merciless steps slowly and cautiously approaching his location and then silence. Suddenly, the intruder peered into the cavity, meeting my father's eyes. The moment stretched into an eternity; it was a Wehrmacht soldier. The soldier looked directly at him, in silence, and then he left just as silently. 'Why…Why had he left without a word?' My father thought. 'Why didn't the soldier raise an alarm?' These questions swirled in his mind, mingling with the lingering fear and confusion.

The soldier's face, partially obscured by the shadows, was a mask of inscrutability. My father had expected a shout, a cold barrel of the gun, or the end of his desperate flight. But instead, there was only silence and the retreating footsteps of the soldier. This unexpected encounter left him both relieved and more anxious than ever.

As the minutes passed, my father wrestled with his emotions. He dared not move, unsure if the soldier might return with reinforcements. The silence around him felt oppressive; the darkness was a blanket that helped to conceal him from the external ominous danger. He strained his ears for any sound, any indication of a threat, but there was none, only the soft rustle of leaves in the night's breeze.

The soldier returned moments later. My father could hear familiar, cautious steps moving closer and closer. Suddenly, the soldier peered again into the cavity, extending his hand to offer a metal cup filled with water. He bent towards my father and whispered, "Wasser?" (English: "Water?"), offering the cup. My father accepted it with obedient hands, eyes wide with trepidation.

The soldier's words were both a warning and an unexpected lifeline. "Ich schlage vor, Sie verlassen das Gelände bald... vor dem Morgengrauen. Übrigens bin ich kein Deutscher; Ich komme aus Österreich; Denken Sie daran; wir sind gute Menschen." (English: "I suggest you leave the grounds soon... before dawn. By the way, I am not German; I'm from Austria; remember that we are good people"). My father, overwhelmed with a complex mix of gratitude and survival instinct, whispered back, "Danke schön."

As the soldier disappeared into the night, my father waited only a few more tense minutes before seizing his chance. Slipping out of the church grounds, he ran under the cover of darkness, his feet pounding a desperate rhythm through Miejski Park and towards the western part of the city. His destination was clear: home.

As the first light of dawn began to creep over the horizon, my father reached his apartment block on Poznańska Street. He knocked softly, his heart racing. The door creaked open, and there stood Leon, a look of immense relief washing over his face. Moyshie, Shmul, and their parents were asleep, oblivious to the night's silent reunion. Leon embraced him, holding him tightly. Despite the odds and the perils, his brother was back. They were all home again, a small sanctuary amidst the chaos, wrapped in the fragile promise of togetherness and hope.

∞∞∞∞∞∞

As the Nazis invaded Poland's western towns, a shadow of terror enveloped Jewish communities, turning their lives into a relentless nightmare. Every day brought fresh horrors; public humiliations were routine, and the physically able were forced into backbreaking labour. Amidst this turmoil, Yosif was one of many forced to perform hard labour. He vanished from dawn till dusk, returning home only late at night. Golda spent those long hours gripped by fear, anxiously awaiting his return. Yosif would stagger in, utterly exhausted, his clothes tattered and his spirit worn thin. Rarely did he bring anything with him. On fortunate nights, there might be a half loaf of stale bread in his hands, a meagre prize that barely alleviated their hunger.

The municipal councils, once symbols of civil order, had transformed into local governing offices of the General Gubernia (German General Government), their authority now a tool of oppression. My father, desperate to find a way out of Kalisz, visited the Bürgermeister's Office at the old Municipal Town Hall. Hope flickered in his heart as he approached the stone building, stepping inside with trepidation and resolve. Facing the stern officer, he requested, "Sir, I need papers to travel safely to Lviv," he stated, trying to suppress the tremble in his voice. The officer's gaze sharpened. "What is your address?" he asked. "2 Poznańska Street," my father replied, barely a whisper. The officer's expression hardened instantly. "That is a Jewish district," he said flatly. "I'm afraid I cannot help you."

My father walked out of the office with profound frustration and entrapment weighing heavily upon him. The walls of his world felt like they were closing in, every door to freedom firmly shut. As he made his way home, the reality of his plight pressed down on him, grim and unyielding. Back home, the familiar faces of Leon, Moyshie, Shmul, and their parents were a reminder of what was at stake. In the darkest of times, their unity was their strength amidst the storm of menace and uncertainty.

As the peril grew increasingly dire for the Jewish community of Kalisz, the need to escape became more urgent and more fraught with danger. Days passed without Leon's return, a chilling silence that spoke volumes of the risks they all faced. It was then that my father, realising the gravity of the situation, made a decision that weighed heavily on his heart.

"Mum, I have to go. I cannot stay here any longer," he voiced his resolve, his words carrying a mix of determination and sorrow. Golda understood the unspoken urgency in his eyes. She decided to walk with him towards the Włodański House, a distance that felt both painfully long and agonisingly short.

The streets, usually bustling with the rhythms of daily life, now seemed to hold their breath in anticipation. Every shadow, every distant sound, was a reminder of the dangers lurking around every corner. Golda walked beside her son, her heart heavy with unspoken fears. The world around them seemed to blur, their focus solely on the path ahead and the bittersweet moments they shared.

In those fleeting moments before parting, my father made a promise born of necessity. "I won't return if I manage to leave Kalisz, but I will write to you. You will know where I am," he assured her, his voice laced with hope and sadness.

Golda, her gaze filled with a mother's love and worry, offered her final words of advice and love. "Go with care, Chaim. Trust your instincts. If the danger becomes too great, come back to us swiftly. If I don't see you return, I will hold onto the belief that you are safe," she said, her voice a tender plea that echoed the depth of a mother's boundless love and concern.

As they reached the Włodański House, the moment of farewell arrived, heavy with the weight of uncertainty and the ache of impending separation. Golda embraced her son tightly; the warmth of her embrace felt like a fleeting shield against the cold reality they faced. My father held her close, drawing strength from her unwavering love.

"Take this," Golda said, pressing a small, worn envelope into his hand. "Inside, there are a few coins and a note. Use them wisely, and remember, my love goes with you wherever you go."

My father nodded; his throat was tight with emotion. "I will, Mum. Thank you. I promise I'll find a way to tell you I'm safe."

With a final embrace, they parted ways. Golda watched as her son walked away, his figure growing smaller in the distance until he was just a shadow on the horizon. She stood there, her heart clinging to the hope that he would find safety and freedom.

As my father made his way through the streets of Kalisz, he felt the weight of his mother's love and the responsibility of his promise. Each step was a step away from the familiar, from the life he had known. Unknowingly, these were the steps towards survival and the possibility of a future free from fear.

The journey ahead was filled with dangers, both known and unknown. As night fell, he found a temporary refuge, a place to gather his thoughts and plan his next move. The envelope his mother had given him was a tangible connection to the home he had left behind. He opened it, finding the coins and the note written in Golda's familiar, careful script. The words were simple, but they carried the weight of her love and the hope for his safety.

"Chaim, my brave son, trust in yourself and the goodness that still exists in the world. We will meet again; I believe this with all my heart. Stay strong and know that you are always in our thoughts and hearts. With all my love, Mum."

He folded the note carefully, tucking it back into the envelope. The coins would help him on his journey, but the note was his true treasure, reminding him why he had to keep moving forward. The darkness around him was vast, but within him, the light of his mother's love burned brightly, a constant source of strength.

∞∞∞∞∞

With a heavy heart and a resolve forged in the fire of necessity, my father embarked on his perilous journey, each step carrying him further away from the familiar streets of Kalisz and toward an uncertain future. His departure marked a physical distance and a gulf of emotions, leaving a family poised on the precipice of unknown trials and tribulations.

As Kalisz fell under the iron grip of the Wehrmacht and SS, clad in their ominous black uniforms, fear lurked in every shadow, and danger prowled the streets like a hungry beast. The soldiers' chilling query, "Jude?" echoed through the air like a death sentence, sending a shiver down my father's spine.

Quick wit and desperation became his armour as he navigated the treacherous terrain of suspicion and hatred. To the soldiers' probing glances and insidious questioning, he calmly replied, "Nix Jude," denying his heritage to ensure his survival. The true enemy, he realised, was not the uniformed Germans but the potential betrayal by his fellow countrymen.

On Wrocławska Street, faced with an approaching army truck, my father's heart raced with fear as he raised his arm to halt the Wehrmacht vehicle. He commanded in Hochdeutsch, "Halt stehen bleiben!" Curious soldiers gazed at him as their truck halted, their scrutiny palpable in the air. One of the soldiers asked: "Is Vas a louse?". My father answered in German: "I am travelling to my cousin in Zduńska Wola". The other soldier said, "You speak Hochdeutsch!? Are there many people like you here?" My father confidently laughed in response. The driver told him to jump in at the back. He confidently climbed onto the truck packed with Wehrmacht soldiers.

As my father spun a tale of a journey to his cousin in Zduńska Wola in flawless German, he felt a surge of adrenaline at his audacity. The soldiers' surprise at his linguistic proficiency in German was his saving grace. In the camaraderie of shared language, barriers momentarily dissolved. With confidence that belied the turmoil in his heart, my father wove a narrative of family ties and filial duty, painting a picture of a beloved uncle's yearning for his German roots, his failing health, and a desperate need for familial connection. The soldiers, touched by my father's story, displayed curiosity and empathy toward him.

The journey with the Wehrmacht soldiers unfolded like a fragile dance of deception and survival. Amidst the truck's rumble and the soldiers' light-hearted responses and laughter, my father's burden felt lighter, his fears momentarily forgotten in the shared humanity of the moment. When the truck halted at Zduńska Wola, he descended amidst warm farewells from the soldiers, their parting gift, a block of German dark chocolate, a small token of kindness in a world consumed by cruelty.

With a mixture of relief and apprehension, my father successfully navigated the steps of his escape from Kalisz, finding temporary sanctuary in Zduńska Wola at the home of an elderly Jewish woman known to his mother. The night offered a brief respite in the tumultuous journey ahead.

As dawn broke over Zduńska Wola, my father mustered his strength and resolve to continue his quest for freedom. Making his way to the office of the local Bürgermeister, he greeted the official in Hochdeutsch, the language of his survival in a world turned upside down. With unwavering determination, he presented a bold request, papers to travel to Lviv under the guise of visiting his ailing German cousin.

The Bürgermeister, a figure of authority amidst the chaos of war, listened to my father's plea with a measured gaze. Recognising the urgency in his eyes and the weight of his words, he nodded solemnly and requested a brief moment of patience.

Returning swiftly, the Bürgermeister presented my father with a document that bore the weight of newfound freedom. The official statement declared: "Heinrich Poznański is of German heritage. All authorities, please enable the holder of this pass to move freely throughout the German General Gubernia." The words, both a shield and a sword in the perilous landscape of occupied Poland, held the promise of safe passage through the shadows of danger and ambiguity.

With a decisive stamp bearing the ominous symbol of the Swastika and the Bürgermeister's authoritative signature above the title, "Bürgermeister, Zduńska Wola," the path to liberation laid open. Armed with his General Gubernia Pass and a heart heavy with the weight of what he had left behind, my father embarked on the next leg of his journey: a train ride from Zduńska Wola to Przemyśl.

After the invasion of Poland by Nazi Germany, roughly two weeks later, on 17th September, the Soviet Union took over eastern parts of Poland as per the Molotov – Ribbentroff agreement between Germany and the USSR [1]. The border between the two occupants ran through the middle of Przemysl, along the San River. My father's journey bore further witness to the horrors that unfolded at the intersection of two occupying forces. Arriving at the Przemysl train station, the blatant reality of occupation unfolded before his eyes. He noticed three Wehrmacht soldiers beating a Hasidic Jew with the butts of their rifles; their faces contorted with hostility and dehumanising hate that fuelled their actions. My father overheard them say in German, "You lied, you filthy Jew! Why did you say you only had 80 Zloty in your fucking dirty wallet? We do not like lying Jews!" The victim fell to the ground unconscious, no longer responding to further blows and kicks, oblivious to the soldiers' hateful words, dripping with disdain and anti-Semitic vitriol.

Despite the gut-wrenching scene, my father pressed on, his steps heavy with the weight of witnessing another senseless brutality. Along the riverbank, a moment of fleeting respite beckoned in the form of a group boarding a wooden boat; their expressions blended hope and desperation, mirroring my father's. He joined them. As the boat got closer to the other side of the river, a Soviet soldier shouted: "Go back, or I will shoot!". The boat continued to move forward. The Soviet soldier fired a shot in the air. The crack of a gunshot shattered the stillness as the soldier's call to retreat was met with defiance by my father and his fellow passengers. As the boat reached the opposite shore, my father and four others stepped onto Soviet-occupied land. Another soldier appeared, armed with a Soviet submachine gun, and ordered them to follow him. With each step they took, they were acutely aware of the fragile line between survival and subjugation in a world ravaged by war. My father and his companions walked in uncertainty, their fate resting in the hands of those who now controlled their lives.

5. Exile to the East

Between October 1939 and July 1943, my father was in exile from his occupied homeland of Poland. He experienced several noteworthy events during this period. Indeed, he spoke about these often, but not as frequently as he talked about his family and life in Poland. Hence, I only have fragments of information drawn from the stories he would speak about concerning this period to inform this section. However, I also have some personal notes scribbled down on a few bits of paper during the last few times I saw my father, when he was at the end of his life, dying from cancer, in our family home in Springvale, Melbourne. In February 1997, he agreed to answer many of my questions, as he was bedridden and physically frail.

∞∞∞∞∞∞

Upon crossing the General Gubernia border into the Soviet Union, my father faced arrest and was subsequently transported to Lviv, where officials processed his illegal status within the USSR. His journey led him to Volgograd, Lisychansk, Odessa, Kiev, Poltava, and Voroshilovgrad. Throughout these places, my father often reminisced about the individuals he encountered, frequently describing them as compassionate souls. Through the narratives he shared during my childhood, I understood that these people extended kindness beyond measure, ensuring his comfort and offering a warm embrace during his travels.

In Volgograd lived Ilya Mirevsky, a hardworking mother of two daughters, Rosa and Paya. Her husband served as the Presiding Member at a local Kolkhoz. When he learned from my father that he had some basic cabinet-making training, Ilya's husband tirelessly sought work opportunities for him. Eventually, he secured a job as a woodwork instructor at a school 18 kilometres away from

Voroshilovgrad. However, due to my father's frequent lateness, he was dismissed.

After leaving the school, Ilya's husband arranged for my father to work at a factory manufacturing wire coils for mattresses. Unfortunately, his output did not meet management's expectations, leading to another dismissal. Despite these setbacks, Ilya's husband persisted and secured a job for him at a furniture factory in Lisychansk. The daily journey across icy, snow-covered fields to reach the factory entrance proved gruelling, especially without proper winter clothing.

One day, after bidding farewell to the Mirevsky family, my father travelled to Odessa. Still, he found it was impossible to secure any work, as he did not have a secure permanent visa. With its bustling port and lively streets, Odessa seemed indifferent to his plight. One of the prospective employers told him to look for a job in the nearby town, Piervomaisk, where the Kirovsky Furniture Manufacturing plant offered a glimmer of hope.

The factory director was Mr Gendelman, a man whose demeanour was as unyielding as the oak they crafted into furniture. Gendelman, himself Jewish, recognised my father's heritage immediately. Yet, instead of offering kinship, he mistreated my father. Gendelman's approach towards my father was harsher than any other worker, a cruel irony born out of fear. He did not wish to be accused of favouring Jews and discriminating against others, so his behaviour towards my father was visibly adverse. The constant humiliation, the harsh words, and the deliberate targeting wore him down. His heart, already heavy with the burdens of displacement, could not bear the added weight of Gendelman's scorn. He decided to resign, leaving him with a bitter taste of anger and disappointment that lingered within him for some time.

Desperation led him to take a reckless chance. He boarded a train to Kyiv without a ticket, a gamble that promised freedom or further trouble. His luck ran out when the ticket master discovered him and forced him off the train at Poltava Station. From the bustling chaos of the train, he was led to the Station Office, an unwelcoming place where he waited for the police to arrive.

At the Poltava Police Station, he spent several nights in remand. The cells were cold and starkly uninviting, the air thick with the despair of countless others who had found themselves in similar predicaments. Each night stretched into an eternity, his thoughts a tangled web of fear and uncertainty. When he finally stood before the Judge at the Poltava Magistrates' Court, the prosecutor recommended a Community Work Order, a sentence that felt like a lifeline amid his growing desperation.

He was sent to the local electricity plant and assigned menial work. The labour was hard and thankless, but it was work, nonetheless. Each day, he toiled, the rhythmic hum of the machines a backdrop to his silent contemplation. The work gave him purpose and sheltered him from the darkness of despair within.

When his Community Work Order ended, he found employment in a toy-making workshop. The shift from the harsh, industrial environment of the electricity plant to the delicate, creative work of crafting toys was comforting. Here, amidst the brightly coloured wood, he found a semblance of peace. Despite the adversity and countless obstacles, he continued to move forward. The journey from Odesa to Piervomaisk, from the humiliation at Kirovsky Furniture Manufacturing to the cold cells of Poltava, and finally to the warmth of the toy-making workshop, was a journey of endurance and hope.

He reflected on his path as he lay in his modest room in the quiet night hours. No matter how painful, each step had brought him to this moment. The future was uncertain, but the present held a promise of renewal. In the simple act of assembling toys, he found a way to reclaim his dignity and humanity. The world outside remained tumultuous, but within the confines of the workshop, he discovered a sanctuary of his own making.

It is not known where my father resided in Poltava. He often spent his free time in the park, walking along the tranquil Vorskla River. With its winding paths and serene atmosphere, the park became a refuge for him, where he could escape the harshness of his daily life. Here, amidst the rustling leaves and the gentle murmur of the river, he met his first love, Ludmila Mozak.

Ludmila was a bright and spirited Pedagogy student at the Poltava National Pedagogical University. Their first meeting was serendipitous, a chance encounter that quickly became deeper. She had a way of bringing light into his world. Her presence was a consolation to his weary soul, and her youthful exuberance starkly contrasted with the heaviness of his disappointing experiences.

My father and Ludmila shared countless evenings in the park. He spoke of her with a fondness that softened his eyes. His voice was tinged with nostalgia as he reminisced about their walks under the canopy of trees. The moonlight would cast silver ripples on the water's surface, creating a magical backdrop for their unfolding romance.

Their conversations were filled with dreams and hopes that young lovers share. With her passion for teaching and her love for learning, Ludmila inspired him to see the world with a renewed sense of wonder. They would sit on a bench by the river, her head resting on his shoulder, discussing their future and shared dreams.

In Ludmila, my father found a kindred spirit, someone who understood his struggles and shared his aspirations. Their bond was forged in the quiet moments they spent together, away from the world's prying eyes. The park became their place, where they could be themselves, free from judgment and fear.

As they walked along the river, hand in hand, my father felt a sense of peace that had eluded him for so long. The hardships he had endured seemed to fade into the background, and the future was no longer a source of anxiety; instead, it was filled with promise.

In the years that followed, my father often looked back on those days with a mixture of longing and gratitude. The park, the river, and Ludmila had been a chapter of his life filled with beauty and hope. And though the world continued to challenge him, the love he had found by the Vorskla River gave him the strength to keep moving forward, ever hopeful, ever resilient. But how far their relationship had progressed, he has never revealed.

One deeply poignant aspect of my father's story was his admission that he received a letter from his mother during his time in Poltava. The letter arrived unexpectedly at his doorstep in February 1941, carrying a weight that shattered the tranquillity of his days. The words were few, but they resonated with an urgency that shook him to the core:

"Dear Chaim, have you seen Leon? We are here at 13 Spokojna Street, in Warsaw. If you haven't seen him, please look for him. Leon is where you are."

The letter, written in Polish, struck my father immediately as it reached his hands. The handwriting was unmistakably different from his mother's. My father had been writing to his parents in Kalisz, but someone had redirected his letters to a temporary address in Warsaw, where Golda, Yosif, Moyshie, and Shmul were staying.

His mind swirled with a mixture of emotions as he read and reread the written words. The letter's cryptic message and the unfamiliar handwriting filled him with many questions and unease. How had his family ended up in Warsaw? And how did they know about Leon's movements? How did they know that Leon was in the Soviet Union? How did they know that he was in Poltava? My father felt perplexed but relieved and encouraged that his parents and two younger brothers were safe in the Polish Capital. The letter's impact was profound. It felt as if the world had shifted beneath his feet, the familiar ground replaced by a landscape of uncertainty. His thoughts turned to Leon, whose fate now seemed intertwined with his own.

The urgency in his mother's written words echoed in his mind, propelling him into action. A renewed sense of purpose marked the days that followed; the serene moments with Ludmila now carried an undercurrent of urgency. His mother's plea resonated deeply, compelling him to find Leon and to understand the mysteries surrounding his family's sudden relocation.

In the quiet moments of reflection, he would reread the letter, drawing strength from his mother's words. The mystery of the unfamiliar handwriting and the unanswered questions about Leon's whereabouts lingered, but they did not diminish the letter's significance.

On reflection, the historical data that came into light approximately 50 years after WWII suggests that if Leon had been near Poltava, there was a grim likelihood that he was no longer alive when Golda's letter reached my father in February 1941. There is a high probability that Leon had been detained in Kharkiv prison during the early months of 1940. During this period, numerous Polish officers, intellectuals, and other illegal Polish refugees were held in Soviet prisons.

On the chilling evening of March 5, 1940, Lavrentiy Beria, the ominous Chief of the NKVD, penned a letter to Stalin. He painted a dire picture, asserting that the majority of the imprisoned Poles were unyielding foes of the Soviet Union. With a cold, calculating tone,

Beria urged Stalin to authorise the execution of all Polish prisoners without the semblance of due process. This, he argued, was a crucial, pre-emptive strike to protect the Soviet regime from these supposed anti-Soviet elements.

Stalin, with his inner circle of loyal confidants. Voroshilov, Molotov, Mikoyan, Kalinin, and Kaganovich swiftly and ruthlessly agreed. They signed the death warrant for thousands, sealing the fate of all Polish prisoners languishing in Belarusian and Ukrainian prisons. This grim decision, rooted in Beria's deeply flawed and paranoid assessment, set in motion one of the darkest chapters of Soviet history.

The executions were carried out with brutal efficiency in Katyń, Kharkiv, and Miednoje. A single gunshot to the back of the head, echoing in the desolate forest, marked the end for each of the 22,000 Polish prisoners. Between April and May 1940, the NKVD, with cold precision, executed these men without charges, without trials, and mercy.

Was Leon one of those countless innocent souls? A 19-year-old young man trapped in the nightmarish gulags of Starobielsk, Ostaszkow, Kozielsk, or perhaps Kharkiv prison? Was Leon among those led to the Katyń forest, where the trees bore silent witness to the massacre? These haunting questions continue to linger unanswered, casting a shadow over history, leaving Leon's fate shrouded in agonising mystery.

The gulags, those bleak fortresses of suffering, were notorious for their brutality and the despair they bred. Kharkiv, Starobielsk, Ostaszkow, Kozielsk, names that resonated with the echoes of countless voices silenced by cruelty. The release of declassified information in 1992 pointed to a very likely possibility that Leon endured unimaginable hardships before he was murdered in the quiet of the Katyń forest, along with thousands of other Polish detainees.

In his heart, my father clung to the hope that somehow, against all odds, Leon had survived. He wishfully imagined Leon finding some small refuge, a place where he could live safely until the storm passed. But, in reality, he would not have suspected that the Soviet NKVD operatives would have murdered Leon and thousands of other Polish men. That thought was simply unacceptable at the time, and for a long time after the war.

Soon after my father received the letter from his mother, another extraordinary event unfolded. One cold evening in late February 1941, my father was working in his workshop when the door burst open, and three ominous secret police officers stormed in. Without explanation, they forcefully arrested him and dragged him to the local detention centre. For the next two harrowing weeks, he was held in custody, bewildered and terrified, with no clue of the reason behind his sudden imprisonment.

In the oppressive confines of his cell, my father found an unexpected ally in his fellow inmate, Ghviruk, the once-influential deputy of Lev Trotsky from the time of the 1917 October Revolution. Ghviruk, who had stood beside Trotsky during the turbulent rise of the Bolsheviks, had witnessed the ruthless political manipulation that followed Lenin's death in 1924. Trotsky, who Stalin outmanoeuvred in the vicious struggle for power, was eventually exiled, and his loyal deputy, Ghviruk, was condemned to life behind bars. Sharing this small cell with Ghviruk was a Jewish engineer who, in a surprising twist of fate, taught my father the intricate game of chess. These moments of intellectual respite provided a brief escape from the relentless oppression surrounding them.

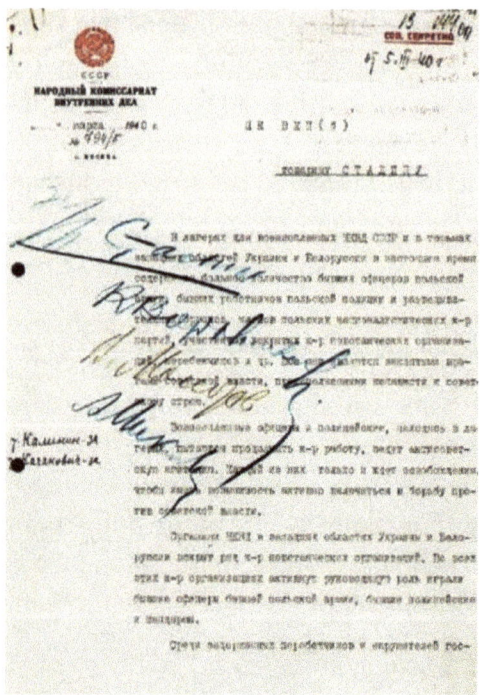

The accepted proposal of Lavrentiy Beria to execute former Polish army and police officers in NKVD prisoner of war camps and prisons. March 1940. [1]

The document is addressed: TOP SECRET – From the CENTRAL COMMITTEE OF THE COMMUNIST PARTY OF THE SOVIET UNION to COMRADE STALIN:

In the NKVD POW camps and the prisons of the western oblasts of Ukraine and Belorussia, there is currently a large number of former officers of the Polish army, former Polish police officers and employees of intelligence agencies, members of Polish nationalist c-r (counterrevolutionary) parties, participants in underground c-r rebel organisations, defectors and so on. All of them are implacable enemies of Soviet power and full of hatred for the Soviet system. POW officers and policemen located in the camps are attempting to continue c-r work and are leading anti-Soviet agitation. Each of them is simply waiting to be freed so they can have the opportunity to actively join the fight against Soviet power. NKVD agents in the western oblasts of Ukraine and Belorussia have uncovered several c-r rebel organisations. In each of these c-r organisations the former officers of the former Polish army and former Polish police officers played an active leadership role. Among the detained defectors and violators of the state…"- (Signatures: In favour – Stalin, Voroshilov, Molotov, Mikoyan) (In margin: Comrade Kalinin – In favour. Comrade Kaganovich – In favour.) [2]

In mid-March 1941, after a harrowing fortnight, my father was transferred to a crowded and stifling room. Here, he found himself in the company of notable figures who shared his plight. Among them were Count Stanislav Szeptycki, the brother of the esteemed Polish Archbishop Cardinal Szeptycki; the Provincial Governor of Lviv, Wojewoda Sikorski; and Professor Zalcer, a lecturer from Lviv University. These distinguished men, each bearing their own tragic stories, spoke Polish, creating a fragile camaraderie amidst the suffocating despair.

The room was so densely packed that any movement was nearly impossible. Bodies pressed against bodies, the air thick with the scent of fear and desperation. My father endured at least two or three days in this overcrowded hell, facing extreme and unimaginable conditions. Once a day, the heavy iron door would creak open, and an oversized aluminium bowl would be passed from the raised hands of one prisoner to another. The bowl was filled to the brim with salty anchovies. Desperate to quench their hunger and exhaustion, the prisoners would grab handfuls of the tiny fish.

My father, driven by starvation, was about to do the same when Szeptycki urgently whispered, "Son, do not eat this stuff, or you will die." Szeptycki was right. The guards provided no water, and those who consumed the salty fish would collapse, succumbing to dehydration and heart failure within hours. The prisoners' hope for survival dwindled with each passing moment in this cruel, suffocating pit.

The shared agony in that room was palpable. Each man's face told a story of lost dignity and shattered dreams. The notable figures, stripped of their titles and status, were now equals in misery. Count Szeptycki, his eyes hollow yet burning with quiet defiance, became a silent leader among them. His whispered warnings and quiet strength gave the men hope in the darkness.

Wojewoda Sikorski (English: Voivode Sikorski), once a man of power and influence, now sat slumped against the wall, his face a mask of exhaustion. Yet, in his eyes, there was a steely resolve, a reminder of the spirit that had once led him. Professor Zalcer, though frail and weakened, would often murmur lines of poetry or fragments of lectures, a poignant attempt to hold onto the world of intellect and beauty amidst the squalor.

In this nightmarish existence, the men found solace in their shared humanity. They spoke of their lives before the darkness descended, of families and homes, of the Poland they had known and loved. My father, younger and perhaps more resilient, absorbed their stories, drawing strength from their resilience and wisdom. The cramped room became a strange sanctuary, where the bonds of camaraderie and the power of memory offered a fragile shield against despair.

Each day blurred into another, each one an eternity of suffering. The ritual of the iron door creaking open, the cursed bowl of anchovies, and the silent vigil against death became the slow rhythm of their lives. My father's body grew weaker, but his spirit, fortified by the whispers of Szeptycki and the murmurings of Zalcer, remained unbroken.

One evening, as the last light of day filtered through the narrow cracks in the walls, Professor Zalcer began to recite a poem. His voice, though weak, carried the weight of unspoken emotions. The verses, woven with themes of endurance and hope, resonated deeply with the men. At that moment, the room, despite its oppressive air, felt lighter, as if the words themselves had the power to lift them from their suffering.

My father closed his eyes, letting the words wash over him. He thought of his family, of the days when life had been filled with simple joys and the promise of tomorrow. The memory of his mother's embrace, his father's steady hand, and the laughter of his siblings filled his heart, giving him the strength to face another day.

In the darkness of that overcrowded room, surrounded by men who had once been pillars of society, my father found the essence of human dignity. The conditions were inhumane, but the spirit of those men, their refusal to succumb to despair, was a light of hope in the abyss.

And so, amidst the darkness and despair, my father survived. The lessons learned in that stifling room, the bonds forged in suffering, would stay with him forever. The names of Szeptycki, Sikorski, and Zalcer remained etched in his memory, symbols of the enduring power of the human spirit in the face of unimaginable adversity.

Finally, my father was brought into the courtroom before the Judge, Presiding Magistrate Kallick. The air was tense, and the room was a sombre theatre where fate was decided. Kallick, his face a mask of stern authority, pronounced in stern Russian that the evidence from secret sources found my father guilty of spying on the Soviet Union.

Desperation laced my father's voice as he proclaimed his innocence, explaining that he was not a spy but a Jew who had fled Nazi persecution. His words, filled with urgency and truth, seemed to bounce off the walls, unheard and unheeded. Kallick, unwavering, reiterated that the evidence before him labelled my father as a spy and a Hitler sympathiser. The Judge's words fell like a death sentence: five years of hard labour in the Far East, Siberia. The hollow accusation of being a "Hitler sympathiser" was eventually dropped, but the damage was done.

The courtroom was silent, the weight of the verdict pressing down like a suffocating shroud. My father stood there, a man condemned by lies, his pleas for justice swallowed by the indifferent machinery of a regime that saw enemies everywhere. The faces around him, stern officials, dispassionate guards, and a few onlookers, blurred together in a tableau of cold detachment.

Judge Kallick's unchanging expression sealed my father's fate with a stroke of his pen. The declaration of five years of hard labour in Siberia was more than a sentence; it was a condemnation of a living nightmare. My father's heart sank; the gravity of the situation settled over him like a leaden cloak. The words "Hitler sympathiser," though retracted, hung in the air, a cruel twist of irony for a man who had fled from the very terror that now ensnared him.

As the guards led him away, my father's mind raced. The icy grip of fear mingled with a fierce determination to survive. He thought of his family, the letter he had received, and the promises he had made to himself. The path ahead was bleak, a journey into the heart of Siberia's frozen wilderness, but he clung to the hope that somehow, against all odds, he would endure.

Count General Stanislav Szeptycki (the documented history shows that Szeptycki survived the war and headed the Polish Red Cross between 1945 and 1950) [3].

Immediately after the judgment was handed down, my father was handcuffed and thrust onto a train bound for Kharkiv Prison. There, he was thrown into solitary confinement. For a week, he endured relentless interrogations at all hours of the night, leaving him mentally and physically exhausted. The shadows under his eyes deepened, and his spirit hung in the balance on the verge of breaking.

The following week, my father was herded onto another train, this time crammed full of prisoners. The train journeyed toward Novosibirsk and then to Bukhta Nakhodka. By a stroke of fate, his short stature allowed him to claim a spot on the top bunk with a small window. Through this tiny portal, he spent countless hours gazing at the sprawling Siberian landscape as the train travelled thousands of kilometres relentlessly.

As the train chugged along, time seemed to stretch and blur. One plain field merged seamlessly into another; dense forests gave way to plain fields and then, more forests. Clear skies slowly turned grey and cloudy, though the exact moment this change occurred was lost in the monotony. The future loomed unpromising, each passing moment a reminder of his precarious journey into the unknown.

The small window offered a fleeting connection to the world beyond the metal confines of the train. My father's eyes, once filled with the light of hope, now stared out with a mixture of resignation and determination. The vast Siberian landscape, with its endless expanse of fields and forests, seemed both beautiful and indifferent. It was a world that existed apart from his suffering, a reminder of the freedom he had lost.

Each night, as the train rattled on, he would lie awake, listening to the rhythmic clatter of the wheels on the tracks. The sound became a sort of lullaby, a constant in the ever-changing journey. In the dim light of the compartment, the faces of his fellow prisoners reflected the same weariness and despair. They were men from different walks of life, now united by their shared fate.

The nights in solitary confinement in Kharkiv had taken a toll on him. The relentless interrogations, the cold, damp walls of the cell, and the absence of human contact had worn him down. He had felt the sharp edges of hopelessness, the creeping sense of being forgotten by the world. But now, surrounded by others, he found a strange solace in their collective presence. They were all fighting the same battle, enduring the same journey into the unknown.

During the day, he would peer out of the tiny window, watching the landscape pass by. With its rugged beauty and harsh environment, the Siberian wilderness seemed to mirror his inner turmoil. There were moments when the train would slow down, and he could catch glimpses of distant mountains or a solitary figure walking along a dirt path with his husky leading the way. These brief snapshots of life outside the train were a bittersweet reminder of what he had lost and what he still yearned for.

As the days passed, the monotony of the journey became a kind of endurance test. The endless expanse of Siberia stretched before him, an unbroken horizon that seemed to promise nothing but more suffering. Yet, amidst the despair, there were flickers of hope. The camaraderie among the prisoners, the shared stories whispered in the dark, and the silent understanding that they were not alone in their struggle gave him the strength to hold his vision of a better tomorrow and to keep hoping.

The train's destination, Bukhta Nakhodka, loomed like a spectre in his mind. It was a place of hard labour where men were sent to be forgotten. But my father clung to the belief that he would survive and endure whatever came his way. The memories of his family and the promise he had made to himself to return to them fuelled his determination.

As the train finally approached Bukhta Nakhodka, my father prepared himself for the next chapter of his ordeal. The future was uncertain, but he faced it with a newfound resolve. The harsh Siberian landscape and the endless days and nights on the train had forged within him a steely determination. He would survive, endure, and one day return to his loved family. The journey was far from over, but he was ready to face whatever came next.

∞∞∞∞∞∞

When my father arrived in Bukhta Nakhodka at the beginning of April 1941, he was immediately assigned to cutting down large birch and pine trees. The crisp and biting Siberian air cut through his thin clothing as he swung his axe, and the rhythmic thud of wood splintering echoed through the forest. His daily sustenance was a piece of densely baked tough bread with a sparse smear of butter and a dollop of honey, a meagre ration that barely fuelled his body for exhausting labour.

After weeks of intense labouring in the open fields of Nakhodka, his body had become a canvas of aches and calluses. One day, he was taken aboard a cargo ship, the iron behemoth groaning as it ploughed through the icy waters. It transported him north to the Chukotskiy Poluostrov, a mere 60 kilometres from Alaska. The cold was relentless, a stark and unforgiving landscape where the ground seemed perpetually frozen.

In this desolate wilderness, his new task was to plant dynamite in the rocks, searching for gold. The work was perilous, and the blasts echoing through the barren land were a harsh reminder of the constant danger. The promise of a glass of Russian vodka and a bowl of 'Soczewica' (Lentil soup) for every gold nugget found was a cruel incentive. Hunger gnawed at him constantly, a relentless companion that sapped his strength and will.

Once, driven by ravenous hunger, he was offered an entire bucket of 'Soczewica'. The sight of the rich and fragrant steaming lentil soup was a moment of sheer unadulterated relief. He ate voraciously, spoon after spoon, his hunger momentarily abated by warmth and sustenance. But in his desperation, he nearly risked a stomach rupture, the pain a sharp reminder of the fine line between survival and succumbing to the harsh conditions.

Each day, the search for gold continued a monotonous cycle of labour and fleeting rewards. The men around him, fellow prisoners, were a silent brotherhood, their eyes hollow with exhaustion and the shared burden of their plight. In the face of such relentless hardship, a grim camaraderie emerged, a bond forged in the fires of their collective suffering.

The landscape, though harsh, was simply beautiful. The snow-capped peaks in the distance, the endless expanse of tundra, and the clear, cold rivers running through the land were all part of a world that seemed both timeless and indifferent to its struggles. My father found a strange peace and harmony in these surroundings, reminding him of the world beyond the labour camps, which still held beauty and wonder.

The vodka, promised as a reward, was a brief respite—a momentary escape from harsh reality. Each glass was savoured, the fiery liquid a small comfort against the cold. The 'Soczewica', though simple, became a symbol of hope, a reminder that even in the bleakest of times, there were moments of reprieve.

My father's body grew leaner as weeks turned into months, and his muscles hardened from the constant labour. Yet, his spirit remained unbroken. In the quiet moments, when the day's work was done, he would sit by the fire, the warmth seeping into his bones, and think of home. The memory of his family, the hope of one day returning to them, seemed like an eternal light in the darkness.

The temperatures in the Chukotskiy Peninsula could plummet to a bone-chilling -40°C. My father had to be meticulously covered to avoid frostbite. Some miners weren't as fortunate, developing facial frostbite with pieces of tissue missing from their faces, the affected areas covered by a darkened, shiny, thin skin. Unlike many of them, he managed to avoid such disfigurations.

One day, while labouring in the cold, unforgiving mine, my father stumbled upon a corpse lying among the jagged rocks. The body, twisted and broken, was a grim testament to the harsh realities of their existence. Someone mentioned, almost in passing, that these were the remains of the renowned Polish literary writer Bruno Jasiński.

My father was familiar with Jasiński's work, his mind immediately conjuring the rich, thoughtful prose that had once provided solace and inspiration. The discovery of his remains disturbed him deeply, more than he could comprehend at that moment. The sight of Jasiński's lifeless body, once so full of intellectual vigour and creative energy, now reduced to a tragic end in the barren wasteland of the mine, was a brutal reminder of the fragility of his own life. The encounter weighed heavily on his heart. Jasiński, a man whose words had danced on the page, exploring the depths of human experience, now lay silent and still, his remains exposed to the harsh elements; his voice extinguished. My father felt a profound sorrow for the loss of such a brilliant mind, an exponent of philosophical humanism, snuffed out by the cruel hand of fate. The fragility of life, so poignantly illustrated by the sight of Jasiński's remains, reinforced his resolve to survive. He was reminded of the preciousness of each moment and the importance of holding onto hope and humanity even in the face of overwhelming adversity. Jasiński's work, though left incomplete by his untimely death, continued to resonate and echo as a source of strength for those who remembered his words. As my father returned to his arduous labour, the image of Jasiński's body stayed with him, a silent companion in his thoughts.

The harsh landscape of Chukotskiy Poluostrov, with its relentless cold and desolate beauty, became a canvas on which he painted his resolve. The discovery of Jasiński's body marked a turning point, a moment of deep reflection that strengthened my father's appreciation for the fragility and resilience of life. It served as a reminder that even in the darkest times, the light of human thought and creativity could still shine, offering hope and inspiration (Jasiński was a committed communist, and it was long believed that he had been sentenced to 15 years of hard labour and perished in a Siberian Gulag. However, in 1992, it was revealed that Bruno Jasiński had been arrested by the NKVD, put on trial, and sentenced to death by firing squad on September 17, 1938. His body was buried in an unmarked grave. In 1955, during Nikita Khrushchev's de-Stalinization efforts, Jasiński was rehabilitated.) [4]

∞∞∞∞∞

On July 30, 1941, General Sikorski, Head of the Polish Government-in-Exile based in London, and the USSR's Minister of Foreign Affairs, Mr. Maisky, signed a pivotal agreement. This agreement included an amnesty, granting freedom to all Poles exiled to the Soviet Union between 1940 and 1941, liberating them from labour camps and kolkhozes. The Sikorski-Maisky agreement allowed all Polish citizens in the Soviet Union to be released from detention centres and gulags, enabling them to volunteer for the Polish Army forming in various parts of Kazakhstan and Uzbekistan. [5]

The dissemination of this political breakthrough, however, was unreliable and varied. NKVD representatives informed some deportees, while others learned about it through local newspapers. Still, others heard the news broadcast on the radio. The local authorities provided special release documents and food rations, often directing the deportees to the nearest railway station. [6]

By late September 1941, my father was free and travelling on a train across Siberia, heading south to the Karaganda region, where he stopped at Akmolinsk (now called Nur-Sultan, the capital of Kazakhstan). In Akmolinsk, he met a contact from the Soviet Voyen-komat (regional military recruitment office). The person gave him the locations where he could join the newly forming Polish military force. These included Lugovoy in South Kazakhstan, Buzuluk in Central Kazakhstan, Pachta in Kirgizia, and Guzar in Southern Uzbekistan. He decided to travel south to Guzar.

My father recalled feeling at home among his Polish compatriots once he arrived at the Polish Army Camp based in Guzar. He soon discovered, however, that to join the Polish Army under General Anders, he had to do three things: Shave his head; Pledge allegiance to Nationalist Democratic Poland; and pledge loyalty to the Polish Army Command by swearing on the Bible's New Testament.

From the outset, my father declared himself an atheist. Disclosing his Jewish heritage might have been more acceptable, but his atheistic stance became a significant obstacle. The army command refused to accept Poles with an atheistic worldview or communist convictions. For a while, he was left in a state of uncertainty, anxiously awaiting the Command's decision. Would they grant him the Polish Army uniform or not? He anticipated a negative response, and with each passing day, his frustration grew more intense.

While stationed in Guzar, he refused to attend the regular Catholic Mass and declined to visit the local military barber to shave his hair off. His resentment deepened as he was kept in the dark for an extended period, not knowing if he would receive his uniform. Upon further inquiry, he was informed that he would get his uniform only after shaving his hair. By then, he had waited long enough. While other enlisting Poles received their uniforms quickly, he felt sidelined and discriminated against. He indicated, "The shaving of the hair will not happen unless I get my uniform."

That day, he was told he would not be accepted into the Polish Army and was asked to leave. With no money in his pocket and no food to eat, he travelled for almost six days by train to Tashkent, the capital of Uzbekistan. He was utterly famished upon his arrival.

The journey to Tashkent was an exhausting odyssey. He felt the gnawing hunger in his belly each day on the train. The landscape outside the window was a blur of desolate plains and distant mountains. Fellow passengers, each carrying their burdens, exchanged weary glances but offered little more than silent companionship.

Arriving in Tashkent, my father was a shadow of his former self. The city's bustling streets, alive with the sounds of traders and the scent of exotic spices, seemed almost surreal. His legs, weak from days of starvation, carried him through the crowded bazaars, where he watched people haggle over fruits and bread he could not afford. The vibrant life around him was a painful reminder of his dire circumstances.

In this foreign land, my father felt both invisible and exposed. While preoccupied with their issues, the people of Tashkent cast curious glances at the gaunt stranger who moved among them like a ghost. His hunger was an ever-present ache, a cruel companion that gnawed at his insides and clouded his thoughts.

Despite the adversity, he found small acts of kindness along the way. A shopkeeper, noticing his desperate state, offered him a piece of bread. The bread, rough and dry, was a feast for my father, who ate it with gratitude that words could not express. Another day, a fellow traveller shared a water flask, the cool liquid reviving his parched throat. These moments of human connection, however fleeting, sustained him through his darkest hours.

Strengthened by these gifts of kindness, my father returned to the bustling Tashkent Railway Station, where he became a baggage carrier for disembarking passengers, desperately trying to scrape together some money. He often gathered just enough to purchase a simple hot drink called Citro, a concoction of hot water with lemon that provided a small measure of warmth and comfort. Each night, he slept on a cold, hard bench at the station, his stomach gnawing with hunger, the unforgiving wood digging into his back and shoulders. Every morning, he presented himself at Tashkent's Voyen-komat, clinging to a sliver of hope.

With a stern yet sympathetic gaze, the official informed him that he could not join the Soviet Forces as he was not a citizen of the Soviet Union. His only option was to join General Anders' Polish Armed Forces, which were forming in the south. My father explained, his voice laced with frustration and weariness, that he had already tried this option.

Seeing the desperation in my father's eyes, the official softened. His hardened demeanour, worn from years of bureaucratic duty, cracked to reveal a glimmer of humanity. He guided my father through various work options, detailing the possibilities with rare patience. Ultimately, he suggested travelling to Semipalatinsk, where employment might be possible.

Weary and discouraged, my father agreed. The official, showing a rare moment of kindness, provided him with a travel pass and some food, advising him to eat slowly to allow his digestive system to adjust. The bread and dried meat were a blessing, and my father accepted them with gratitude, promising himself that he would savour each bite.

The journey to Semipalatinsk was another gruelling chapter in his odyssey. The train, filled with the weary and the needy, chugged through the endless expanse of the Soviet landscape. My father sat quietly, the food parcel clutched in his hands, a precious lifeline in his struggle for survival. He ate sparingly, each morsel a careful calculation to stave off hunger while preserving his meagre provisions.

In mid-October 1941, after a difficult 16-hour journey by train from Tashkent, my father arrived at Semipalatinsk Station in Kazakhstan. On the platform, a man already aware of his arrival approached him. Introducing himself as Babin, he informed my father that the Tashkent Voyen-komat had instructed him to meet him and take him to a temporary lodging.

The station was a hive of activity, starkly contrasting my father's experience of desolation during his journey. The air was sharp and cold, a biting reminder of the approaching winter. With a demeanour that hinted at duty and kindness, Babin guided my father to a small, cramped hostel. For a few days, this would be his refuge. The room was bare, the bed was hard, but it was a shelter. During this time, Babin arranged food rations and secured membership at a canteen that was usually reserved for factory workers in the area. Each day, without fail, my father attended the canteen for his main meal, feeling the pangs of hunger slowly subside. The food was simple but filling, a much-needed boost for his weary body.

After several days, Babin found longer-term accommodation for my father with a family whose husband had been conscripted into the Red Army. The woman, her two children, and her elderly mother welcomed him into their modest home with a warmth that momentarily softened the harshness of his reality. The house was small, with thin walls, but the spirit of hospitality was robust. The children's laughter, the elderly woman's gentle humming, and the mother's kind eyes made the place warm and welcoming.

As he settled in, he anxiously awaited further news from Babin regarding employment opportunities. The days passed slowly, each one a blend of waiting and adjusting to his new environment. The family treated him with kindness, sharing their meagre meals and offering companionship in the evenings. The mother, a resilient woman, would often speak of her husband with a mix of pride and sorrow, her words a reminder of the countless families torn apart by the war.

When Babin finally returned, his news was far from what my father had hoped for. He informed him that the Soviet Union was preparing for war, and the best he could offer was a small piece of land on the outskirts of town. My father could plant strawberries, watermelons, and vegetables there to sell at the local market. However, winter was coming, and he would have to wait until spring the following year for any planting to be done. With a heavy heart, he accepted the offer. It was not the future he had envisioned.

The plot of land was a humble expanse of soil, bordered by a few scraggly trees and the distant silhouette of the town. After a long, cold winter, in early March 1942, my father set off to work. The days were long and laborious, his hands becoming rough and calloused from the toil. Yet, there was something quietly fulfilling about the work. The act of planting, of nurturing life from the earth, provided a slight sense of control, which was often taken away from him along his journey in exile.

He would rise before dawn each morning when the sky was still dark. The children sometimes joined him in the fields, their laughter a bright counterpoint to the laborious work. As the weeks turned into months, my father's small plot of land flourished in June. The strawberries ripened to a deep red, the watermelons grew heavy and sweet, and the vegetables thrived. In the evenings, he would return to the family, exhausted but with a sense of quiet accomplishment. The mother, her children, and the elderly woman had become his surrogate family, their lives intertwined by the shared experience of war and survival. Their home, with its simple comforts and genuine warmth, was a sanctuary amid uncertainty. The small blossoming piece of land and the family that took him in became the cornerstones of his new life. It was not the life he had planned, but it was one he could build upon.

During his 18-month 'family placement' in Semipalatinsk, my father immersed himself in the daily chores of his host family, helping with shopping, cooking, cleaning, and home maintenance. All was well until July 1942. That month, my father's world was shattered when he became severely ill. The local doctor diagnosed him with malaria, and for 20 agonising days, he was bedridden, feverish, shaking, sweating, and plagued by vomiting and diarrhea. The family, with whom he had formed a bond, cared for him with their unwavering support.

After his recovery in August 1942, my father's thoughts turned to his family. He had not received any letters from his mother since February 1941, and he had no idea of his brother Leon's whereabouts. Determined to reconnect, he wrote to his parents at 13 Spokojna Street, Warsaw, but weeks passed with no reply. He tried again and again, but each attempt was met with silence. As 1942 turned into 1943, my father's hope began to wane, and the uncertainty about his family's fate weighed heavily on his heart.

Notes

1. https://katyn.ru/index.php?go=Pages&in=view&id=6
2. https://en.wikipedia.org/wiki/Lavrentiy_Beria
3. https://en.wikipedia.org/wiki/Stanisaw_Szeptycki
4. https://en.wikipedia.org/wiki/Bruno_Jasinski
5. https://en.wikipedia.org/wiki/Sikorski_Mayski_
   Agreement

6. Gehenna

In mid-July 1942, the Judenrat, the established Jewish Council within the Warsaw Ghetto, grimly informed the inhabitants that deportations would begin on July 22, 1942. The announcement hung over the ghetto like a death sentence, each word a harbinger of impending doom. Any resistance to leaving their homes would likely be punishable by death. The sense of dread was palpable. A chilling wind swept through the narrow, crowded streets, leaving fear and despair in its wake.

Around that time, the Chairman of the Judenrat, Adam Czerniakow, received an order from the SS command on Stafki Street to organise the Ghetto's Jewish Police to manage the deportations. The command was as cold and unyielding as the steel from which it was delivered, a demand that turned Czerniakow's heart to lead. Faced with this horrifying directive, Czerniakow found himself at a harrowing crossroads. The weight of this moral dilemma pressed down upon him, each breath a laborious task as he grappled with the enormity of the decision.

Rather than comply and draw up lists of those to be deported, Czerniakow made an agonising choice. On July 23, 1942, he chose to commit suicide. In his final act, he sought to reclaim the sliver of humanity that the Nazis sought to strip away. His death was a silent protest, a refusal to be complicit in the machinery of genocide. Czerniakow's passing was a tragic example of resistance, a testament to the excruciating choices faced by those caught in the maelstrom of cruelty and oppression.

The news of Czerniakow's suicide spread through the ghetto, a grim whisper that ignited both sorrow and sombre respect. His decision became a poignant symbol of the ultimate sacrifice, a stark reminder of the inhuman conditions under which the Jews of the

Warsaw Ghetto lived. In their cramped, decaying quarters, with hope dwindling like the light of a dying candle, Czerniakow's final act was a flicker of defiance against overwhelming darkness.

Through this act, Czerniakow communicated what words could not: the profound depth of his compassion for his people and the unbearable burden of his role. His suicide was not a retreat but a stand against the impossible choices imposed by the Nazi regime. It was a moment of profound sorrow that underscored the tragedy of the times, capturing the essence of a man who, even in death, sought to protect the dignity of his community. [1]

By late July or early August 1942, Spokojna Street fell within the section of the Warsaw Ghetto designated for deportation. The oppressive heat of summer did little to alleviate the growing sense of dread among the residents. SS soldiers stormed the area, forcing the inhabitants from their homes and herding them to a specific gathering point. The air was thick with fear, and the sounds of shouted orders, the clatter of boots, and the cries of children.

Yosif, Golda, Moyshie, and Shmul were among those who had to step outside and join the throngs of people who had already been uprooted from neighbouring buildings. The moment was surreal, a heart-wrenching blend of chaos and resignation. Each step they took was heavy with uncertainty and despair, their hearts pounding with a mix of terror and disbelief.

The SS soldiers, brandishing machine guns, escorted the crowd along Warsaw's Zamenhof Street, their presence a grim reminder of the iron fist that controlled their fate. The soldiers' expressions were hard, devoid of any trace of humanity, as they barked aggressive orders and pushed the crowd forward. The march to the Umschlagplatz (Transport Point) was relentless, the heat and dust only adding to the misery of those forced to walk this path.

As they trudged along the cobblestone streets, the city they once knew so well seemed to transform into a hostile landscape. The familiar buildings and alleyways, now silent witnesses to their suffering, blurred into a background of oppressive uncertainty. The Umschlagplatz loomed ahead, a place of dread and unknown horrors, the gateway to an unfathomable destination.

Yosif clutched Shmul's hand tightly, trying to impart some semblance of strength and comfort. Golda clasped Moyshie's hand, keeping him closely beside her. Both boys' youthful faces etched with fear and confusion. The family moved as one; their steps synchronised in a desperate dance of survival. The weight of their shared fear was almost palpable, a silent testament to the bond that held them together in the face of unimaginable adversity.

Each step toward the Umschlagplatz felt like a step away from life itself. The crowd's collective despair was a living thing, a heavy, suffocating presence that seemed to sap the strength from their limbs. The journey was a cruel reminder of their powerlessness, a march orchestrated by the hands of fate and the whims of the merciless Nazi regime.

In those harrowing moments, the essence of their humanity was tested. The sight of elderly neighbours struggling to keep pace, mothers trying to soothe their crying infants, and men with haunted eyes marching stoically—all these scenes were etched into the collective memory of those who walked that path. The Umschlagplatz, merciless and unforgiving, awaited them, a symbol of their displacement and the starting point of their forced exodus to oblivion.

Through the terror and confusion, Yosif's mind clung to fleeting fragments of faith and hope, desperately seeking some divine intervention. Golda's presence beside him was a lifeline, a reminder of the love and strength that still bound them together. Moyshie and

126

Shmul, though young, embodied the resilience and spirit that Yosif hoped would somehow carry them through the nightmare unfolding around them.

As they reached the Umschlagplatz, the reality of their situation began to crystallise. The crowd pressed closer together, seeking solace in numbers, their collective breath a prayer for survival. The Umschlagplatz, a symbol of their captivity, was a place where dreams were shattered and lives were irrevocably changed. The SS soldiers herded them with mechanical efficiency, their cold eyes reflecting a world devoid of compassion.

At the Umschlagplatz, the frightened and weary crowds were instructed to wait. The air was thick with dread, every breath laden with the collective fear of those gathered. The sound of a locomotive's ominous arrival, its brakes screeching to a halt on the other side of the ghetto wall, pierced the oppressive silence. The harsh, metallic noise seemed to herald their impending doom, each screech a reminder of the iron grip of fate that held them.

After an agonizingly long wait, the guards finally opened the gate. The heavy clang of metal against metal echoed through the air, a jarring prelude to the chaos that followed. Pointing their submachine guns, the guards barked orders at the parched and starving crowd, commanding them to move through to the other side. The authoritative voices were sharp and unyielding, cutting through the numbing exhaustion that gripped their terrified captives.

On the other side, freight train wagons (Güterwagen) awaited them, their dark, cavernous interiors promising no comfort, only more suffering. The sight of these wagons, stark and foreboding, drained whatever remaining hope the people might have clung to. The train's sheer physical presence, the wagons' iron and steel frames, felt like prison bars closing in around them.

The people, already drained of hope and strength, were herded into the cramped, suffocating wagons. The guards showed no mercy, their gestures and shouts propelling the crowd forward with ruthless efficiency.

Inside the wagons, the air was stifling, the space confining. The crowd pressed together, bodies overlapping in a desperate attempt to find some small measure of comfort. The air grew thick with the scent of fear and despair, every breath a struggle in the sweltering heat. There was no room to sit or lie down, only the oppressive weight of human bodies crushed against one another. The floor was covered in lime, adding to the discomfort and stinging their eyes and throats. It was a cruel irony, a substance meant for preservation, now adding to their misery.

As the doors of the wagons slammed shut, plunging them into near darkness, the reality of their situation became starkly apparent. After two excruciating hours of standing in this suffocating confinement, the train began to move slowly, inching its way out of Warsaw. The initial lurch of the train was jarring, causing the tightly packed passengers to sway and stumble against each other. The rhythmic clatter of the wheels on the tracks became a monotonous, oppressive soundtrack to their suffering.

Inside the wagon, the darkness was almost complete, broken only by the occasional sliver of light that managed to penetrate the small, barred windows. The lime dust in the air made it hard to breathe; each inhale brought a searing pain to passengers' lungs. The heat was unbearable, sweat mingling with the dust to create a sticky, suffocating layer on their skin.

In this moving prison, the essence of every person's humanity was tested. The strength of their spirit, the depth of their love, and the bonds of their family became their only refuge. Yosif's silent prayers,

Golda's soothing murmurs, and the children's fragile hope were all they had to cling to as the train carried them toward an uncertain fate.

This harrowing journey was a microcosm of a much larger tragedy that was unfolding before them. Each moment of despair was met with a quiet defiance, a refusal to let go of their dignity and humanity. And as the train rattled on through the dark night, their collective strength, their silent endurance, became a faint hope in the impenetrable void of their suffering.

Yosif tried to create a small barrier around Golda, Moyshie, and Shmul, using his body to shield them from the worst of the crush. His efforts were futile against the sheer number of bodies, but it was an instinctive act of protection, a father's desperate attempt to offer some comfort to his family. Golda's eyes, streaked with tears, reflected both fear and a fierce determination to survive.

The train's slow progress felt like a cruel mockery, each minute stretching into an eternity. The noise and vibration of the moving train were disorienting, adding to the sense of dislocation and helplessness. The physical discomfort was relentless, every muscle aching from the enforced stillness, every breath a struggle against the oppressive heat and lime dust.

For the children, the experience was particularly harrowing. Moyshie and Shmul, their faces pinched with fear and discomfort, clung to their parents. The normally spirited boys were subdued, their young minds unable to fully grasp the horror of their situation but keenly aware of the palpable fear surrounding them. In the suffocating darkness, the wagon became a cauldron of shared misery. The occasional murmur of prayer, a whispered word of comfort, or a stifled sob punctuated the oppressive silence. Each passenger was trapped not only by the physical confines but also by the weight of their despair and the uncertainty of their fate.

It was impossible to know where the train was heading, shrouded in the thick uncertainty of nightfall. The only light that penetrated the oppressive darkness of the Güterwagen came from small, barred window openings on either side, barely illuminating the sea of desperate faces. The barbed wire over these openings seemed like a cruel reminder of their entrapment.

Fear and hopelessness weighed heavily in the stale air, mingling with the faint light that seeped through. Every jolt of the train brought Yosif, Golda, Moyshie, and Shmul closer; they clung to each other, trying to draw strength from their shared presence. Voices of anguish, pain, and terror jammed the cramped Güterwagen as people lost strength. Some collapsed where they stood, while others remained upright, supported by the bodies of their fellow companions.

After four to five hours of this relentless movement, the train stopped. Night enveloped them, and a heavy, oppressive silence fell over the wagon. The people inside no longer had the energy to express their anguish or pain. Unbeknownst to them, the train had arrived at Treblinka Station with its sixty freight wagons. Sixty wagons crammed with children, babies, men, and women of all ages, waiting in silent agony beyond pain and exhaustion. They stood like this through the entire night, unaware of the horrors that awaited them at dawn. They did not know that what lay ahead was pure hell. They did not know that the gates of this hell were temporarily closed because the operators of this inferno were asleep, regaining their strength for the morning's atrocities.

As the night dragged on, hope and despair intertwined in the hearts of Yosif, Golda, Moyshie, and Shmul. The darkness outside was a mere shadow compared to the abyss they felt within, each moment bringing them closer to the unimaginable fate that awaited them.

Morning arrived with a jarring whistle, piercing the heavy silence that had settled over the night. There was a noise of some movement, but the Güterwagen that Yosif, Golda, Moyshie, and Shmul occupied remained motionless. Every two hours, perhaps less or more, the silence was broken by commotion somewhere outside and that relentless piercing whistle.

Suddenly, there was a firm bump—a steam engine had just connected to their Güterwagen. Like everyone else, Golda felt a momentary relief as the train began to move again. The slight shift in their surroundings offered a sliver of hope, a promise of the end to their stifling entrapment.

But Golda had no way of knowing that their freight wagon was now attached to a small locomotive pulling only eight or ten Güterwagens. The remaining wagons, still loaded with despairing souls, were left idle at Treblinka station, seemingly abandoned to an unknown fate.

As the train slowly pulled away, Golda's fleeting relief was soon overshadowed by a gnawing sense of dread. The uncertainty of what lay ahead weighed heavily on her, each bump and rattle of the train amplifying her fear. The passengers, clinging to the faint hope that movement meant salvation, were unaware that their journey led them deeper into the abyss of no return.

The name "Ober-Majdan" loomed on the station's building as the freight train stopped. The SS soldiers swiftly unlocked the doors, and a blinding burst of light flooded the cramped, dark interior of the Güterwagen. A rush of fresh air mingled with the aggressive bark of orders: "Everyone out, now!" (German: "Alle raus, jetzt! ")

In the best scenario possible under these horrific circumstances, Golda and Yosif, with Moyshie and Shmul in tow, would have followed the crowd of people before them, disembarking as smoothly as possible in such chaos. The sudden influx of light and air was almost disorienting after hours of suffocating darkness. As they moved carefully towards the opening, their senses were assaulted by the chaotic scene around them. It was the sight of lifeless bodies sprawled on the floor of the wagon that froze their hearts. The reality of their situation crashed down on them with brutal clarity. The SS soldiers' shouts and the frantic pouring of the crowds out of the wagons seemed distant, muffled by the sheer weight of the horror that was unfolding before their eyes as they carefully disembarked down onto the ramp.

Historical accounts painfully record that many people perished during the torturous journey between Warsaw and Treblinka. Adding further to this tragedy, anyone who was slow to get out of the Güterwagen or who clumsily tripped over a dead body would be yanked down forcefully onto the ramp and beaten. Those struck with the butt of a rifle and who couldn't get up would be shot in the head in front of everyone else, their lives extinguished with barbaric brutality. The SS men, accompanied by armed Ukrainians, shouted like enraged vicious dogs. Their barks of orders and curses filled the air, amplifying the terror and chaos. They dragged the frail and weakened from the wagons, beating them savagely. The sight of the frail elderly men and women seemed to infuriate them the most, and their frustration was unleashed mercilessly.[2]

The ramp became a scene of indescribable horror as these cruel enforcers showed no mercy. Yosif, Golda, Moyshie, and Shmul were thrust into this nightmare, witnessing the brutality first-hand. The heart-wrenching cries, the desperate pleas for mercy, and the cold, unfeeling commands of their tormentors created an atmosphere of pure shock. Golda gripped Moyshie's hand tightly, her heart pounding with fear and shock as they stood with the others, mortified.

They stood numb on the ramp, exposed to the elements of nature, feeling the cold morning air and the touch of the chilly breeze on their tired, petrified faces. They would notice the fog in the distance, hiding

132

the trees that stood silent and frozen. Perhaps they were puzzled by the yellowish colour smudging the surfaces of the surrounding Treblinka grounds. Thankfully, they did not know that it was the colour of human ash mixed with sand and spread across the sombre, serene landscape. The fresh air was a cruel reminder of the life they had been torn from. The once-simple pleasures of nature now held a sinister undertone, a backdrop to the trauma witnessed in the present and the trauma yet to be experienced. Yosif kept a protective arm around Shmul, his eyes scanning the area, trying to grasp any sense of what was happening and what was to come.

The moments dragged on, each minute feeling like an eternity. The cold seeped into their bones, but they were beyond shivering, beyond reacting to the physical discomfort. Yet, even in this abyss of despair, the faintest glimmer of hope persisted—a hope that somehow, by some miracle, this hellish ordeal would end. As they stood on the ramp, their feet felt cold and dead. They were part of the crowd, a crowd of physically and mentally broken people, a sad crowd devoid of any agency or capacity to act. In front of them stood a dozen men dressed in dark SS uniforms, carrying whips and submachine guns, each standing roughly a few meters from each other. Behind them was a wall covered with blankets and quilts of different colours. Who did these blankets belong to? Anyone might wonder. But there was no energy left to seek any answers [3].

The SS men had little patience for the anguished cries of toddlers, held tightly and anxiously by their petrified mothers. For any baby or toddler, the horrendous trip was both physically and emotionally distressing. All too often, an SS man or a Ukrainian collaborator would locate the source of a child's woeful cry, march over, and, with brutal force, grab the toddler by their tiny feet. Ripping the child from their mother's embrace, he would swing the child violently, smashing their fragile body against the panel of the freight wagon.

The people gathered on the ramp would hear the anguished cries of horrified mothers, their horror-stricken voices merging with the fierce protesting cries of their precious children. Then, there would be a sickening thump, followed by another and another. A momentary, chilling silence would ensue, only to be shattered by the sharp crack of the gunshots. Golda clutched Moyshie's hand tight, her heart breaking with each scream, each thud, each gunshot. Yosif held Shmul close, his eyes filled with fear, anger, and helplessness.

Such scenes were heartbreakingly common during the disembarkation of the deportees at the Ober-Majdan station ramp. In the aftermath of these horrific acts, an eerie silence would settle over the entire crowd of deportees, standing motionless, terrified, and disoriented. The air was thick with despair and the oppressive weight of death. The landscape around them, once perhaps a symbol of life and continuity, was now a backdrop to the worst of humanity's atrocities. The yellowish tint of human ash mixed with sand smeared the grounds, a silent testament to the countless lives extinguished here. The cold morning air, once refreshing, now felt like a cruel mockery of their suffering. [4]

Suddenly, there would be a loud, aggressive order: "Everyone move forward" (German: "Alle kommen voran"). The crowd would begin to walk as the oppressors, armed with guns, would gaze upon them with their cold eyes and occasional sinister smiles. Golda could barely process the horror around her. Her heart pounded in her chest as she maintained a tight grip on Moyshie's hand, desperately trying to shield him from the worst of the violence. Yosif, with Shmul close by, kept his eyes forward as he walked ahead. The sight of brutalised motionless bodies fuelled his determination for his family to survive. His steps were lined with apprehension, vigilance and hope that none of his loved ones would fall victim to the SS's indiscriminate violence.

As they were moving slowly across the ramp, they could see the vast expanse of the camp ahead. The sun, climbing higher in the sky, cast harsh shadows on the bleak landscape. The reality of Treblinka—a place designed for death—began to sink in. The smell of burning flesh filled the air, a grim indication of the fate that awaited them and thousands of others.

In this moment of sheer terror, amidst the shouting and brutality, Golda whispered to her children, trying to impart a sense of hope and strength. "We must stay together, no matter what", she urged, her voice trembling but firm. Each step was a defiance against fate that seemed all but certain. The determination to protect each other and remain together gave them a flicker of resilience and a fragile thread of hope that, somehow, they might survive this hell.

As they approached the first point, the 'Station Square', they noticed a sign in Polish and German:

"Attention Warsaw Jews! You are in a transit camp from which the transport will continue to labour camps. To prevent epidemics, your baggage is to be handed over for disinfection. Gold, money, foreign currency, and jewellery are to be deposited at the 'Cash Office' against a receipt. They will be returned later upon presentation of the receipt. For physical cleanliness, all arrivals must have a bath before travelling on." [5]

The truth was that the sign was misleading. There were no 'receipts' and no 'Cash Office'. In the 'Station Square,' an SS man stood who addressed the new arrivals in a firm, direct, and loud voice: "Listen carefully. You are to leave all your baggage and belongings where you are standing. Take your documents, valuables and toiletries with you, and follow through this gate to the reception area. You have a minute or two to collect the things I mentioned. Do not ask questions. Follow your way through."

People gathered their documents, valuables, and toiletries, clutching onto the last remnants of their former lives. They made their way through an opening in a barbed-wire wall, camouflaged by green branches, each step heavy with dread. They walked past strange contraptions and coiled barbed wire strewn across the ground, a sinister labyrinth leading them to another open square known as the 'Reception Area.'

By then, it was a gathering of doomed souls, dispossessed of their belongings, standing petrified and helpless, overwhelmed by a suffocating sense of entrapment. They were surrounded by armed SS men and wachmänner (watchmen) stationed in distant watchtowers strategically positioned along the perimeter of this macabre 'settlement.' One thing was painfully clear: there was no way to escape.

Suddenly, a harsh voice cut through the oppressive silence, drawing their heads towards the speaker—an SS man with an Alsatian dog sitting obediently by his tall leather boots. "Achtung! Women are to remain where they are. Men are to go to the barrack on the right, where they are to undress and wait for further instructions."

Golda's eyes filled with tears as she was forced to separate from Yosif, Shmul, who was almost 19, and Moyshie, who was nearly 12. Her heart shattered as she watched them disappear into the 'male reception' barrack on the right, never to see them again. [6]

Inside the barrack, a single loud voice commanded, "Everyone undress! Leave your clothes where you are and proceed to the left!" The voice repeated these simple words over and over, echoing off the walls. The SS men then rushed the naked crowd of men and boys out of the barrack into a narrow pathway, enclosed on both sides with thick barbed wire intertwined with green branches. This path, known ominously as the "Tube to Heaven," was lined with SS men stationed two to three meters apart, their vicious dogs straining at their leashes, ready to tear into the passing bodies.

As the naked prisoners were herded forward, the SS men wielded whips and iron bars, striking their victims to spur them on, ensuring they pressed forward into the so-called 'showers' as quickly as possible. The air was thick with the stench, fear, and the cries of pain; a grim symphony of suffering. Each strike, each bark of the dogs, and each step forward was a descent deeper into the depths of hell.

The prisoners, stripped of their dignity and humanity, moved in a terrified, desperate mass, their skin exposed to the biting cold and the brutal blows. The barbed wire and green branches, which might have seemed incongruous in another setting, added to the surreal horror of their final journey here. The relentless drive towards the 'showers' was a march towards inescapable doom, each moment laden with terror and despair. [7]

The women still standing in the 'Reception Area' heard the screams of pain and horror. They listened to the barking of the vicious dogs and the SS men screaming at the petrified running men and boys: "Faster, faster, the water will get cold. Others still have to go under the showers!" To escape from the blows and dog bites, Yosif, Shmul, and Moishe would have had to run as quickly as they could. At the end of this grotesque path, there were two men at the entrance to the chamber, one on either side; one armed with an iron bar and one armed with a sharp machete. They drove the men and boys with blows to their bodies as they passed the entrance into the chamber. As soon as the chamber was full, the two men closed the doors. Inside, the trapped victims were overcome by the horror of their experience. There was no light, no shower appliances. This was not a communal shower room. Instead, they heard a harsh engine noise. The external loud engine conveyed its thick fumes through several pipes connected to the four sections of the chamber. Carbon Monoxide filled the dark, bleak, packed room, bringing life to its end for every person present. [8]

In the Warsaw Ghetto, established in November 1940, thousands of people died of hunger between January 1941 and July 1942. Between July 23 and September 15, 1942, over 95% of the inhabitants who remained alive were transported to Treblinka as part of Operation Reinhard. It is impossible to know if 19-year-old Shmul was part of the Jewish underground resistance (Żydowska Organizacja Bojowa). One can only speculate about these possibilities.

The most likely scenario is that all three—Yosif, Moyshie, and Shmul—died together. Yosif would have prayed through the terrifying sounds of screams that merged with the deadly engine noise. All three of them would have stayed close, sensing each other's touch as their consciousness faded into oblivion. No longer would they hear the anguished cries as they merged into a single soul, reaching the end of its existence.

Yosif, a loving and peaceful father, in his last moments, would have tried to create some space for Moyshie and Shmul so that they could breathe a little more. It was his final gesture, a gift of love to his dear sons before he could no longer be. As their breaths became shallower, they would have felt each other's presence, a small comfort in their final moments. Yosif's prayers, mingled with the desperate cries around them, would have been his final plea for mercy and a final testament to his enduring love and faith.

The horror of their end is unfathomable, but in such terror, the bond of their family offered a fleeting solace. Together, they faced the unimaginable, their spirits intertwined in a final act of love and unity.

This 'Gehenna' now awaited Golda, who would have to make her way with all the other women. First, they undressed; then, their hair was roughly cut with four or five swift snips of sizable scissors, each woman processed in the span of 20-30 seconds. Finally, they were ordered to run along the same tortuous path all the way to the gas chamber.

In her last moments of terrifying consciousness, Golda would hold on to her deepest hope of being reunited with all of her sons and Yosif. Perhaps, in those final, fading moments, before time stood still, she saw them all: Abram, Chaim, Leon, Shmul, Moyshie, and Yosif. Her heart, though filled with dread, clung to the solace of these beloved faces, finding a brief respite in the midst of unimaginable horror.

Golda's final thoughts were a desperate plea for togetherness, a wish that their spirits might find each other in the 'beyond'. The echoes of their love, their shared memories, were the last flickers of light in the encroaching darkness.

∞∞∞∞∞∞

Some 20-25 minutes later, an SS man looked through a glass spy window in the door. They noticed the image that by now was familiar to them. The victims held on to one another; they all stood upright, like one single block of human flesh abandoned by its soul. [9]

As the gas chamber's side doors opened, the Sonderkommandos began to unload the room filled with a mass of contorted bodies. The bodies tumbled out down the heavily sloping floor along the side of the chamber. The faces of the dead were jaundiced; many had blood around their noses and mouths. SS men looked closely at the corpses brought outside. If there was a groan, a single shot to the head ended the unconscious suffering. There was a team of Sonderkommandos who were armed with dental pliers. Before the corpses were loaded onto the trolleys, they made sure to extract any gold teeth they could spot. When this was done, the Sonderkommandos loaded the bodies onto the trolleys. They then pushed these along the narrow-gauge tracks towards the gravel pit that was 50 meters long, 25 meters wide, and up to 10 meters deep. They laid the tormented bodies of the dead in rows, packed closely together. The vast pit was not filled in. It was still waiting for another three or four thousand victims, who were to arrive that very day at the Ober-Majdan ramp. People carrying suitcases and holding children on their way to the 'Station Square'. And like previous arrivals, they too would experience the horror of disembarkation, and they too would fearfully wonder, where were they? What was going to happen next? [10]

It is not known if Shmul was spared from death by being selected at the 'Reception Area' to 'work' at the Treblinka-I camp. Due to his age, it is possible that he would not have been chosen for Treblinka's gas chamber (Treblinka-II). Instead, he would likely be selected for the hard labour option. If so, he would work in the vast gravel pit or in the forest, where prisoners cut wood to fuel the cremation pits. Also, a small number of Jewish young men who were not killed immediately upon arrival became members of the Sonderkommando. Their job was to unload the gas chambers, load trolleys with dead bodies, push them along the track to the nearby pits and bury the victims in their open mass graves. The prospect of Shmul coming across the bodies of his mother, father, or his 12-year-old brother, Moyshie, is a contemplation of horror. But in Treblinka, all imaginable hell was possible. For the victims of Treblinka, death was a relief from immense suffering. Young men assigned to these horrendous 'duties' died from exhaustion within a maximum of two months. Otherwise, if they lived but could no longer cope with the demands of what was required of them, they were taken to an enclosed 'Lazaret' area, which they entered through a small building marked with a Red Cross sign. Once inside the "Lazaret", they stood on the edge of yet another large pit. The SS man would fire a gun at the back of the victim's head. The lifeless body would tumble down to the bottom of the pit. If these victims were still labouring past April 1943, they would be shot and cremated on the pyres instead. [11]

In April 1943, the Germans discovered mass graves of Polish officers and civilians in Katyń near Smolensk. Himmler did not wish for similar findings to occur in Treblinka. He ordered the exhumation of the dead victims' bodies, so they could be burned on large pyres constructed on the eastern side of the gas chamber. [12] These large cremation pyres were constructed with railroad rails laid as grates on thick concrete blocks. The bodies were placed on rails over the wood underneath, splashed with petrol, and burned. Jankiel Wiernik, one of the very few survivors of Treblinka, wrote: "It was a harrowing sight, with the bellies of pregnant women exploding from boiling amniotic fluid. The heat radiating from the pits was maddening. The bodies burned for five hours; the pyres operated 24 hours a day. Once the system had been perfected, 10,000–12,000 bodies at a time would be incinerated daily. These open-air burn pits had to be refuelled at 5-hour intervals. Regularly, the human ashes were mixed with sand and spread over the surrounding area of 5.4 acres." [13]

Notes

1. https://en.wikipedia.org/wiki/adam_czerniak
2. Keller Niss, Caren (date unknown). Treblinka.
3. https://www.jewishgen.org/Frogottencamps/Camps/Treblinka/Eng.html)
4. Wiernik, Jankiel (1945). A year in Treblinka. Verbatim translation from Yiddish. The first ever published eye-witness report by an escaped prisoner of the camp.
5. Ibid.,
6. Ibid.,
7. Ibid.,
8. https://en.wikipedia.org/wiki/Treblinka Extermination_camp
9. Wiernik, Jankiel (1945). A year in Treblinka. Verbatim translation from Yiddish The first ever published eye-witness report by an escaped prisoner of the camp.
10. Ibid.,
11. Ibid.,
12. Ibid.,
13. Ibid.,

7. Lenino

In late April 1943, Babin visited my father with unexpected, good news. My father was in the field, tending to his plantation, when Babin's surprise visit caught him off guard. The sun began casting long shadows across the rows of ripening strawberries and watermelons, a testament to my father's labour. After exchanging greetings, Babin did not waste any time and explained that a new Polish Army was forming in the Russian village of Sieltzy (Polish: Sielce). The formal name of this new force was the "1st Infantry Division of Tadeusz Kościuszko."

Babin offered my father an opportunity: a train ticket from Semipolacinsk to Ryazan if he wished to enlist in the newly forming Polish military service. The news was like a gust of fresh air, carrying with it a sense of purpose and a glimmer of hope. My father's hands, still dirty from the soil, trembled slightly as he took handwritten instructions from Babin, the paper feeling both weighty and fragile in his grasp.

Babin detailed the process: once my father arrived in Ryazan, he would be picked up at the Voyen-komat and transported northwards to Sieltzy, across the River Oka. Babin emphasised that the Kościuszko Infantry Division was under General Berling's command, adding prestige and importance to the opportunity. General Berling was one of the three central members of the Union of Polish Patriots established in the Soviet Union; Moscow's equivalent of General Sikorski's London-based Polish Government-in-Exile.

The significance of this opportunity was not lost on my father. As Babin spoke, his mind raced through the possibilities and the implications. The chance to wear a uniform, to stand with his countrymen, to fight for a cause greater than himself—it was a chance filled with hope and aspiration of returning home, in the midst of a tumultuous time. The mention of General Berling, a name associated with patriotism, only heightened the sense of urgency and possibility.

Babin's visit felt like a turning point. For so long, my father had been rooted in the soil of his vegetable patch, finding solace in growing life from the barren ground. Now, he was offered a chance to fight for his homeland and reclaim a part of his identity that the war and displacement had overshadowed. The prospect of joining the Kościuszko Infantry Division stirred something deep within him, a resurgence of the spirit that had carried him through many trials. He accepted Babin's offer.

The night before he left, my father sat with the family that had taken him in, sharing a simple meal. The children's laughter, the warmth of the small home, and the quiet strength of the woman who had opened her doors to him all filled his heart with gratitude and sadness. He knew he'd miss them, but the call to arms was one he could not ignore.

As he boarded the train early in the morning, the weight of his decision settled over him like a cloak. With its rhythmic clatter and the hum of conversations around him, the train became a vessel of hope and determination.

In Ryazan, as promised, he was met by representatives of the Voyen-komat and taken north to Sieltzy. The landscape shifted as they crossed the Oka River, the vast stretch of water a silent witness to the passage of countless soldiers before him. The camp at Sieltzy bustled with activity; the mobilisation of a fresh force ready to carve its name into history was clear. As he watched young men training hard, his past hardships seemed to fade in the light of this new chapter, replaced by a sense of duty and the hope of returning home as a soldier fighting for his homeland and a brighter future.

My father's heart swelled with pride as he stood in line to register for military service. In early May 1943, he was accepted into the newly formed 1st Division of the Polish Infantry. Within days, he donned the uniform of the Kościuszko Army. The fabric, rough against his skin, was a reminder of who he was and where he belonged. Standing among his fellow soldiers, he felt a profound reconnection to his roots and his heritage. The name Tadeusz Kościuszko, emblazoned on the banners, was a reminder of the enduring spirit of resistance and the fight for freedom.

Sieltzy Camp, near Ryazan in Russia – My father (fourth in line for the registration) patiently waiting for enlistment in the newly forming Polish Infantry Division of Tadeusz Kościuszko. [1]

He soon discovered that General Berling was a communist of Jewish heritage. This revelation added a layer of complexity and camaraderie to his sense of purpose. The shared heritage and ideology created within my father an unspoken commitment that transcended the uniform he wore.

The Infantry Division consisted of three regiments, and my father was assigned to the 1st Battalion of the 1st Infantry Regiment. His battalion was scheduled to lead the initial offensive on October 12, 1943. Knowing he would be part of the vanguard filled him with pride and anticipation of the challenge ahead. Each day leading up to the offensive was filled with rigorous training, the physical demands pushing him to his limits, while the camaraderie among his fellow soldiers grew stronger. They shared stories, hopes, and fears; their bonds forged in the crucible of impending battle.

General Berling with his soldiers of the 1st Division of Polish Infantry of Tadeusz Kosciuszko. [2]

My father often spoke with immense pride about being part of an army with a singular aim: to march forward and liberate Poland. He reminisced about his Polish military uniform and the Division's characteristic 'Rogatywka' military hat. He took pride in fighting under the Polish flag, adorned with the white eagle emblem, which symbolised the Division's deep Polish heritage and unwavering commitment to combating the German Nazi oppressors.

He often mentioned that he became a member of the Union of Polish Patriots, and his official military role was defined as the Officer of Political Education ("Polwych"; English: "PolitEd"). His position fuelled his sense of duty and reinforced his belief in the cause he was fighting for. The blend of military discipline and political education gave him a profound sense of purpose and responsibility in the struggle to free his homeland.

On 15 July 1943, my father stood with 11,500 soldiers to take the Oath at the Military Ceremony in the open field outside Sieltzy. The date of the oath ceremony coincided with the anniversary of the Battle of Grunwald, where Polish King Władysław Jagiełło and his armies defeated the German Crusaders on 15 July 1410.

Above: Three presiding leaders of the Union of Polish Patriots established in the Soviet Union, from left: Wanda Wasilevska, Alfred Lampe; and Gen. Zigmund Berling. The Union of Polish Patriots was Moscow's equivalent of General Sikorski's London-based Polish Government-in-Exile. Wanda Wasilewska and Alfred Lampe participated in the creation of the 1st Tadeusz Kościuszko Infantry Division. These three individuals defined the sociopolitical topography of post-war Poland. Two months after the battle of Lenino, in December 1943, Alfred Lampe died in Moscow following a massive heart attack. After the war, his ashes were interned at the Powązki Military Cemetery in Warsaw. He was posthumously awarded the Order of the Cross of Grunwald, 1st class. [3]

My father was ready to commence his duties in the Infantry Division; however, he faced a problem—his thick hair was an unwelcome sight among the Regiment's command. All soldiers who volunteered for the Kościuszko Infantry Division were required to shave their heads or keep their hair short. My father had an issue with that. He resisted cutting his hair and ignored several reminders to visit the army barber.

One day, a Russian sergeant named Vozniakov, flanked by his two offsiders, approached him. Vozniakov stated directly, "Pozniak! You need to have your hair cut right now! I order you; do you understand?" My father, with a stubborn glint in his eye, turned his back on Vozniakov, who quickly followed and commanded his men: "Tie him up and take him to the barber!"

My father at the time of the Oath Ceremony

As soon as he heard these words, my father spun around, stepped forward, and delivered a solid blow to Vozniakov's face, knocking the Russian soldier to the ground with blood gushing from his nose. Vozniakov, dazed and furious, raised his head and shouted, "Zviazee; Yob tvoyu matc!" (English: "Tie him up! Motherfucker").

He was taken into custody for disobeying the Russian sergeant's order. The incident sent ripples through the regiment. Late that night, the Regiment command advised the Soviet command that their soldier was an Officer of Political Education and demanded his release. He was released immediately, and the issue of his hair was never raised again.

This incident, a blend of defiance and unexpected resolution, became a defining moment for my father. The struggle over his hair was more than a matter of personal pride; it was a stand for his individuality in a world that demanded conformity. The altercation with Vozniakov was a flashpoint, revealing his stubbornness and courage.

In the days that followed, my father carried on with his duties, his hair a symbol of his silent rebellion. The other soldiers, having witnessed the confrontation, regarded him with a mixture of respect and curiosity. The tale of his defiance spread through the ranks, becoming part of the regiment's lore. He continued to prepare for the impending offensive, the tension of the battlefield mingling with the newfound camaraderie among his comrades.

The days were long and exhausting; each drill and manoeuvre was a step closer to the reality of combat. My father found assurance and confidence in the routine, the repetitive motions of preparation providing a semblance of control over the looming battle ahead. The presence of General Berling, a man whose background mirrored his own, was a source of inspiration.

As October 12th approached, the atmosphere within the battalion was charged with anticipation. The air was thick with the unspoken thoughts of what lay ahead, the weight of responsibility resting heavily on their shoulders. My father's thoughts oscillated between pride and fear, the duality of his emotions reflecting the uncertainty of their mission.

On the eve of the offensive, the soldiers gathered for a final briefing. The night was filled with quiet conversations and moments of introspection. General Berling's words, filled with conviction and empathy, resonated deeply with each soldier, reinforcing their commitment to the cause. My father felt a surge of determination, a steely resolve that cut through his anxiety.

As dawn broke on October 12th, the battalion stood ready. The first light of day cast long shadows on the field, the air crisp and cold. Standing among his comrades, my father felt a deep sense of unity and purpose. They were not just individuals facing a battle, but a collective force bound by their shared history and the fight for a common cause. The overall plan was for the Division to approach and break through the German defence line between Trigubova and Polzukhy. The 33rd and 290th Soviet armies were then meant to assist the Kościuszko Division in reaching the Dnieper River. [5]

At 5:55 in the morning, when the dawn light barely pierced the horizon, the 1st Battalion, where my father was stationed, began their push towards the Mireya River. Above them, Polish artillery unleashed a relentless barrage, the thunderous explosions reverberating through the air, a symphony of war echoing in the early morning stillness.[6]

The soldiers, adrenaline coursing through their veins, made their way across the Mireya River. The cold water biting at their legs starkly contrasted with the heat of battle that awaited them. Each step was a testament to their determination, the collective breath of anticipation mingling with the mist rising from the river.

The German trenches loomed about 200 meters away as they reached the western bank. The distance seemed both vast and perilously close. The ground between them and the enemy was a no-man's land, a stretch of earth that the fury of combat would soon scar.

My father felt the moment's weight amidst his comrades' ranks. The artillery barrage above created a deadly canopy designed to suppress the German forces and pave the way for the infantry's advance. The sky was a canvas of fire and smoke, each burst of artillery a brushstroke of destruction.

The order to move forward arrived, and the battalion charged ahead. The chaos of war nearly drowned out the sound of boots pounding the ground. My father's heart thudded in his chest, the weight of his rifle a reassuring weight. The faces of his mates, hardened with resolve, reflected his own determination.

They moved in coordinated bursts; the training and preparation were now second nature. The German trenches were a maze of fortifications and barbed wire, a fortress that they had to breach. Each step forward was met with the crack of enemy fire, bullets whizzing past, finding targets among the advancing soldiers.

My father pushed on, the air thick with smoke and the sharp smell of gunpowder. The ground under his feet was rough, scarred with craters from the artillery attack. The shouts of orders and the cries of the wounded filled the air as the battalion kept moving, driven by the collective will to break through the enemy lines.

As they closed the distance to the German trenches, the intensity of the battle escalated. The initial shock of the artillery had given them a momentary advantage, but the Germans were regrouping, their resistance fierce. My father found himself in the thick of the fight, his rifle a constant companion. The noise was deafening, a relentless barrage of sound and fury. The faces of the enemy soldiers, glimpsed through the smoke, were a stark reminder of the human cost of war. Each shot fired, each step taken, was a dance with death. The air was thick with the sounds of warfare: the deafening roar of artillery, the staccato bursts of machine gun fire, and the shouts of soldiers. Amidst this turmoil, my father and his comrades fought fiercely, driven by the hope of breaking through and pushing the enemy back.

As they reached the edge of the German trenches, hand-to-hand combat ensued. Once a place of relative safety for the enemy, the trenches became a battleground of life and death amidst chaos and desperation. My father fought with a ferocity born of necessity, his instinct guiding him through each deadly encounter, a bloody fight for survival. [7]

By the time the sun was fully in the sky, the 1st Battalion had secured a foothold in the German trenches. The cost had been high, the ground littered with the fallen, both friend and foe. My father, exhausted but resolute, looked around at his comrades, their faces a testament to their shared sacrifice. The bravery and determination of the 1st Battalion had carved a path through the enemy lines. Standing amidst the battlefield's ruins, my father felt a profound sense of accomplishment and loss, realising at the same time that the fight was far from over.

The German counterattack was severe and far more potent than expected. The Polish 1st Battalion maintained its position, awaiting the advance of the battalions from the 1st and 2nd Regiments. As part of their counterattack, German artillery began to pound the 1st Battalion. About half of the battalion's soldiers perished under the barrage of German artillery and infantry. [8]

At around 9:20 a.m., a barrage of fire from Katyushas (Soviet multiple rocket launchers) began to hammer the German defences as the 1st and 2nd Regiments launched their main assault. The noise was like thunder cracking all around. The offensive broke through the German positions, and Polish soldiers attempted to seize control of Trigubova and Polzukhy. By 11:00 a.m., the Polish Tank Division had approached the constructed bridges across the Mireya River. Five tanks got stuck in the muddy terrain, and another two suffered mechanical failure. Only three tanks managed to cross to the other side of the river.

By 2:00 p.m., both the 1st and 2nd Regiments had taken control of Trigubova and Polzukhy—but not for long. Minutes later, the Germans launched their second counterattack, accompanied by artillery and advancing tanks. The German Luftwaffe also appeared in the sky from the southern and northern directions. The Polish Infantry maintained their resolve to hold their positions, but ultimately, they were pushed back out of Trigubova and Polzukhy.

The 3rd Regiment began its counterattack, but Polish artillery was weakened as their ammunition supplies quickly diminished. [9]

German counterattacks from both ground and air were decimating the Polish battalions. The sky was a grim theatre of death, with low-flying Messerschmitts and Stuka bombers screaming overhead, adding to the chaos on the ground. The relentless barrage of fire was overwhelming. Some soldiers, gripped by fear and desperation, began to retreat. The ground shook with the fury of German artillery, and the air was thick with the acrid smell of gunpowder and smoke.

Amidst the turmoil, my father noticed a few soldiers breaking ranks, retreating in panic as the firestorm intensified. His heart pounded not just from the fear of the enemy but from losing control, of seeing the line collapse. At that moment, something primal surged within him—a fierce determination to hold the line, to stand firm against the tide of destruction. He raised his gun, his voice cutting through the loud discordance of battle, "You! Get back to your positions! Right now! Or I will put a bullet in your head!"

The soldiers hesitated, caught between the terror of the advancing enemy and the authority in my father's voice. For a brief moment, order was restored, and they turned back to face the oncoming assault. But the reality of the situation was dire. Despite their attempts to hold the line, the onslaught from German artillery and the relentless advance of Panzer Division tanks was too severe. The ground trembled as the tanks rolled forward, unstoppable juggernauts of steel and fire.

The 1st Regiment, battered and outgunned, was forced to withdraw entirely. It was a retreat not born of cowardice but of necessity—a strategic pullback to avoid complete destruction. The soldiers found themselves isolated, cut off from reinforcements, and poorly supported by artillery. Their ammo dwindled as the enemy pressed ever closer, with each shot a desperate effort to hold back the advancing tide.

My father's heart ached with frustration and helplessness as they pulled back. The retreat starkly contrasted with the pride and determination they had felt at the start of the offensive. The sight of their comrades falling, the realisation that they were being pushed back by an enemy that seemed insurmountable, weighed heavily on their spirits.

Yet, even when faced with overwhelming odds, their hearts refused to surrender. The retreat was not a defeat but a regrouping, a moment to gather strength and find another way to fight. My father, though battered and weary, was not broken. The fire that had driven him to command his fellow soldiers to hold their ground still burned within him. In the battle for Trigubova, they faced the worst that the German war machine could throw at them, and although they had been pushed back, they were not defeated.

In the days that followed, my father reflected on the retreat and on the faces of the soldiers who had stood with him, fought, and bled for a cause greater than themselves. The memories of that day, the sound of his own voice commanding the retreating soldiers back to their positions, would stay with him as a reminder of the thin line between courage and despair, between holding the line and being overwhelmed by the tide of war. [10]

The 1st Regiment, originally made up of 2,800 soldiers, was whittled down to just 500. Out of the 450 soldiers in the 1st Battalion, where my father was based, only a few remained. Miraculously, he was one of them. At 19:20, the 2nd and 3rd Regiments, supported by 16 Soviet tanks, launched a renewed attack. Despite their efforts, they couldn't retake Trigubova and Polzukhy. The gunfire continued late into the night. [11]

That night, clouds obscured the moon, making it difficult to distinguish a friend from a foe. At times, the distance between Polish and German soldiers was minimal, with just a few meters separating them. Machine gun fire consumed the entire battlefield, a relentless barrage of bullets and explosions. Sometime after 2:00 a.m., silence finally descended over the ravaged land. The occasional bursts of gunfire, here and there, interrupted the peace of the dark, sleepy terrain. [12]

Strangely, my father's army coat was full of holes. The command of the 1st Regiment gathered its remaining soldiers and announced that volunteers were needed to collect the machine guns and mortars left on the battlefield among the fallen soldiers. My father volunteered. Under the cover of night, a handful of volunteers ventured out onto the battlefield to retrieve the military equipment. He recounted performing this task several times. He crawled very close to the German defence line during his last attempt. On the ground, he saw the bodies of dead Wehrmacht soldiers. He picked up a Wehrmacht helmet and, in complete darkness, entered the German-occupied area. He could see the silhouettes of soldiers keeping watch. One isolated Wehrmacht soldier stood out in the cold of the night and lit a cigarette. My father positioned himself behind him and casually asked in Hochdeutsch, "Have you got a spare smoke, partner?" The soldier did not turn around but said, "What? You've run out?" By then, my father was next to him. He placed his army knife against the soldier's throat and dug the barrel of his pistol into his back. He then whispered into his ear, "Not a squeak, Fritz, or I cut your throat… Move."

They slowly moved across the battlefield; my father kept the Wehrmacht soldier close at gunpoint. Upon reaching the Polish side, the soldier was immediately tied up and taken for interrogation.

On the morning of October 13, 1943, despite the formidable presence of the Wehrmacht's 337th Army stationed in the area, the

Kościuszko Infantry Division launched another attack. Two brigades of tanks supported them, while the third tank brigade failed to engage as its tanks got stuck in the thick mud extending southwards along the swamps lining the banks of the Mireya River. [13]

The 2nd Regiment, bolstered by six tanks, managed to take control of Polzukhy. However, the day followed a similar harrowing pattern. The Wehrmacht bombarded Polish positions with heavy artillery, mortars, and gunfire from swooping German Luftwaffe warplanes. Once again, after moving into Polzukhy, the 2nd Regiment was forced to retreat. [14]

Tensions ran high as General Berling sought to take command of the Soviet 33rd Army, leading to heated arguments with General Gurdov. Ultimately, in the late afternoon at 17:00, General Berling received an order: on the coming night of October 14, 1943, the entire Kościuszko Infantry Division was to retreat from combat and be replaced by the Soviet 164th Infantry Division. [15]

In the early hours of October 14, 1943, the Polish regiments retreated over the Mireya River, their spirits weary but unbroken. The haunting echoes of artillery fire and the relentless cries of battle lingered in the air as they made their way to safety, leaving behind a battlefield soaked with blood and sacrifice. [16]

On October 16, 1943, during roll call, only 4,600 soldiers remained from the original cohort of 11,500. Many soldiers were wounded, some never to be fit to serve again. Much blood was spilled in those two days, and the losses were heavy. Yet my father was one of the soldiers who survived the fierce battle, miraculously without any wounds. [17]

During many reflections, my father would say, "Many soldiers fought bravely with a burning passion. Instead of succumbing to fear, they maintained a determined resolve to confront and destroy a far more powerful and well-organised enemy. These courageous soldiers were Polish patriots who deeply harboured their hope—to return to their homeland and liberate their villages, towns, and farms, bringing safety to their loved ones."

He continued, "They did not know that belonging to an army that had arisen in the communist Soviet Union would one day be held against them, devaluing their gallant efforts, patriotism, love, and longing for a return to the distant family homes they cherished. They could not have foreseen that, years later, historians and politicians— many of whom had never smelt the gunpowder or felt the heat of battle—would dismiss and disregard them, their sacrifices swept aside to fit the prevailing socio-political Zeitgeist."

It is true that many Kosciuszko Army soldiers, who fought with courage, would find themselves caught in the cruel machinery of history, their deeds viewed through the distorting lens of political ideology. They fought not for a political doctrine but for the simple and profound desire to free their homeland and to protect the people and places they loved. They did not ask to be part of a controversial chapter in history; they were thrust into it by the circumstances of their time, by the desperate need to resist an overwhelming enemy.

These soldiers' courage and dedication deserve to be honoured without political bias, for they fought and died with the hope of a free and safe Poland in their hearts. Their struggle, their willingness to lay down their lives for a cause greater than themselves, is a testament to the enduring spirit of the Polish people. They were not perfect men or saints; they were soldiers, caught in the tides of history, doing what they believed was right.

The Battle of Lenino was not just a military engagement; It was a crucible in which the hopes and dreams of countless Polish soldiers were tested. Their legacy is not one of victory or defeat but of the unwavering resolve to fight for what they believed in, no matter the cost. [18]

Monument at the Powązki Military Cemetery in Warsaw for the Fallen Polish soldiers [19]

Notes

1. https://historia.interia.pl/historia-na-fotografii/1-dywizja-piechoty-im-tadeusza-kosciuszki-zdjecie, iId,1488715, iAId,118350

2. Ibid.,

3. Ibid.,

4. Ibid.,

5. Ibid.,

6. Ibid.,

7. Ibid.,

8. https://en.wikipedia.org/wiki/Battle_of_Lenino

9. Hubert, Henryk (1959). Lenino. Wydawnictwo Obrony Narodowej (Publisher: National Defence of Poland, Warsaw); page 86

10. https://historia.interia.pl/historia-na-fotografii/1-dywizja-piechoty-im-tadeusza-kosciuszki-zdjecie/18350 id/

11. Ibid.,

12. https://pl.wikipedia.org/wiki/Bitwa_pod_Lenino

13. Ibid.,

14. Ibid.,

15. Ibid.,

16. Ibid.,

17. Hubert, Henryk (1959). Lenino. Wydawnictwo Obrony Narodowej (Publisher: National Defence of Poland, Warsaw); page 223

18. https://historia.interia.pl/historia-na-fotografii/1-dywizja-/piechoty-im-tadeusza-kosciuszki-zdjecie/id-488715

19. https://pl.wikipedia.org/wiki/Bitwa_pod_Lenino

8. Return to Homeland

On the 23rd of July, 1944, the Kościuszko Infantry Division crossed the Bug River (pronounced 'Boog'), a crossing that marked not just a geographical boundary but an emotional one as well. It was a moment that signalled their relentless push toward the heart of Poland, the land they longed to reclaim. At the end of their long march, from the 15th to the 27th of July, the Division reached the banks of the Vistula, the great river that flowed like a vein through the nation's soul.

The battles that followed along the Vistula River in the Masovian Voivodeship were fierce and unforgiving. The earth was scarred with trenches and defensive structures, each a stubborn barrier that had to be overcome inch by inch. The fighting raged across this eastern-central region, with every step forward paid for in blood and sweat.

On one occasion, my father moved steadily along a narrow trench, abandoned in haste by the retreating German infantry. The trench, a lifeline for those who had fled, was now a silent, mud-slicked passageway. As he advanced, his senses heightened by the closeness of death, he suddenly came across a Wehrmacht soldier. The man was severely wounded, lying on his back, his breath coming in shallow, pained gasps. His hands, stained with blood, were raised in a gesture of surrender, a last plea for mercy in a world where such a thing had all but vanished.

In a desperate tone, the soldier repeated two words relentlessly, like a broken spell: "Hitler Kaput... Hitler Kaput." The words lingered in the air, a testament to the collapse of the ideology that had caused so much destruction. My father stepped closer, his submachine gun steady in his hands. For a moment, he stared at the man intensely, his eyes burning with a complex mix of emotions. The soldier's face, twisted with pain and fear, reflected the many faces that haunted my father's dreams—the faces of the lost, the dead, the betrayed. But at that moment, no mercy remained in my father's soul. The war had stripped it away, layer by layer, until only hardened resolve was left. He snapped sharply in Hochdeutsch, the words cold and precise: "Du Kaput!" Then, he fired a short burst of bullets into the Wehrmacht soldier's chest.

The man's body jerked violently, then went still, his last breath escaping into the air like a whisper. The trench, once a place of refuge, now became a grave. My father stood there, the gunfire still echoing in his ears, mingling with the distant roar of battle. The deed was done, and yet there was no satisfaction, no release from the anger and pain that had driven him to pull the trigger. Only a heavy silence remained, pressing down on him like the weight of all the lives lost in this brutal, horrific war.

As he moved on, leaving the lifeless body behind, deep inside him, the echoes of that encounter would stay, a reminder of the darkness that war had brought upon him and the cost of survival in a world that had lost its way.

When the Kościuszko Division and other Polish Army units reached the outskirts of Warsaw on August 26, 1944, they came within a breath of their ultimate goal—liberating the city that had endured so long under occupation. Yet, they were ordered to halt just 10 kilometres from Warsaw's perimeter. The soldiers, exhausted from battle but burning with determination, consolidated their troops and munitions, preparing for the next phase of their campaign.

It wasn't until September 9th that the order finally came to move into the offensive once again. The Red Army, bolstered by the Polish attachments, surged forward to take control of Praga, the suburb situated on Warsaw's eastern bank of the Vistula. This push was crucial; Praga was the gateway to Warsaw, and its capture would bring them one step closer to liberating the city.

Between the 10th and 14th of September, bloody battles erupted in the streets of Praga. The fighting was fierce, a deadly game of cat and mouse as my father and his comrades navigated the war-ravaged streets. The buildings, once homes and businesses, were now crumbling fortresses of brick and mortar, offering both cover and peril. Every step forward was careful and deliberate; the soldiers moved from one building to the next, using the ruins as shields against the relentless enemy fire.

Crossing the streets was a deadly gamble. My father had to find the right moment to dash across the open spaces, relying on his fellow soldiers to provide "fire cover." The sound of gunfire echoed off the walls, mingling with the distant roar of artillery and the screams of the wounded. Praga was burning, the flames licking at the sky, casting a hellish glow over the battlefield. The air was thick with smoke and the stench of death.

The cobblestone streets, once paths of daily life, were now littered with the bodies of soldiers from both sides. The blood-soaked ground was heavily covered with debris—rubble from the shattered buildings, disintegrated army equipment, and the remnants of lives torn apart by the relentless advance of war. The war machinery belonging to the German 73rd Division was burning, the twisted metal carcasses of tanks and trucks adding to the chaos and destruction that enveloped Praga.

Amidst this inferno, my father pressed on, driven by the same resolve that had carried him through battles before. Each fallen comrade and each destroyed building only hardened his determination to see this fight through. In the streets of Praga, the harsh truth of war was laid bare—there was no glory, only survival. My father and his fellow soldiers fought not for praise or recognition but for the hope of reclaiming their homeland, of bringing some measure of peace to a world torn apart by chaos. The battles they fought in Praga were not just for a patch of land but for the future of a free Poland. [1]

My father was with a group of soldiers, steadily and strategically approaching the eastern bank of the Vistula, hoping to secure a bridgehead despite the intense enemy fire that emerged from various levels of the abandoned apartment buildings lining the smoky streets. Each building was a fortress, and each window was a potential deathtrap. With every step forward, they moved with calculated precision, knowing that one false move could mean the end. Building by building, floor by floor, corridor by corridor, they confronted their enemy with deadly machine-gun fire or the concussive blows of grenades, pushing onward to the next street and the next building. Death lurked in every shadow, hiding behind every corner, waiting patiently to claim another life.

As they advanced, the tension in the air was palpable, the very atmosphere charged with the electricity of impending violence. The streets were choked with smoke and debris, the sounds of battle echoing off the shattered walls. The soldiers moved as one, their senses heightened, their minds focused on the task. There was no room for fear, only the cold determination to survive and to press forward.

While quickly crossing the street under the cover of machine-gun fire from his comrades, my father suddenly caught sight of a flash of submachine-gun fire, bursting with a vengeance from a window to his left, aimed directly at him. In that split second, instinct took over. He reached for his grenade, his fingers trembling slightly as they found the cold metal. With a swift, practised motion, he threw it as far as he could toward the source of the deadly gunshots. As he raised the grenade and cast it at his enemy, he shouted with fierce defiance, "Jak umierać to z muzyką!" ("If death must come, let there be music!").

The grenade raced through the air, a harbinger of death, and exploded with a thunderous roar. The force of the blast shook the ground, sending a shockwave through the narrow street. For a moment, time seemed to stand still, the chaos of battle reduced to a single, defining moment. But in the next instant, everything changed. He felt a dry sensation in his mouth as if the very moisture of life had been drained from him. His hands, which moments before had gripped a submachinegun with steady resolve, were no longer holding a weapon. Instead, they were cradling his belly, blood spilling from the gaping wound in his abdomen. The sight was surreal, a nightmare made real. He tried to walk, his body bent over in a desperate attempt to contain the injury, forcing himself to take two or three faltering steps before the strength drained from his legs.

He stumbled and collapsed, the cobblestones cold and unforgiving beneath him. The world around him faded, the sounds of the raging war that filled the air receding into the distance. The screams, gunfire, and explosions became muffled as if heard through a thick shroud. His vision blurred, the edges of his sight darkening until nothing was left to see. He fell into the numb abyss of nothingness, the black void that consumed all thought, all feeling. The cobblestone street became his final resting place, his body still amidst the chaos, a silent testament to the brutal reality of war. In those final moments, he was alone, suspended between life and death, the music of his defiant cry echoing in the silence of his mind.

And then, there was only darkness…an oblivion.

∞∞∞∞∞∞

There was a dim, faint light, and a mixture of human voices echoed everywhere as if coming from a distant, unreachable place. Shadows danced on the edges of his consciousness, vague silhouettes that seemed both familiar and strange. The sounds of people calling, their hurried footsteps, the rustle of cloth and the clinking of metal floated through the haze. Where was he? The cold seeped into his bones, yet his body was burning, his skin feverish and damp with sweat. His mouth was parched, a desert of dryness that begged for relief.

"Pić… Woda…" ("Drink… Water…"), his mouth softly whispered the words, over and over, a plea born from instinct rather than thought. But there was no response, no hand to offer him a sip, no voice to comfort him. The echoing voices ignored him, their conversations swirling around him like a distant wind. "Pić… Woda…" The words fell from his lips, more breath than sound, as the darkness tugged at the edges of his mind, threatening to pull him under.

Then, a flashback—a sudden searing memory of the submachine-gun fire, the burst of bullets cutting through the air with deadly precision. The sharp crack of gunfire, the explosion of the grenade, the sensation of his blood pouring from his body, and then… nothingness. The intrusive episode was brief, a flash of pain and fear that quickly faded back into the void.

After a while, the echoing voices returned, but this time, they were clearer and more insistent. The world around him became more defined, the shadows resolving into shapes, the voices into words. The noise of chaos grew more vigorous and explicit: "It's Dr Piwko here." The voice was firm and authoritative, a lifeline in the swirling confusion.

"Can you hear me, soldier?" The question cut through the fog in his mind, a command as much as a query. "We cannot give you water." The words stung, deepening the already unbearable thirst. But there was also a hint of compassion in the voice, a recognition of his suffering. "You lost a lot of blood. Stay calm; we are arranging your blood transfusion."

The words felt strange and distant, yet somehow, they still reached him. Blood transfusion. The term drifted through his mind, foreign and clinical but filled with the promise of life. He wanted to speak, to ask for water again, to make them understand how dry his mouth was and how much he desperately needed a drink. But his voice was gone, swallowed by the exhaustion that held him and the fading grip of consciousness.

He was drifting, caught between the world of the living and the dark void that threatened to take him. The voices of the doctors and nurses became his anchor, pulling him back from the brink. He tried to focus on them, the words they were saying, and the sensations of hands working quickly and efficiently over his body.

There was pain, yes, a deep, throbbing pain that seemed to pulsate with every beat of his heart. But there was also a strange numbness, a detachment from his body as if he were watching himself from afar. The cold steel of the stretcher beneath him, the sterile smell of antiseptic, the muffled sounds of the war outside—they were all part of a world that felt increasingly distant, like a dream he could not fully wake from.

Dr Piwko's words continued a steady stream of instructions and reassurances. They were arranging his blood transfusion, doing everything they could to save him. But could they? A part of him wondered if it was already too late, if the damage done was beyond repair. He felt his consciousness slipping again, the edges of the world blurring into darkness.

But he held on, clinging to the sound of those voices, to the faint hope they offered. "Pić... Woda..." The words became a mantra now, a rhythm that kept him tethered to life, even as darkness pressed in from all sides. He could not let go, not yet. There was still a battle to fight, a life to reclaim. If only he could survive this moment; if only he could stay awake long enough to feel the warmth of blood returning to his veins.

The light dimmed again, the voices fading into the background as the numb abyss of nothingness once more began to take over. But even as he slipped away, Dr. Piwko's words lingered in his mind, a faint echo of the world he was struggling to remain a part of.

My father continued to flicker in and out of consciousness. Each time he regained a small bit of self-awareness, his parched lips would form the words, barely a whisper: "Pić... Woda." But the response was always the same—a firm yet gentle voice, softer now than before, repeating, "Wody nie można!" ("Water not allowed!"). The words were a lifeline and a restraint all at once—comforting in their consistency yet denying him the one thing he craved most.

He was in a large military hospital, hastily set up behind the battle lines, somewhere on the outskirts of Praga. The building, once perhaps a normal place, had been turned into a refuge for the wounded, where the fine line between life and death was carefully navigated. The room was vast, filled with rows of beds occupied by Polish Army soldiers, each one a testament to the brutal toll of war. The air was thick with the scent of antiseptic, blood, and the faint, lingering smoke from the nearby battlefields.

Nurses moved quickly, their faces masked by the urgency of their tasks. They carried water, first aid kits, bandages, gauze, and intravenous blood plasma packets—anything and everything that could stave off death for a few more hours or minutes. Though gentle, their hands moved with the precision of those who had seen too much, who had learned to put aside their emotions for survival.

My father was too weak to notice what was happening around him. His eyes, when they opened, were glassy and unfocused, and he appeared to be gazing at something far beyond the hospital walls. He was oblivious to the organised chaos surrounding him, unaware of the constant hum of activity as life and death played out in equal measure. Yet, he was alive, though barely. He could feel the dryness in his mouth with an intensity that overshadowed almost everything else. His body was burning with pain, a searing heat that seemed to radiate from every nerve, yet at the same time, he felt numb and paralysed by exhaustion and injury.

Where was he? How had he gotten here, and why? These questions drifted through his mind like leaves on the wind, there for only a fleeting moment, before being swept away by the fog of his pain and confusion. The memories of the battle, of the flash of the submachine gun fire, flitted in and out of his consciousness like a cruel replay that his mind couldn't switch off, a relentless loop that offered no escape. And then, the darkness would claim him again. The world would fade, the voices and the pain receding into a distant murmur as he slipped back into unconsciousness. It was a merciful oblivion, a place where he didn't have to think or feel, where the pain was absent, and the thirst that gnawed at him could be forgotten, if only for a little while. Inevitably, consciousness would return, dragging him back to the vague clutter of noises and the echoing voices surrounding him. The hospital, with its busy nurses and rows of wounded men, would come into focus for a moment, only to blur again as his strength ebbed away. The cycle repeated itself endlessly, a torturous rhythm of awareness and oblivion.

In those brief moments of clarity, my father grasped at the few things he could understand: the dry, burning thirst, the pain that never entirely left him, and the constant, unyielding presence of the hospital around him. It was a place of healing but also a place of waiting— waiting to live or waiting to die.

"What is your name?" The words drifted through the haze, blending with the faint noises that seemed to rise and fall in his mind. The sounds were distant, like echoes in a vast, empty hall, and he couldn't quite understand their meaning. "Can you hear me, soldier?"

The question was relentless, tugging at the edges of his hazy awareness.

Then, suddenly, the voice sharpened, cutting through the fog with a clarity that startled him. "What is your name, soldier?" His half-lidded eyes, heavy with exhaustion, slowly turned toward the source of the voice. The effort was immense, as though his eyelids were weighted with lead. His unfocused and dim gaze finally settled on the figure leaning over him.

"Chaim… Hen… Henryk… Henryk Poznański," he managed to whisper, his voice barely more than a breath. The name felt foreign on his tongue, as though it belonged to someone else—someone distant and far removed from the battered body lying on the bed.

"Henryk," the voice continued, firm yet gentle. "We gave you much blood… but cannot give you water. Do you hear me?" The words cut through the fog, reaching him with authority and compassion. "The doctor will see you very soon. You need to lie still… You are doing well."

The voice was a lifeline, anchoring him to the present, to the reality of the situation. He tried to hold onto it, to let it pull him back from the dark depths threatening to consume him. The mention of blood, of the life they were trying to restore to him, was a faint comfort, a reminder that he was still among the living, still fighting, even if that fight now took place within the confines of his own body.

He wanted to respond, to tell them he understood, but the words wouldn't come out. His mind was a swirling mix of pain, emotion, and confusion, and all he could focus on was the unbearable thirst that kept tormenting him. The voice had said no water, and although he understood the reason and the logic behind it, it did nothing to ease the gnawing need.

But the voice was calm and reassuring. It told him he was doing well and that he needed to lie still, so he tried. He forced his body to relax, to stop fighting the pain and the thirst, and to surrender to the care of those around him. The voice was right; he had to trust them, trust that they knew what they were doing and that they were doing everything they could to save him.

As the words faded back into the hospital's background noise, his eyes fluttered shut once more. The darkness, always lurking at the edges of his awareness, began to close in again, but this time, it felt less terrifying, more like a blanket being gently pulled over him. The voice had promised that the doctor would see him soon, that he was doing well, and that was enough for now.

In the quiet moments that followed, as he drifted between wakefulness and sleep, between pain and numbness, the voice's echo stayed with him, a small beacon of light in the darkness. It reminded him he was not alone, that others were fighting to keep him alive, to bring him back from the edge. And as long as he could hear that voice and hold onto those words, he knew he had a chance to live.

My father was becoming more aware of his circumstances. His mind was slowly clearing, allowing him to grasp the reality around him. "Henryk…" a male voice unexpectedly broke through the fog, catching him by surprise. "Henryk, it's Dr. Piwko here," the voice continued. "You've lost a significant amount of blood. We've given you a good amount of plasma and a blood transfusion. We currently plan to use a saline solution to wash away your wounds. Henryk, we must do this to prevent infection; you understand, don't you?"

He could not muster the strength to respond verbally, but he understood. The words reached him clearly, and he grasped the gravity of the situation. He was still here, still fighting, and the battle had shifted from the battlefield to his severely wounded body.

The man spoke in a tone that was both apologetic and firm. "Unfortunately, we do not have any anaesthesia. Before we can use a proper antiseptic, we need to wash off your wounds. You hear me, Henryk?" The words served as a warning, preparing him for the pain to come.

He vaguely nodded, the movement slow and weak but enough to show he understood. His body was too weak for anything more, but inside, his will to survive had not wavered.

"Okay, I will be back," Dr. Piwko said, his voice softer now, almost reassuring. With those words, he disappeared from view, leaving him alone once again with his thoughts and the throbbing pain that radiated through his upper body.

As he lay there, my father's mind wandered to the words he had just heard. The thought of enduring the procedure without an anesthetic filled him with dread, but he knew it was necessary. The infection was an enemy just as deadly as the battlefield, and he had to fight it with whatever strength he had left.

His awareness continued to sharpen, bringing a deeper understanding of his precarious situation. The voices, the pain, the endless thirst—they all pointed to the fragility of his condition. Yet, there was a flicker of hope, a sense that he was being cared for, that his life was worth saving.

He concentrated on that hope, letting it ground him as he prepared for what lay ahead. The darkness still lingered, hovering at the edges of his mind, but now it was mitigated by Dr Piwko's firm words, filled with a resolve to see him through this ordeal.

As long as voices guided him, hands worked to heal him, he would keep fighting. He closed his eyes, readying himself for the next step, and clung to the promise that had been made—that he was doing well, that he would make it through. And in that fragile hope, he found the strength to carry on.

A nurse appeared by his trolley, starkly contrasting with the chaos inside him. "Henryk, I'm Jadźka; I am going to wash off your wounds," she said, her voice firm but not unkind. She held a folded square of thick gauze in front of his face. "I want you to bite on this. Open your mouth and keep biting on it."

His jaw clenched reflexively as if bracing for the torture that awaited. He could do nothing else but bite down on the gauze to somehow endure the pain.

"Henryk, I have to do this," Jadźka's voice came again, a young, steady tone tinged with urgency. My father could barely register the words, his mind overwhelmed by the searing pain. It was like nothing he had ever experienced before, a pain so sharp it felt as if it would tear him apart. His body was already crying out in pain, a cutting, intense agony that seemed to pulse from every fibre of his being. Where was it coming from?

"Wounds... it will not... long," Jadźka's voice broke through the fog, but it sounded scattered, fragmented, like a radio signal fading in and out. And then, the flashback came again, the horrific memory of the machine-gun fire pounding in his mind. The sounds, the flashes of light, the terror — it all came crashing down on him, dragging him back into the darkness.

He faded into unconsciousness once more, the pain and fear receding into merciful oblivion. But it was short-lived. He woke again to the loud, chaotic noises of the hospital surroundings, the cacophony of sounds pressing in on him from all sides. The dim light, the hurried footsteps, the muted cries of the wounded—it all swirled around him in a dizzying blur.

"Henryk... Can you hear me?" A man's voice broke through the noise, steady and clear. My father tried to focus, to pull himself out of the haze and onto the voice. "We have disinfected your wounds; we should be able to avoid any pus leaking from them."

The words reached him, though their meaning took time to sink in: "disinfected," "wounds," "pus." The language of war and survival, clinical and cold, yet filled with the promise of life. "Henryk... we cannot stitch you up yet," the man continued, his tone urgent but calm, a lifeline in the sea of confusion. "We will be applying antiseptic from time to time to make sure you will not develop any infection; critical, Henryk. You understand."

Did he understand? The words were clear, but their significance was muddled by the pain and exhaustion that consumed him. Infection. Antiseptic. Critical. The words felt heavy, loaded with meaning he could not grasp.

He understood enough. The fight was not over, and his body was still a battlefield. Infection was the enemy now; the doctors and nurses were his comrades in this new fight for life.

The antiseptic was applied to the wound many times, each time an ordeal of agony that seemed to stretch the boundaries of what he could endure. Each time, they handed him the thick gauze and each time, he bit down on it with all the strength he could muster, his teeth grinding against the fabric as he braced himself for the vicious pain that would inevitably follow.

What my father did not yet know was the extent of his injuries— the full scope of the damage that had been inflicted on his body. His entire abdomen, from the sternum down to his pubis, had been opened in a desperate attempt to remove several bullets that had lodged deep within his flesh. The surgeons had worked methodically, their hands steady despite the chaos around them, extracting bullets from the centre of his abdominal area and one bullet perilously close to his heart. His left hand, too, had been severely wounded, mangled by the ferocity of the gunfire.

The enormity of the task was daunting. The abdomen had to be kept open for at least 9 to 12 hours, a gaping wound that needed to be meticulously maintained free of any infection if there was to be any hope of healing the internal injuries. The doctors and nurses were fighting a race against time, against the relentless march of sepsis and other infections that could so easily take hold in such conditions.

My father lay stretched across his trolley, motionless all this time. His mind drifted in and out of consciousness, a half-aware state where time seemed to lose its meaning. He could no longer feel the passage of hours, only the intermittent bursts of pain as the antiseptic was applied, each one a reminder that he was still alive, still fighting.

Nurse Halina, one of the many tireless figures moving through the dimly lit ward, would moisten his lips from time to time with a cotton bud submerged in distilled water. The gesture was a small mercy in the midst of his suffering, a brief relief from the relentless thirst that gnawed at him. The cool touch of the water against his parched lips was almost enough to make him believe that the pain might one day end—that he might emerge from this ordeal with his life intact.

But for now, there was only the present—only the pain, the antiseptic, the gauze between his teeth, and the hands working tirelessly to keep him alive. My father remained motionless, his body stretched across the trolley as if suspended between life and death, between the horrors of the battlefield and the fragile hope of recovery.

On September 15, 1944, Dr. Piwko faced the unimaginable task of performing an operation that was both unthinkable and necessary. The circumstances were dire; resources were scarce. My father lay on the trolley, his body weakened yet braced for what was to come. Minutes before the procedure, Nurse Jadźka stood beside him, her presence a beacon of warmth in the cold clinical atmosphere of the hospital. She leaned in, her face softened by an empathic smile that spoke of shared strength and concern. "You are a brave man... Henryk. I know you are brave and tough, aren't you?" Her words were gentle, almost a whisper, but they carried the weight of conviction. In that moment, she offered him not just comfort but a reminder of the courage that had carried him this far through battles and tribulations.

Those words echoed in my father's mind as Dr. Piwko, with the help of another nurse, began to stitch his belly. There was no narcosis, no anaesthesia to numb the pain—none were available in the makeshift hospital, where every resource was stretched thin by the demands of war. The pain that followed was unlike anything he had ever known, a searing agony that tore through him as the needle pierced his flesh again and again.

He tried his best not to scream, to keep the agony locked within, but it was a battle he was losing with each passing second. The fire in his abdomen was all-consuming, a relentless torture that pushed him to the brink. He could feel every stitch, every pull of the thread as it worked to close the gaping wound that had been left open for so long.

At the head of the trolley, Jadźka sat, her strength finally giving way to the unbearable sight before her. She had seen so much suffering and had steeled herself against it, time and time again, but this was too much. Tears welled in her eyes and began to spill down her cheeks as she whispered, "Oh Matko Boska... Nasi chłopcy tak bardzo cierpią" (English: "Oh Saint Mother... Our boys suffer so much"). Her voice was a tremor in the air, a quiet cry to the heavens that seemed to echo the silent screams locked within my father's throat. The room was filled with the sounds of the procedure—the sharp intake of breath, the muted sobs of the nurse, the methodical movements of the doctor—yet it was her words that lingered, a poignant reminder of the shared pain and the shared humanity that bound them all at that moment.

It was a pain no man should have to bear, yet here he was, enduring it because there was no other choice. After all, survival demanded it. His body shook with the effort to stay silent, to keep the pain from spilling out, but it was a losing battle. As the final stitches were placed, the room seemed to hold its breath. The ordeal was over, but the echoes of it would linger long after the physical wounds had healed. My father's body, marked by the crude yet life-saving stitches, was a testament to the resilience of the human spirit, to the ability to endure even the unendurable.

Jadźka's tears, her quiet prayer to the Matko Boska, served as a reminder of the true cost of war—covering the pain that extends beyond the battlefield into the hearts of those caring for the wounded and witnessing the suffering of fellow humans. In that room, amid the pain and tears, there was also a deep sense of connection—a recognition of the shared burden they all carried, a burden that could only be faced with courage, compassion, and a heart still strong enough to call out to the heavens.

∞∞∞∞∞

Later in life, my father would often talk about that traumatic surgery, recalling how it had taken away his will to live. The memory was a dark shadow that stayed with him—a moment when the pain was so fierce, so all-consuming, that the thought of death felt like a kind relief. As his body was painfully stitched up, every fibre of his being begged for the suffering to end. He wanted nothing more than to escape the agony, to let go and find peace in the silence of death. But despite his despair, despite the crushing weight of the pain, he survived.

After a week of slow, agonising recovery, he was transferred to a Field Hospital, where he spent at least two months convalescing. The days in the Field Hospital were long and difficult, but they were also a time of connection and camaraderie. My father got to know many

177

of the soldiers who had fought on the Belorussian front, men who, like him, had faced the horrors of war and lived to tell the tale.

One of these comrades was Aaron Hekelman, a man whose presence brought a sense of calm and solace to the hospital. My father often saw him sitting at the piano, his fingers gently coaxing melodies from the worn keys. Something about Hekelman's music soothed the soul, offering a brief respite from the memories of battle and the pain of healing.

Once, my father saw Hekelman singing a new song he had written, titled "A Song About My Warsaw" (Polish: "Piosenka o Mojej Warszawie"). The room went silent as Hekelman started to play, his voice rising and falling with the haunting melody. The lyrics, simple yet profound, captured the longing and love many soldiers felt for their distant homeland—a homeland they fought for, suffered for, and would never forget.

The words of the song resonated deeply with my father, touching a chord that had been buried beneath the pain and the trauma. It was a reminder of what they were fighting for, of the city that still lived in their hearts despite the distance and war. As Hekelman sang, the music filled the room, enveloping each of the men in a warm, shared memory of home.

The lyrics of "A Song About My Warsaw" were more than just words—they were a lifeline, a connection to the past and a beacon of hope for the future. At that moment, as the song filled the air, my father felt a glimmer of the will to live to return. The pain, the despair, the trauma—they were still there, but so too was the love for his homeland, the love that had sustained him through the darkest of times.

With its poignant melody and heartfelt lyrics, the song became a symbol of resilience for my father and his comrades—a reminder that even in the darkest of times, there was something worth fighting for, something worth living for. And so, as he lay in that Field Hospital, surrounded by men who had seen and endured so much, my father began to heal—not just physically, but in spirit as well.

It took a long time for my father to recover sufficiently, for the wounds to close, and for his spirit to mend. The journey back to himself was slow and arduous. The simple acts of talking, smiling, walking, and conversing—things that had once come so easily—had to be relearned, each step forward a tiny victory over the shadows of pain and despair that lingered in his memory.

On January 10, 1945, he was finally discharged from the Field Hospital; his body had healed enough for him to rejoin the army. The war was still raging, but as Berlin fell on April 20, 1945, my father found himself increasingly thinking about his family. His thoughts were dominated by a burning question: Where were his parents and brothers? He still remembered the address on the back of the letter he had received from his mother while in Poltava: 13 Spokojna Street. With its simple, hopeful words, the letter had been a fragile link to the family he longed to see again. But what would he find when he reached Spokojna Street? Would the building still be standing, or would the flames of war have consumed it? And more importantly, would his loved ones still be there? The questions haunted him, each one a painful twist in his heart.

A Song About My Warsaw

Like the smile of a beloved girl,
Like the poem of a spring awakening,
Like the chirping of swallows at dawn,
Youthful feelings, still unknown,
Like dew sparkling on the grass,
A poem of love being born,
So does the heart rejoice in singing this song,
The song about my Warsaw.

How I wish, with a carefree step,
To trace the paths of my wanderings,
To stroll aimlessly down Marszałkowska
To gaze at the Vistula from a bridge,
To ride the number nine to the Avenues,
And weave into the crowd on Nowy Świat,
And to see, as I once did in my youth,
How you, Warsaw, smile at me.

I know you are not the same today,
That you have lived through bloody days,
That despair and pain weigh heavily on you,
That I must shed tears for you.
But the way you live in my memory,
I will restore with the sacrifice of my blood,
Believe me, Warsaw, beyond song and tears,
I am ready to give my life for you.

Aaron Hekelman, 1944

It was spring, sometime in late April 1945, when my father decided to take a walk towards Spokojna Street. The air was still cool, but the first signs of new life began to stir, with buds appearing on the trees and a gentle breeze carrying the faint scent of blossoms. By then, he had heard about the Warsaw Ghetto and the whispers of places called concentration camps, though the full horrors of these sites were still only vaguely known to him.

As he made his way through the streets of Warsaw, his mind was heavy with uncertainty. The city was beginning to wake up from its long, war-torn slumber, but the scars of destruction were everywhere. Buildings lay in ruins, and the streets were filled with people trying to piece their lives back together. Yet, despite the devastation, there was a resilience in the air, a feeling that life would carry on, no matter how deep the wounds.

The contrast was striking when my father turned onto Spokojna Street from the busier Okopowa Street. Spokojna Street (In English: Quiet Street), true to its name, lived up to its promise of quietness. The street was lined with old trees, their branches arching overhead to form a canopy of shade. The leaves rustled softly in the breeze, and a calm atmosphere felt almost out of place in a city still reeling from the war's aftermath.

On the right side of the street, a weathered brick wall encircled the historic Powązki Cemetery, a place that had seen generations of Warsaw's dead laid to rest. The wall was worn, its red bricks chipped and aged, yet it stood firm, a silent protector of the memories within. On the left side, remnants of buildings showed the scars of war—crumbling facades, broken windows, and piles of rubble here and there. The buildings bore odd numbers, each a remnant of the life that once thrived in this area.

My father, 1945.

Finally, my father's steps slowed as he approached the building he had been searching for; the address that had occupied his thoughts long before he came to Warsaw. He paused, facing a badly neglected structure, its walls streaked with grime and its windows either broken or boarded up. The building bore the number he had been looking for—number 13.

Number 13 Spokojna Street. The address had been etched into his memory, a thread that connected him to his past, to the last communication he had received from his mother while he was in Poltava. Now, standing before it, the building seemed to hold the weight of all that had been lost. It was a shell, a shadow of what it once was, its exterior battered by forces of war and time.

My father approached the entrance cautiously, his heart pounding in his chest. The door hung askew on its hinges, the wood splintered and rotting. He pushed it open, the sound of creaking wood breaking the stillness of the street. The building's interior was dark and musty, the air thick with the scent of decay. The floors were littered with debris, and the walls were covered with marks of neglect and abandonment.

He stepped inside, his breath catching as he called out softly, "Is anyone here?" His voice echoed through the empty rooms, but there was no answer. The silence was deafening, starkly contrasting to the bustling life that must have filled these halls. He wandered through the rooms, each one empty and holding a memory of what could have been.

He stood in what had likely been the main room, the light filtering through a broken window casting long shadows across the floor. He tried to imagine his parents here, living their lives, holding onto hope even as the world around them crumbled. But the images in his mind were fleeting, dissipating like smoke in the wind.

Suddenly, a voice called out from an adjacent room, startling my father from his thoughts. "Can I help you?" The voice was steady and matter of fact, yet it carried a weight that seemed to cut through the silence of the deserted place.

My father followed the call, stepping into the room where the voice had come from. Inside, he saw a man standing on a ladder, busily painting the wall, his brush moving methodically as if trying to cover up the past with each stroke. The man looked down at my father from his perch, his expression curious yet guarded. My father approached him, his steps slow and deliberate. "Excuse me," he began, his voice steady despite the turmoil in his heart, "do you know what sort of place this was?"

The man paused, the brush hovering in mid-air as he considered the question. He glanced at my father, then back at the wall he was painting as if searching for the right words. Finally, he answered, "Well, from what I know, before the Hitlerites attacked us, this was a School of Photography. Sometime after the Hitlerites took control of Warsaw, this building became part of the Ghetto... you know, the Hitlerites created the Ghetto for the Jews."

My father's breath caught in his throat, but he remained silent, letting the man continue.

"Lots of Jews lived in this building for a year, maybe longer," the man went on, his voice tinged with a distant sadness. "But then they were taken away, in cattle trains, never to be seen again."

My father's heart pounded in his chest as he stared intensely at the man's face, trying to read the emotions behind the words. "What do you mean: never to be seen again?"

The man sighed, his expression darkening as he met my father's gaze. "Panie... (Sir...), they were all killed, that's what I mean. That is what people say. All the Jews from the Ghetto were taken out on the cattle trains, and they never came back. People say... they all got killed."

The words hit my father like a punch, but he pushed himself to stay calm, though the deep lines on his forehead showed the tension. "So, who were the people that stayed here in this building?" he asked, his voice steady but edged with a tension he couldn't fully mask.

The man looked around the room as if seeing it anew before returning to him. "What people? Panie... Entire families with kids. A family would cram into each room along the corridor," he said. "They had to share the space with many other families. Szwaby (the Krauts) didn't care if the Ghetto was overcrowded or not; many people died of starvation or typhus. But there is nothing left now. They viciously flattened almost every building after the Jews put up their resistance."

The man's voice softened as if he were sharing a terrible secret. "Panie, no one was left alive. None of those Jews that were here escaped death; none of them survived."

My father felt the words sinking into him, heavy and cold. He stared at the man, unable to speak, his mind reeling from the implications of what he had just heard. The image of his parents, of the life they might have led here, mingled with the stark reality that the man was describing.

"None of them survived," the man repeated, his voice barely more than a whisper. The room, once filled with the echoes of lives lived and lost, now seemed unbearably silent. The man on the ladder returned to his work, the brush moving once more in steady strokes. My father watched him for a moment longer, his heart heavy with the knowledge he had sought but dreaded finding. He had come looking for answers, and now that he had them, they felt like a weight too great to bear.

My father stood there, rooted to the spot, his thoughts a chaotic whirl of disbelief, grief, and anger. The calm that had marked Spokojna Street, the peace he had felt moments earlier upon arriving, was shattered by the truth. His parents, the people who had stayed

184

here, who had fought to hold on to life amid unimaginable suffering, were gone. The building, city, and world had moved on, but the pain and loss remained.

With a nod of thanks that he wasn't sure the man even noticed, my father turned and walked away, leaving the room and heading along the long corridor towards the exit. As he stepped outside the building, the burden of what he had learned pressed down on him with every step. The calm aura that had once defined the street was now a cruel reminder of the stolen peace and the lives that had been erased.

As he walked back down the street, the old trees still offering their shade, my father knew that this place, once filled with the hopes and dreams of so many, was now a graveyard of memories. He had found what he was looking for, but it was not the closure he had hoped for— only a deeper understanding of war's loss and the knowledge that some wounds would never heal.

∞∞∞∞∞∞

Sometime later, in 1945, with a heavy heart filled with unspoken fears and a flicker of faint hope, my father travelled from Warsaw to Kalisz. A part of him—irrational and stubborn—clung to the idea that perhaps, through some miracle, his family might still be living in the small, familiar ground-floor apartment at 2 Poznańska Street. The thought of it kept him moving, one foot in front of the other, through streets that seemed completely unfamiliar in the shadow of war.

When he finally arrived, the reality was harsher than he had prepared himself for. The apartment was no longer theirs. The warmth of his mother's presence and the comforting hum of daily life were gone, replaced by a cold, empty void. Tomasz, the old caretaker, met him at the door, his face marked by years of hard living and the toll of witnessing too much suffering.

Warsaw vanished after the October 1944 bombing, before which SS-
Obergruppenführer Bach-Zelewski removed Frederik Chopin's heart from its
resting place to add it to his personal collection of curiosities. Eventually, this
much-loved city rose again, and Chopin's heart was returned to its original place.
[3]

Over 400 hectares were assigned by German Nazis to contain 450,000 Polish Jews in Warsaw's Ghetto. The zone consisted of 73 streets and 27,000 dwellings, closed off by an 18-kilometre-long and three-meter-high continuous wall. At least 160,000 people died of starvation and widespread epidemics. From 22 July to 15 September 1943, 265,000 Polish Jews were transported to their death in Treblinka. Above this is what was left of the Warsaw Ghetto after the October 1944 bombing, when the German Luftwaffe levelled the entire area, purposefully leaving a Catholic Church intact [4]

Tomasz shook his head slowly as he recounted to my father the events that had unfolded in his absence. "Many letters arrived from the USA and Switzerland during the war," Tomasz said, his voice tinged with regret. "They came from Sarah Gotboim, through the Red Cross, from 1939 to 1944. But every one of them was returned to the sender. The Poznańskis were taken away from Kalisz to Warsaw in early 1941. All Jews were taken out of Kalisz and transported to Warsaw. Your parents, Chaim, and your two youngest brothers have never returned since."

The words fell like stones into a bottomless well, the echo of them reverberating in my father's soul. He stared at the caretaker, trying to make sense of the loss that seemed too vast, too incomprehensible to absorb in one moment. It wasn't just the apartment that was no longer theirs; it was the life, the history, the very essence of who they were that had been stripped away.

As my father's eyes wandered through the familiar space that was no longer his, he noticed how different it looked. The old walls, once adorned with the signs of his family's life, now bore the marks of strangers. A new Polish family had moved in, their presence a silent testament to the relentless march of time and the brutal reality of war.

"The Germans who lived in your apartment during the occupation removed all of the Poznańskis' belongings," Tomasz added, in a tone that was a mix of sympathy and resignation. "Now, as you can see, a new Polish family is living here."

The caretaker's words lingered in the air, but my father could hardly reply. He nodded absentmindedly; his mind adrift in a whirl of memories and what-ifs. The burden of it all felt overwhelming—this realisation that the threads linking him to his past had been cut, that the life he knew had vanished, leaving only an empty shell behind.

Standing in the spot that was once his home, he felt an overwhelming sense of dislocation. He was an untethered man, drifting in a world that no longer recognised him, living a life that was now irreparably changed. The hope that had driven him to Kalisz—the faint, desperate hope he might reunite with his family—had faded, replaced by a bleak, numbing sorrow.

But even in that moment of despair, a quiet, steely resolve was forming within him. He had survived when so many had not, and with that survival came the responsibility to carry forward the memory of those who were lost. The apartment, the city, and even the people who now occupied the space that had once been his were all part of a world that had moved on. I know my father carried the past with him, in his heart, in his memories, in every step he took from that day forward.

As he bade him farewell, the caretaker's voice was a distant murmur, lost in the whirlwind of thoughts and emotions that filled his mind. As my father turned to leave, he took one last look at the building, at the place where his family had lived, loved, and struggled. Then, with a heavy heart, he walked away, the weight of history pressing down on him, but determined to honour the life that had been lived within those walls, even if it was gone forever.

While residing in Warsaw (33 Rakowiecka Street, Mokotów), my father encountered individuals who claimed to have seen his brother Leon in a Soviet Gulag in Chelyabinsk. The news, though fragmentary and uncertain, ignited a fragile hope within him—a hope that perhaps, against all odds, Leon had survived the horrors of the war. The possibility that his brother might still be alive, languishing in some distant, frozen corner of the Soviet Union, spurred him into action.

Determined to uncover the truth, my father began writing letters to the Red Cross in 1946, pleading for any information they could provide about Leon. Each letter was penned with a mixture of desperation and hope, the words carefully chosen, as if by sheer force of will, he could pull his brother back from the void. He recounted every detail he could remember, clinging to the belief that somewhere, someone might recognise the name and might have seen the face that had been seared into his memory.

But as the weeks turned into months, there was no response. The silence was deafening; each day that passed without news deepened the ache and disenchantment in his heart. He waited; the hope that had flared so briefly slowly began to dim. The uncertainty gnawed at him, the not knowing almost worse than the finality of death. Where was

Leon? What had become of him in that vast, merciless expanse of Siberia?

Then, after many long months, a letter finally arrived. My father tore it open with trembling hands, his heart pounding with fear and anticipation. The words inside, however, were stark and unforgiving. In a straightforward statement, the letter advised that the search of available data had not yielded any positive findings regarding a person named Leon Poznański.

The sentence, so blunt and devoid of emotion, felt like a blow. The hope that had sustained him through those long months of waiting was shattered in an instant. The possibility that Leon might still be alive, that he might one day walk through the door, was gone. In its place was a void, a deep, unyielding sorrow that no words could fill.

Yet, even in his despair, my father clung to the belief that Leon had not simply vanished. The thought of his brother lost in the frozen wastelands of a Soviet Gulag haunted him. It was a spectre that would linger in the corners of his mind, a wound that would never fully heal. Though the Red Cross had found no trace of Leon, my father refused to let his memory fade. He continued to search, ask questions, and keep alive the hope that one day he might learn the truth about what had happened to his brother.

In October 1946, a sombre reunion took place in Warsaw. Aunt Regina and Arek Jakubowicz, accompanied by their son Samuel, made the journey to visit my father. The visit was heavy with the weight of the past and the uncertain future ahead. During the war, Arek Jakubowicz held a crucial and burdensome responsibility as the Head of Labour within the Judenrat of the Lodz Ghetto. His role in the Administration of the Jewish Authority had placed him at the heart of the Ghetto's harrowing existence, a position fraught with impossible choices and unrelenting pressure. Meanwhile, Regina and her son Samuel, known affectionately as Mula, had endured the unimaginable horrors of Ravensbrück, the largest concentration camp for women within Germany's prewar borders. Somehow, against all odds, they had survived.

The war had left deep scars on each of them, scars that no time could fully heal. The visit was bittersweet, a brief moment of reconnection amidst the ruins of their lives. They spoke of the past in hushed tones, memories flickering like shadows across their faces. There was so much to say, yet words felt inadequate, unable to bridge the gap between what they had lived through and the new world they were trying to navigate.

By 1947, it was clear that the Jakubowicz family's future lay far from the ashes of Europe. They had decided to immigrate to the United States, a place that held the promise of safety and a fresh start, far from the horrors they had endured. My father, who had so few familial bonds left in the world, accompanied them as far as he could. Together, they took the train south, the journey filled with both hope and sorrow, knowing that this parting would be their last.

As the train approached the border with Czechoslovakia, they had to bid each other goodbye. My father was unable to travel beyond that point. They stood together on the platform, the weight of their shared history hanging in the air. Regina, Arek, and Mula looked at my father, their eyes reflecting the pain of yet another separation, another loss. They embraced, the moment heavy with unspoken words, and then they parted. My father watched as the train carried them away, taking with it the last of his close family.

The knowledge that he would never see them again was a quiet agony, one that he carried with him in the years that followed. Letters from America, a potential lifeline across the vast ocean, were routinely sent back to the sender by the new communist authorities in Poland, sealing off yet another connection to his past. The iron curtain of the post-war world had descended, and with it, the final thread of his connection to the Jakubowicz family was cut.

The memory of that parting lingered with my father, a bittersweet reminder of the family he had lost and the resilience they had shown. The pain of separation and the loneliness of being left behind were ever present, but so too was the knowledge that somewhere across the ocean, his family was alive, starting anew. It was a small comfort, a glimmer of light in an otherwise dark and fractured world.

In the years that followed, my father would often think of them—of Regina, with her strength and dignity; of Arek, burdened by his past; and of Mula, who had survived Ravensbrück and now faced a new future. He would wonder what their lives had become, how they had adapted to a world so far from the one they had known. But those questions would remain unanswered, lost in the silence that followed their departure.

Mula: one of the very few children who survived the Lodz Ghetto

Regina and Arek Jakubowicz – circa 1947

The Jewish Authority Council (i.e. Judenrat) of Lodz Ghetto, Chairman
Rumkowski (seated in the centre), poses with members of the Council and four
couples at a joint wedding celebration in the Lodz Ghetto. In the front row from
right to left: Arek Jakubowicz, David Gertier, Regina Jakubowicz, Mordechai
Rumkowski, Dora Fuks, Leon Rosenblat, and David Warszawski – circa 1943 [5]

Notes

1. Bacyk, Norbert (2006) Operation Eastern Front 1944. Leandoer & Ekholm Publishing, Stockholm 2006. p. 125

2. United States Holocaust Memorial Museum collections.ushmm.org

3. Ibid.

4. Ibid.

5. Ibid.

PART – II

DISILLUSIONMENT

9. Sanctified Anti-Semitism

Since 966 AD, when Poland began and officially embraced Christianity, the Catholic faith has been the cornerstone of Polish national identity. Catholic Poles' identity is encapsulated in a profound and unwavering love for Jesus Christ (Polish: Pan Jezus Chrystus). This devotion is more than just a religious faith—it is a collective unconscious, deeply embedded in the very psyche of Polish society. In the minds of the faithful, Pan Jezus is not merely a figure of worship; he is the Son of God, the Holy Spirit, the immaculately pure sufferer of human pain. His suffering, borne with divine grace, is seen as a direct result of the evil forces that sought to destroy him—forces that, according to deeply rooted beliefs, include primarily the Jews who supposedly betrayed him and caused him to suffer on the cross.

These core beliefs have been instilled in Polish Catholic society by the clergy over the centuries through subtle yet pervasive indoctrination. From the earliest days of Christianity in Poland, the dictums of the New Testament were taught with a focus on the narrative of Jesus's betrayal and crucifixion. This narrative placed the Jews in the role of the betrayer, synonymous with Judas. This message was not overtly hateful as it was subtly woven into the fabric of religious education and reinforced through generations of worship.

The clergy, who wielded immense influence over the nation's spiritual and moral life, ensured these beliefs were passed down through the ages. Throughout the Dark, Middle, and Modern Ages, the teachings of the Church were the primary source of moral guidance for the Polish people. At every Eucharistic liturgical service, whether in the grand cathedrals of major cities or the humble chapels of rural towns and villages, these subtle messages embellished with tacit meanings, were voiced in sermons that effectively promoted an implicit social understanding that Jews were the representatives of evil, they were the ones who had turned away from the divine light of Christ and, therefore, did not belong to Poland.

Even as Poland moved through the ages, modernising and changing in many ways, these beliefs remained a constant undercurrent, shaping attitudes and actions. The image of Jesus as the ultimate sufferer, betrayed and crucified, was a powerful social instrument used to draw a stark line between those who were seen as part of the Polish nation and those who were not. The suffering of Jesus has always been a collective memory; it was felt as a wound that never fully healed, and it could be reopened whenever there was a need to reaffirm the boundaries of national Polish identity.

For centuries, this narrative has been a part of the Polish Catholic consciousness, a way of understanding the world that has had profound implications for how Jews were viewed and treated. The idea that Jews did not belong in Poland was not just a prejudice; it was a deeply held belief rooted in the teachings of the Church and reinforced by the very structure of Polish society. The weight of these beliefs continued to influence how Polish people saw themselves and their place in the world. The love of Pan Jezus is not just a personal faith; it is a national creed that defines who is welcome in Poland and who is not. There was always little room for those who had rejected the love of Pan Jesus, namely those who were seen as the betrayers of all that was good and holy.

This dialectic has long been the hallmark of the Christian Catholic mindset, not just in Polish society but across the entirety of the European continent. From its earliest days, the Catholic value system has found expression in a set of beliefs and judgments that, at their core, were deeply anti-Semitic and profoundly demoralising, and finding their justification in the very text of the New Testament, which among the Gentiles is not read from the originally intended perspective of Judaic tradition but from the tradition of the Great

Roman Empire going back to Constantine and the Council of Nicaea, the first ecumenical council of the Christian Church in 325AD.

One need only turn to the Gospel of Matthew, where the infamous words are recorded: the Jews, in a moment of collective self-judgment, declare that they will never be able to wash away their guilt —"His (Jesus') blood will be on us and our children." This passage, charged with the weight of millennia, has been instrumentalised for both nationalistic and religious purposes—in Poland, creating an apparent and dangerous dichotomy: 'us'—the faithful believers in the righteousness and goodness of Pan Jezus, and 'them'—the ungodly, deceitful Jews who refuse to believe, and who are forever marked by their betrayal of Pan Jezus.

∞∞∞∞∞∞

After his visit to Spokojna 13, my father fully grasped the harrowing reality of his family's fate and the devastation that had befallen the Jewish communities during the German Nazi occupation of Poland. The weight of this understanding settled over him like a shroud, inescapable and suffocating, as the stories of what had happened came to light, piece by agonising piece.

However, even before the German invasion, my father was no stranger to the darker currents that had long been stirring beneath the surface of Polish society. He was already aware of the right-wing nationalistic waves that swept across Poland in the wake of Marshal Piłsudski's death. This seismic shift had agitated the embers of traditional, historical Polish anti-Semitism, fanning them into flames once again.

Polish nationalism has always been allied with the Polish Catholic Church. Historically, it was always a powerful alliance that shaped the nation's soul. As already stated, in Poland, the Church was not just a religious institution but the bedrock of identity, heritage, and the vision for the country's future.

In the Second Republic of Poland, when the Church and the Nationalists led by Roman Dmowski joined forces, their vision for Poland left little room for those who did not share in the bloodline and the faith that had come to define what it meant to be genuinely Polish. To them, an ideal Poland was a nation untainted by diversity, where the richness of Jewish life and culture was seen not as a thread in the national tapestry but as a stain that had to be scrubbed away clean.

My father saw these undercurrents with a sense of unease before and after the war. He saw how the rhetoric of purity and exclusivity seeped into the public consciousness, how the alliance between the Church and the Nationalists created a climate where anti-Semitic sentiments could flourish with tacit approval.

With its immense influence over the hearts and minds of the Polish people, the Church became a conduit for these nationalistic ideals. The Nationalists, in turn, drew on the Church's authority to legitimise their vision of a Poland purified of those who did not belong—Jews, who had lived alongside Poles for eight centuries since the 1200s. For my father, this confluence of religion and national identity was deeply troubling. He understood all too well the dangers of such a union, how it could turn neighbours into strangers and strangers into enemies. He saw how the threads of Polish identity, once interwoven with Jewish life, were being unravelled, leaving behind a vision of Poland that was narrow, insular, and hostile towards those who did not fit the prescribed integral aspect of Polish Catholic identity.

As the Nazi occupation took hold and the full extent of the horror was revealed, my father's fears were confirmed. The very forces that had once quietly agitated for a homogenous Poland had now found a brutal ally in the Nazi regime, which conducted its vision of racial purity with merciless efficiency. The fate of the Jewish communities was sealed in the ghettos, the concentration camps, and the mass graves that scarred the land.

In Poland, the alliance between the Catholic Church and nationalists created a fertile ground for open Jew-hatred. The idea of a unified Poland, free of Jews, was achieved not by Poles but by more militant nationalist forces of Nazi Germany, in the most brutal way—through the total extermination of an entire people. As my father understood his family's fate and the Jewish communities in Poland, he also recognised the deeper forces that had shaped that destiny. It was a lesson that stayed with him throughout his life, a reminder of the dangers of letting fear and prejudice take control.

For Polish Nationalists, the world was starkly divided, with no room for Communists, liberals, or any other ideological perspectives that diverged from their Catholic worldview. There was only space for a militant form of Catholicism, one that fused faith with fervent Nationalism and left no room for dissent or difference. In their envisioned Poland, the Church was a fortress of identity, its walls impenetrable to any influence that did not align with its theistic and nationalistic ideals.

After the war, as Poland staggered to its feet, bruised and battered by years of Nazi occupation and the subsequent imposition of Communist rule, there was a silent, unspoken blessing that many would have felt within the Polish Catholic Church and the ranks of the Nationalists—most of the Jews had disappeared from the Polish landscape. The Jewish communities that had once thrived in towns and cities across the country were gone, with more than 3,000,000 Polish Jews, erased by the horrors of the Holocaust. For those who had long harboured anti-Semitic sentiments, this tragic void was felt as a phenomenon of purification, a return to Poland that was more authentically Polish.

In the years that followed, as Polish society struggled to recover from the 'shellshock' of war and occupation, conversations about the nation's future were dominated by the heroism and sacrifices of Polish Catholic heroes. The narrative of resistance, of a country that had endured unspeakable suffering at the hands of the Nazis, took centre stage. In the public discourse, there was little room for the stories of those who had been systematically exterminated and little acknowledgment of the Jewish suffering that had occurred alongside the Polish suffering. The focus was on the resilience of the Polish spirit, embodied in the Catholic faith and the nationalist fervor that had survived the darkest days.

As the nation tried to 'move on' from its trauma, most people looked to the Church for healing and direction. The Church, though stripped of official State power under the new Communist regime, retained a profound influence over the hearts and minds of the people. It offered solace and a sense of continuity in an upended world. Even in its extinguished political role, the Church found ways to propagate its message, subtly but powerfully, reinforcing the bonds between faith and national identity.

The standard view espoused by the clergy was one of divine protection—a narrative that offered comfort to a people in need of hope. Pan Jezus had risen to protect His followers, to shield them from the world's evils. In their pain and hardship, the Polish faithful had a place to turn to: the Church. It was a haven, a sanctuary where they could come to pray, lay their burdens at the foot of the Lord's cross, and feel the spirit of Pan Jezus fill their hearts and souls.

Within this sacred space, they were reassured of their safety and their place in a world that had been violently shattered. The message was clear: those who remained steadfast in their faith and clung to the Church's teachings would be protected from all that was evil. Subtly, almost unnoticed, the message extended beyond spiritual protection. It served as a reminder of the old division between those who accepted Christ and those who rejected him. The Jews, whose absence from Poland was now a grim reality, were cast as the other, as those who had turned away from the divine protection offered by the Church through Pan Jesus.

The Monument of the Warsaw Uprising

In this narrative, the Church offered not only a spiritual solace but also a confirmation of moral superiority and a reassurance that the Polish people, in their faith, were aligned with the divine will. Their suffering was seen not just as a consequence of war but as a test of their faith, which they had passed by remaining faithful to Pan Jezus and the Church's doctrine. The absence of the Jews, the silence left by their disappearance, was woven into this narrative as an implicit affirmation of the righteousness of the Polish Catholic identity.

As the nation rebuilt itself, these subtle messages reinforced the idea that the future of Poland lay in its Catholic roots, in a vision of the country that was homogenous, faithful, and unyielding in its commitment to the Church. The wounds of the war were deep, but the Church offered a balm—a narrative that sanctified the suffering of the Polish people while quietly erasing the suffering of those who did not fit into its vision of a Catholic Poland.

In Polish society, those subtle, theistic messages permeated daily life, quietly shaping the social fabric and dictating what was considered acceptable. Just as it was deemed appropriate for a fallen mortal to seek absolution within the privacy of the confessional from a compassionate and forgiving priest, it was equally acceptable to harbour and express anti-Semitic sentiments. These sentiments, often cloaked in a veneer of pity, were woven into the community's tacit understanding of who followed moral faith and who did not.

In this worldview, where the memory of its Jewish citizens was buried alongside the ruins of the war, it was socially acceptable to pity the Jews, but this pity was not born of compassion; instead, it was driven by a sense of moral superiority. The Jews, after all, had betrayed and killed the merciful Pan Jezus, who, in the hearts of the faithful, remained eternally alive. This belief, deeply embedded in the collective unconsciousness, positioned the Jews as people forever marked by their rejection of Christ, a rejection that had, in the eyes of many, justified their disappearance.

The story was clear: while it was a moral duty to forgive neighbours' sins through the sacrament of confession, it was also acceptable to see the Jews as people who had lost their place in the moral order by turning away from Pan Jezus. This wasn't seen as hatred but as a simple, undeniable truth repeated in sermons, stories, and the subtle, everyday interactions that shaped the community's culture and folklore.

In this context, anti-Semitism was not just tolerated; it was, in many ways, regarded as sacred. It was integrated into the very identity of what it meant to be Polish Catholic and part of a community that had endured so much but had stayed strong in its faith. The Jews, by contrast, were considered outsiders, and their disappearance was seen through the lens of their alleged betrayal of Christ.

This deeply ingrained belief allowed for the expression of anti-Semitic values to coexist with a sense of pity and righteousness. The boundaries of morality were stretched to allow for the coexistence of faith and prejudice, purity and exclusion. The confessional, a place of forgiveness and redemption, stood in stark contrast to the social norms that allowed for the marginalisation of an entire people. Yet, in the minds of many, there was no contradiction—only a reaffirmation of a deeply held belief that the survival and purity of the Polish soul depended on its steadfast adherence to a vision of identity that left no room for those who did not share in its faith.

Thus, the idealistic messages preached from the pulpit were smoothly translated into socially acceptable customs and actions. The Church's teachings, combined with the strong currents of Nationalism, fostered a society where anti-Semitism was not just tolerated but became part of the cultural identity. It was viewed as a natural extension of the faith, a reflection of the firm, unwavering belief that to be Polish was to be Catholic, and to be Catholic was to be aligned with the divine will—a will that, in the eyes of many, had marked the Jews as a people to be pitied but never fully accepted as Poles with a different faith.

∞∞∞∞∞∞∞

The Jews and their communities, long since absent from Polish soil, somehow remain the eternal scapegoats, their absence only amplifying their role as the repository for the nation's unspoken sins. Combined with the indoctrinated value system that Jews should be viewed as people that one would pity, in contrast to superior, godly Poles, is the uncomfortable envy that arises when the notion of superiority is challenged. Should any Jew be wealthy, highly educated or financially secure, these cannot be signs of his wisdom or virtuous qualities, but signs of his inherent greed and exploitative nature.

Through tacit remarks, offhand comments, and deeply ingrained social mores, anti-Semitic expressions continue to echo through Polish society. The notion that American Jews are robbing Poland is not new. The old conspiracies that Jews outside Poland control the world's governments have intensified, as the Jewish communities that once thrived in Poland are no more. The final exodus of the last remnants of the Holocaust survivors occurred between March 1968 and December 1969, when the remaining 30,000 Jews were driven from Poland during the so-called 'anti-Zionist campaign.' This campaign, politically framed to disguise its true intent, was nothing less than a continuation of the 'final solution' to the 'Jewish problem.' It was a move that appeased both the Church and the Nationalistic elements within Poland, a tacit agreement that allowed the last vestiges of Jewish life in Poland to be erased.

The tragedy of this campaign was not just in the loss of these remnant Jewish families but in the way it was accepted and quietly endorsed by a society that had been conditioned over centuries to see its Jews not as fellow citizens but as eternal outsiders. The Church, though stripped of its official power in the Communist State, still held immense sway over the moral and spiritual direction of the nation. Its quiet approval of the anti-Zionist campaign signaled to the faithful that this was a righteous move, a necessary step in purifying the devout Polish nation.

Individual values and core beliefs are stable human characteristics that are resistant to change and deeply rooted in both personal and collective identity. Similarly, a society's collective unconscious, especially one steeped in cultural and theistic values, evolves slowly in a deeply pervasive and durable manner. In the case of Polish Catholic society, it is highly likely that the implicit anti-Semitic attitudes, which have been durably woven into its fabric, will persist for centuries to come.

∞∞∞∞∞∞∞

While these thoughts may seem like offensive sweeping generalisations, they reflect a deeper, nuanced understanding of Polish culture—one that is difficult to define objectively yet can be described through its folklore, arts, sentiments, and the subtleties of its collective psyche. Polish culture, after all, is complex and multifaceted, embodying both the highest ideals of humanity and the darker undercurrents that have shaped its history.

Objectively speaking, Poland holds a prominent place in history as the country with the highest number of registered "Righteous Among the Nations" at Yad Vashem in Israel. This honour reflects the remarkable bravery and moral strength of many Polish individuals who risked their lives and their families' lives to save their Jewish neighbours during the Holocaust. Many of these Polish heroes never sought reward or recognition for their courageous, compassionate actions; they acted out of a strong sense of moral duty, guided by their conscience and faith.

Indeed, among Polish Catholic worshippers from all walks of life, one would quickly find many morally virtuous men and women who refused to stand idly by while their neighbours were subjected to horrid forms of victimisation. These individuals embodied the highest principles of their faith, demonstrating a profound compassion and empathy that transcended the prejudices of their time. Their actions serve as a potent reminder that some rise above the collective biases within any society and act under the true essence of their beliefs.

In the 1200s, under the reign of Casimir the Great (Kazimierz Wielki), the historical founders of Christianity—the Jews—were formally invited to settle in Polish lands. This moment in history, while seemingly a gesture of inclusion, had laid the groundwork for the duality that would come to define the relationship between Polish Catholics and Polish Jews in the centuries to come. While individual acts of heroism and moral integrity illuminate Poland's history, the broader societal attitudes remain under the shadow of this long-standing Catholic doctrinal position. The pressing question is whether Polish society can urgently reconcile these two aspects of its identity—the deep-seated anti-Semitic sentiments that have been nurtured over centuries and the undeniable legacy of moral courage displayed by so many of its people.

As Poland continues to navigate its complex history, the crucial challenge will be to acknowledge and confront these dualities, to honour the legacy of those who acted with moral clarity while also addressing the darker aspects of its past. Only by facing these truths can a society hope to move beyond the prejudices that have so long shaped its collective consciousness towards a future where the moral compass is guided not by exclusionary doctrines but by a deeper understanding of the shared humanity that binds us all.

10. My Communist Poland

On 2nd April 1945, the Polish Army regional command posted my father in the position of Section Manager within the Mokotów Prison, which incarcerated mainly German prisoners of war and Polish Nationalists opposed to the newly established Polish Communist Government. Throughout the 1947 – 1948 period, a large proportion of Polish Nationalists were identified as members of the Freedom and Independence (Polish: 'Wolność i Niezawisłość' "WIN"), an organisation established on 2nd September 1945 and vehemently opposed to the Polish United Labour Party ('Polska Zjednoczona Partia Robotnicza' "PZPR").

WIN initially identified itself as a peaceful organisation ideologically opposed to the Soviet Union and PZPR. However, in time, WIN became armed and highly disciplined in their intention to fight the established communist government of the Polish People's Republic "PRL." WIN's anti-Semitic values underpinned their strong belief that the established new Polish regime was not only communist but also dominated by Jews, who, even after Hitler's Final Solution, managed to infiltrate and rule Poland. [1]

The history of WIN includes close ties with the Ukrainian 'Pollisian Sich', that is, the Ukrainian Nationalist Army, which was formed with financial help from Nazi Germany in 1941. The aim of the Ukrainian 'Pollisian Sich' was to fight against the Soviet forces. The 'Pollisian Sich' at a later stage changed its name and became known as the Ukrainian Insurgent Army ('Ukrayinska Povstanska Armiya' "UPA"). In August 1941, the UPA, led by its founder, Taras Bulba-Borovets [2], committed a massacre of defeated and retreating Soviet soldiers. This massacre took place after the UPA took control of the small Ukrainian town of Olevsk. Many Jews living at Olevsk were subjected to pogroms, forced labour, and various acts of public humiliation. In November 1941, the UPA killed approximately 3,000 Jews. The Ukrainian Nationalists also committed mass murder against Polish civilians in several regions of Poland. In Wołyń, the Ukrainian Nationalists killed approximately 60,000 innocent Polish residents. In Lwów (English: Lviv), 24,800 Polish women, children, and men were viciously killed. In Stanisławów, 18,000 were murdered; and in Tarnopol, 27,600 were murdered. [3]

The Polish communist government had intelligence pointing to the close collaboration between WIN and UPA, specifically involving joint guerrilla attacks (e.g. Hrubieszów assault). [4] During the trials, the members of WIN were offered no clemency from the Polish Head of State, Boleslaw Bierut. They were all executed at Mokotów Prison. [5]

My father's post at the Mokotów Prison was within the Ministry of Public Security (Polish: 'Urząd Bezpieczeństwa' "UB"). Joining the Polish United Workers' Party (PZPR) was a formality, a necessary step in becoming part of the government apparatus that he believed would usher in a new era. Though foreign and fraught with complexities, this world represented the fulfilment of his youthful ideals. He often thought of his parents, wondering if they would have shared in his satisfaction if they could have lived to see the Poland for which he fought—a Poland reborn, a Poland where the old, oppressive Dmowski's Endecja had been swept away.

Yet, beneath these thoughts, there was a persistent undercurrent of grief, a sorrow that gnawed at him in quiet moments. His mind would drift back to 2 Poznańska Street in Kalisz, to the single-room home where his family once lived. In the silence of his new life, he would imagine stepping through the door, hearing the familiar voices, feeling the warmth of their presence. This profoundly personal fantasy was a refuge from the harsh realities of his daily existence— a broken Warsaw struggling to rise from its ruins.

77 years after the Wolyń massacre. Between 1943 and 1945, Ukrainian nationalists attacked 99 Polish towns and villages in Wolyń, a Nazi-occupied region of Poland that is now part of Ukraine. It is estimated that around 100,000 Poles were slaughtered with utmost cruelty at the hands of Ukrainian Nationalists. The killings were initiated and directed by a radical Ukrainian Nationalist, Stepan Bandera, and his Organization of Ukrainian Nationalists and its military arm, the Ukrainian Insurgent Army. Ukrainian villagers eagerly participated in the massacre. Their goal was to purge all non-Ukrainians from a future Ukrainian state. [6]

There was a future ahead, bright with the promise of reconstruction, but it was a future that did not include the people he loved the most. He knew that they were gone; that they had perished in his absence. This knowledge weighed heavily upon him; the guilt lurked in the corners of his mind. He asked himself over and over: Could he have saved them? Should he have stayed? Was there a way to protect them from their terrible fate, which he did not consider?

Now, he was living in 'Communist Poland', a place he had always wanted to be, a place he had earned through his sacrifices and his belief in a better world. But with this achievement came an incomparable loss: the tragic death of his mother, father, and innocent brothers. The joy he should have felt was tainted by his loss, by the memories of a time when Poland was overrun by the SS and Gestapo, when the country had become hell on earth. Millions of people, Jews like his family, had been transported to this inferno, where they were gassed and cremated, their ashes scattered across the land, mingled with the soil and rivers or lakes of a country that had once been their home.

And now, after all that horror, there was peace. The terror had ended, and the communists were in power, a power he had fought for and believed in. He no longer had to fear the rise of the Polish Nationalist Democratic Front (Endecja); many of them were in jail. He no longer had to worry about the hate they incited against Polish Jews. He no longer had to fear being incarcerated for his underground communist activities and for the secret cells he had formed as a teenager in Kalisz when he was on the cusp of becoming an adult.

But this new life, this victory, felt hollow. His price was too high, and the losses were too significant. The Poland he had fought for was now his, but the family he had hoped to share it with was gone. He was caught between the triumph of his ideals and the sorrow of his reality, unable to reconcile the two. How could he allow himself to enjoy his life in his communist Poland, knowing that his family had suffered so much—that they had been consumed by a tragedy that he could not prevent?

These thoughts haunted him, a constant reminder of the complexity of his existence. He was a man who had achieved what he had set out to do, but at a cost that left him forever questioning, forever grieving. The bright future he had envisioned was now shadowed by the past, by the memories of a family that would never see this 'New Poland', and by the guilt that he carried with him every day as he walked through the broken city that was now his home.

My father saw German Nazism and the Polish National Democratic Front (Endecja) as two sides of the same coin. To him, both aimed for exclusion, oppression, and ultimately the destruction of those who didn't fit their narrow ideas of 'national identity'. The horrors he associated with Nazism echoed in his mind with Endecja's hatred and exclusionary tactics, a group that, like the Nazis, aimed to create a homogeneous society at the expense of anyone considered the 'other.'

Conversely, many Polish nationalists viewed communists not as the liberators of Poland, but as the new occupants. It did not matter to them that the newly established Polish Government was composed of Polish communists rather than Soviet nationals. In their eyes, Polish and Soviet communists were indistinguishable—they were all agents of a foreign power, puppets of the Soviet Union, and worse, traitors of Poland.

This distrust was deeply ingrained. For the nationalists, the idea that the communists could be trusted was unthinkable. The presence of a communist government in Poland was seen as a continuation of foreign domination, a betrayal of the Polish nation's sovereignty. The fact that these communists were Polish made little difference; they were seen as collaborators, complicit in the subjugation of their people.

On the other hand, one could argue that the London-based Polish Government-in-Exile, revered by many nationalists, was itself a puppet—this time of the British Government. The Polish exiles, clinging to the hope that Winston Churchill would come to their aid, placed their faith in a promise that was never fulfilled. The British military support they so desperately needed did not materialise, and perhaps it was never truly intended. Even if Stalin had allowed British planes to land in Ukraine or Belarus, it is doubtful that it would have made any difference. The British Government, driven by its own strategic interests, turned a blind eye to Poland's suffering.

History is full of these bitter ironies. The British, who had once stood as a beacon of hope for the Polish exiles, had already shown their willingness to appease aggressors when they ignored the annexation of Czechoslovakia. They were equally indifferent to the detailed reports sent to them by the brave Witold Pilecki, who had infiltrated Auschwitz to gather intelligence on the atrocities being committed there. Pilecki's courage, his desperate attempts to alert the world to the horrors of the extermination camps, went largely unanswered. [7]

My father worked at Mokotów Prison for three full years whilst attending regular monthly meetings of his local PZPR Mokotów branch. He was part of the UB apparatus and a firm adherent to political proponents like Lenin, Engels, and Lev Davidovich Bronstein (Leon Trotsky). The Mokotów Prison was located at 37 Rakowiecka Street, and therefore, it was within walking distance from his apartment block, which was guarded by two soldiers at the main entrance, 24 hours a day, seven days a week.

In his apartment, where the shadows seemed longer and the nights more restless, my father lived with the constant tension of the past creeping back into the present. Just in case of an ambush or a home invasion by anti-government secret underground groups or individuals, he kept his army revolver, and three or four grenades strategically placed atop his wardrobe. These cold, hard objects of war were more than just weapons—they were his security. Without them, he felt exposed, as if the very walls that sheltered him were made of glass, ready to shatter at the slightest pressure.

The war left him with both physical and mental scars. The latter were not visible—wounds deep within his soul. These were the injuries we now understand as the trauma of war—what today might be termed as the Chronic Post-Traumatic Stress Disorder—but back then, war trauma had no name. The concept was hardly understood, and admitting to any mental disturbance carried a stigma that could isolate a man from his mates and undermine his sense of self-worth.

33 Rakowiecka Street, Mokotów today

Because of his PTSD, he lived in a state of vulnerability and vigilance, always alert and expecting danger. The smallest disturbance could trigger an intense reaction; his patience had worn thin by the constant strain of keeping his guard up. His anger would flare suddenly when stress mounted, like a fire ignited in dry grass, burning bright and consuming all in its path.

But it was in the quiet of the night, when the world outside his window was hushed and still, that the real battle began. Nightmares haunted his sleep, pulling him back into the horrors of war. He saw his parents, gone forever but never forgotten, mingling with the memories of battle—memories that played out in stark, terrifying detail. The most troubling were the flashbacks, those cruel intrusions that pulled him back to the front lines, where the rapid-fire of submachine guns echoed in his mind. He could feel the bullets entering his body, not as sharp pain but as something hot and insidious, like molten lead searing his flesh. These memories, though faded with time, had not vanished. They lingered, persistent and disturbing, kept alive by his unconscious psyche that refused to let him fully escape the past.

During the day, his thoughts were no less troubled. They came unbidden, intruding in moments of quiet, filling his mind with the faces of his parents and brothers, of the life they had before the war and the life that was stolen from them. He thought of the war itself, of the things he had seen and done—things that could never be undone. These thoughts were like ghosts, ever-present, haunting him in ways that words could never capture.

My father carried these burdens alone, his pain hidden behind a stoic exterior. War had taken more from him than just years of his life—it had taken his peace, his sense of security, and perhaps most tragically, his ability to fully live in the present. The past forever marked him; his heart was weighed down by memories too painful to bear yet too profoundly ingrained to forget.

There was no joy in his work at Mokotów Prison. The walls of that place, stained with the suffering of so many, seemed to mirror his inner turmoil, amplifying his hidden emotional pain that he could never escape. His soul, never free from torment, was held captive by the memories that haunted him. In his Rakowiecka Street apartment, with grenades and a revolver hidden in discreet places, he was always ready, prepared to protect himself from his enemies—those anti-Semitic nationalists, the collaborators and the UPA sympathisers.

As far as my father was concerned, enemies surrounded him on all sides in his new Poland. He could not forget those who had been indifferent to the anti-Semitic boycotts of the past, those who had never wanted Jews or communists in their midst, and who still harboured that quiet, festering resentment. He could not forgive those who saw no significance in remembering the concentration camps, where millions had been exterminated, as if the horrors that took place there were just another chapter to be forgotten. He could never forget those who had betrayed their Jewish neighbours in Jedwabne or those who had murdered survivors in Kielce, their hatred still burning even after the war's end. And he could not let go of the bitterness toward those who were indifferent to the suffering at Bereza Kartuska, where his brother Abram had been tortured and sent home to die.

These were not abstract antipathies mixed with anguish; they were the source of his ongoing grief and anger, the fuel that kept the fire of his resentment internally burning. My father spoke of these enemies often, his words heavy with the weight of disgust that time had not eased. The anguish in his voice, a raw and visceral sound that cut through the air like a knife, was unforgettable. When he recalled the Warsaw Ghetto Uprising, his voice would tremble with pain. "When the clouds of smoke were rising above the Warsaw Ghetto," he would say, his eyes distant, "the anti-Semitic Poles would joke, Ah... the flies are burning."

Those words, cruel and callous, were seared into his memory, a reminder that the hatred he had fought against was still alive, lurking beneath the surface of the society he had returned to. It was this indifference that haunted him as much as the atrocities themselves. For all the horrors of war, the true horror lay in the hearts of those who could laugh at suffering or remain indifferent.

In his vision of a brave new communist world—his Poland—he believed he still had to protect himself. The scars of war and the deep-seated sense of vulnerability lingered like a dark cloud above him. Yet, despite his outward resolve, there was a part of his life he rarely spoke of—a shadowy chapter of his post at Mokotów Prison shrouded in discomfort and unease. He never divulged much about his role

217

within Mokotów Prison and never opened up about that period of his life with the same candour he displayed when recalling his other jobs. It was as if he carried a weight of discomfort; a burden of secrecy; or perhaps deep unresolved conflict implicating feelings of shame, that he was unwilling or unable to share. He felt uncomfortable admitting that he was a "UB man" (Polish: Ubowiec), a member of the Ministry of Public Security, an institution feared and loathed by many.

On a more joyful note, my father would sometimes reminisce about the young women drawn to him during his days as a Polish soldier. He spoke with pride about how his charisma seemed to attract them, how some would linger in the corridor outside his office at the Mokotów Prison. As the day drew to a close, their eyes hinted at the possibility of a romantic evening together. These memories, tinged with a fleeting warmth, were like rays of sunlight piercing through the otherwise dark clouds of his past.

Yet even these light-hearted moments could not compete with the shadow that loomed over his time spent within the prison's oppressive walls. The smiles and flirtations of those young women, though cherished, paled in comparison to the weight of the experiences he carried from his work. The laughter of those evenings was drowned out by the echoes of despair that haunted the corridors of that place, where his soul felt the heavy burden of the suffering around him.

It was as if the fleeting joys of youth and romance were swallowed whole by the vast, consuming darkness of his memories—the memories of a time when the line between duty and moral compromise blurred into something almost unrecognisable. Those brief, tender encounters with the women who admired him were like delicate flowers struggling to bloom in his life's harsh, unforgiving landscape. They offered him a momentary respite, a glimpse of what might have been, had his life taken a different path. But in the end, they were just that—moments, quickly overshadowed by the inescapable realities of the world he inhabited.

On one rare occasion, he hinted at what his work might have entailed, mentioning almost offhandedly that part of his duties involved training for a possible role as a secret counterintelligence agent. "That is why," he said, "I learned English—it was a prerequisite to becoming a secret counterintelligence agent." But even as he spoke those words, there was a hesitation, a reluctance that suggested a deeper conflict. Ultimately, he confessed that he had never felt comfortable with such a role. "Being a spy," he admitted, "ideologically did not feel right for me."

And that was all he ever said about his first government job at Mokotów Prison on Rakowiecka Street. The details of what he did, his decisions and the moral dilemmas he faced remained locked away, buried beneath layers of reticence and perhaps guilt. Clearly, this part of his life was a source of internal conflict, a chapter he would rather forget than relive.

In his silence, I sensed a man who had been torn between his ideals and the harsh realities of the world he found himself in—a world where the line between right and wrong may have been blurred, where survival sometimes required compromises that left deep, invisible wounds. His reluctance to speak of his time at Mokotów Prison was not just about protecting himself from judgment, but about grappling with the dissonance between the Poland he had dreamed of and the Poland that existed in reality. He was a man who had survived the war, only to find himself embroiled in another, a more insidious battle within his soul.

Today, the historical lens through which we view the Mokotów Prison offers a stark contrast to the perspective my father held during his time there. To him, it was a stronghold where Nazis and anti-government 'traitors' were justly incarcerated, a necessary evil in the chaotic aftermath of war. But history has since reframed that narrative. The records now paint Mokotów Prison not merely as a prison but as a place where suspects were subjected to harrowing interrogations. They were tortured, often without mercy, for their alleged anti-communist activities. Among these so-called "traitors" were the "cursed soldiers" of the Home Army, individuals who had once been revered as heroes in the fight against Nazi occupation but were now branded enemies of the State. The prison, which housed approximately 950 inmates, was also a holding place for recidivist alcoholics and those deemed antisocial or dangerous, tucked away in its more obscure corners.

During the war, Mokotów had been under the iron grip of the Gestapo, a place where the very notion of justice was perverted. Innocent civilians swept up in random street roundups were imprisoned alongside resistance fighters, all held as pawns in a deadly game of retribution. The prison became a black hole, where most never emerged alive, their fates sealed by the ruthless efficiency of the Nazi reprisals.

In the early days of the Warsaw Uprising, when the Home Army managed to breach the prison's defences and liberate 300 prisoners, their victory was met with brutal retaliation. Nearly 500 inmates were slaughtered by the SS and Wehrmacht, a grim reminder that Mokotów Prison was a place where death held dominion. Yet, despite the widespread destruction that engulfed Warsaw, Rakowiecka Street and the Mokotów Prison remained relatively unscathed, a sinister testament to the German General Government's control over the area.

During my father's tenure, from the 2nd of April 1945 to the 20th of May 1948, Mokotów Prison was more than just a place of incarceration. It was a nerve centre for the Polish Secret Police and Secret Intelligence, where the walls whispered secrets and the floors bore the weight of countless tortured souls. Among the prisoners was Jürgen Stroop, the infamous German war criminal who orchestrated the liquidation of the Warsaw Ghetto and the massacre of the remaining 50,000 Jews. But Stroop was not alone in his infamy. The prison also held members of the Polish underground, the Home Army, and others who were seen as threats to the established government—the Bierut government, which had risen from the ashes of war and had no tolerance for Jew-hating nationalists and anti-communists.

However, the stark truth is that many of these Polish prisoners were not criminals but patriots—men who fought bravely against the Nazi occupation. They were individuals who risked everything during the Warsaw Uprising—men with strong moral convictions whose only crime was believing in a different vision for Poland's future. It was their right, after all, to hold their beliefs, even if that put them at odds with the ideology of the communist government.

But what about those who collaborated with the pro-Nazi militias, like the UPA? What about those whose actions blurred the line between patriotism and betrayal? These questions cast long shadows over the memories of those who suffered and died in Mokotów Prison, shadows that stretch across the decades and challenge our understanding of justice and morality itself.

In this dark context, the comparison between Mokotów Prison and Mauthausen becomes unavoidable. Both were sites where humanity was stripped away—where men were starved, tortured, and murdered in the name of ideology. So, how could my father reconcile his work at Mokotów Prison with his understanding of humanism? How could someone who had endured so much, who had lost everything, find himself in a place where such horrors were carried out? The answer is straightforward: he did not choose to be there. It was his first posting during his military service in liberated Poland. Was his work there a way to cope with his grief, to channel his pain and anger against those he saw as anti-Semites, anti-Soviets, and anti-Communists? Did he see them all as one and the same—bullies, Jew-haters, and traitors—deserving of the terrible fate that had befallen his family? I do not believe so. My father loved Poland and regarded himself as a Polish patriot.

The thought of my father grappling with the legacy of Witold Pilecki, a man who risked his life to expose the horrors of Auschwitz, is a painful one. Pilecki was a hero, an exponent of moral courage in a world gone mad. How could my father, a man who had seen the worst of humanity, come to terms with the fact that he worked in a place where men like Pilecki were condemned? Perhaps it is no surprise that he spoke little of his time at Mokotów Prison. He left his post just five days before Pilecki's execution on the 25th of May 1948, a move that speaks volumes.

My father's reticence about his work at Mokotów Prison was not just a matter of professional discretion; it reflected the inner turmoil that troubled him. The man who had once fought for a different vision of Poland, who had dreamed of a future free from hatred and tyranny, found himself caught in a system that upheld the very harms he had sought to dismantle. How does one reconcile such a reality with one's aspirational ideals? It is a question I imagine haunted my father for the rest of his life, a question that may never have had an answer.

∞∞∞∞∞∞

On May 20th, 1948, my father was demobilised from military service, marking the end of his tenure at the Mokotów Prison. It was a significant day, not just because it signalled the conclusion of his military duties but also because it marked a new chapter in his life— a transition from the rigid structure of military service to the murkier, more ambiguous realm of civilian governance. As a civilian, he was transferred to the Central Committee of the Polish United Workers' Party (Polish: Komitet Centralny "KC" Polskiej Zjednoczonej Partii Robotniczej "PZPR").

What exactly his role was during this brief period in the Central Committee remains a mystery. My notes from past discussions with my father reveal nothing about his duties during this time. It is as if this chapter of his life was shrouded in a quiet ambiguity, a gap in the narrative that he either could not or would not fully explain. He was there for only a short time, approximately two months, from May 21st until July 15th, 1948—a fleeting presence in the vast and complex machinery of the government.

Given the brevity of his tenure, I can only presume that this period was one of transition, perhaps a time of training and preparation for his next role within the Central Office of Press Control, a position within the Worker's Co-operative Publicity, the central apparatus of Polish media (Polish: Robotnicza Spółdzielnia Wydawnicza "RSW" Prasa). This post, which he commenced on July 20th, 1948, would place him at the heart of the State's control over the flow of information—a role that would force him to navigate the delicate balance between duty and social conscience.

In the quiet corridors of the Central Office of Press Control, where the walls seemed to absorb the weight of countless suppressed words, my father found himself entangled in a new role—one that brought him closer to the machinery of power, within the political system he dreamed and fought to establish. As the Chief Inspector within the Main Bureau of Control of Press and Publications, his duties were clear, yet they carried a heavy burden that weighed on his conscience. His task was to oversee the meticulous examination of unpublished material submitted by writers, journalists, and intellectuals across Poland. These submissions were to be dissected, scrutinised, and purged of any content that strayed from the Party's stringent guidelines.

This role demanded a delicate balance between loyalty to the state and the uneasy awareness of censorship's profound impact on a nation's soul. My father's responsibility was to ensure that the Regional Inspectors—those scattered throughout the various Bureau of Control branches across Poland—had performed their duties with the necessary rigour. He was to confirm that the 'political correctness' of every piece of material had been sufficiently sanitised, to ensure that no word or idea slipped through to endanger or challenge the tightly held narrative of the State.

It was a job that demanded precision, a keen eye for the tiniest nuances, and an unwavering commitment to the ideology that had shaped his life and was now shaping the nation. Yet, as he probed deeper into his work, it became clear that he couldn't ignore the suffocating reality of his role. He was not just an enforcer of guidelines; he was a gatekeeper, watching over the flow of information and deciding what the Polish people could see, hear, and read.

The extent of censorship infiltrated all aspects of life in Poland, including politics, social relations, the economy, culture, and even seemingly innocent areas like sport and health. Every article, book, and news report reaching the public had to pass through the iron grip of the Main Bureau of Control of Press and Publications. The local censorship offices, spread out like silent outposts across the country, sent their recommendations to his desk, where he was to review them diligently. Should a line be altered here, or a phrase cut there? Should a piece be entirely banned, with its content deemed too dangerous for the minds of the people?

As the days went on, the reality of this suppressive apparatus weighed heavily on him. The same ideals that once filled him with hope now felt like chains, binding him to a machine that stifled the very essence of life—freedom of thought, freedom of expression, freedom to question and to dream. Each recommendation he signed off on, each piece of text he approved for alteration or eradication, left a small wound on his spirit. He could feel the ideals he had once cherished were slipping away, replaced by the cold, hard mechanics of control.

This was not the Poland he had envisioned, nor the Poland he had hoped to rebuild. Yet there he was, a cog in the machine he once believed would create a fair and equal society. The irony was not lost on him; the power he had helped to forge was now the same power demanding silence, conformity, and unquestioning obedience.

In those moments, alone in his office, surrounded by the papers and files that dictated the boundaries of thought in his country, my father grappled with the dissonance between his duty and his conscience. He was not blind to the moral cost of his work. Each decision to censor, to erase, to silence was like cutting away a piece of his own soul. He could feel the darkness of this work settling into him, an insidious presence that threatened to consume what little remained of the idealism that had once driven him.

And yet, despite the growing unease, he carried on. War had taught him the cost of resistance, the price of standing against the tide. He had fought too hard, lost too much, to turn back now. The revolution had promised a new world, a better world, and he had no choice but to believe that this work, however dull or uninspiring, was a necessary part of that promise. But in the quiet of the night, when the shadows in his apartment seemed to stretch longer, and the silence grew thicker, he wondered if the Poland he had fought for had been lost somewhere along the way, buried beneath the layers of control and censorship that now defined his life.

These thoughts, like ghosts, haunted him, reminding him of the distance between the man he had been and the man he was becoming. The inner conflict fumed within him, a battle between the ideals of his youth and the harsh realities of his present. And though he never spoke of it, the weight of this internal struggle was always there, pressing down on him, a reminder that the fight for a better world had come at a cost he was still struggling to pay.

The Main Bureau of Control of Press and Publications was more than just a gatekeeper of permissible thought; it was a vigilant watchdog, constantly refining its methods to ensure that nothing slipped through the cracks of its intricate censorship system. My father, as Chief Inspector, was tasked with overseeing not only the initial vetting of unpublished material but also addressing any lapses that had occurred after publication. If a piece of writing made it past the censors with content later deemed inappropriate or ideologically risky, it was his duty to identify the failure, propose new rules, and tighten the existing regulations to prevent future breaches.

The stakes were high, especially when it came to sensitive subjects like Polish-Soviet relations. My father knew all too well that any published material had to adhere strictly to the narrative dictated by the State. This narrative absolved the Soviet Union of any wrongdoing, particularly regarding the infamous massacre of 22,000 Poles, including military officers, refugees, and members of the intelligentsia, in the Katyń Forest. Shrouded in ambiguity and silence, this dark chapter of history was a delicate issue, and any hint of Soviet culpability was to be erased or, better still, never acknowledged at all.

The rules surrounding Polish-Soviet relations were explicit: no publication could ever burden the USSR with responsibility for the massacre. Hence, the truth about Katyń was to remain obscured, a shadowy secret buried beneath layers of official denial and strategic omission. Moscow had not formally admitted guilt until 1990, so the matter was kept in a limbo of deliberate vagueness, not to be addressed openly or questioned in print for almost five decades.

This aspect of his work troubled my father deeply. He understood that the censorship system was not just about controlling information; it was about shaping reality itself. Was he complicit in constructing a national memory that deliberately distorted the truth, silencing the voices of the dead and the grieving? No. My father always believed that the Nazis perpetrated the Katyń atrocity. Yet it is true today that in 1948, the Katyń massacre— a scar on the collective soul of the Polish people— was treated as an inconvenient detail to be swept under the rug, rather than a tragedy that deserved acknowledgment and mourning. When the truth came out, it was a bitter pill for my father to swallow. By then, he was in a completely different part of the world: Australia. Even then, it was easier to believe that it was simply Western propaganda trying to smear and demonise the collapsing Soviet Union. Even then, my father did not let his ideals be eroded by growing disillusionment and regret.

The tension between his duty and his conscience grew with each passing day. He knew that he was playing a part in a grand deception, one that kept the people in the dark about the true nature of their history and their relationship with the Soviet Union. While he carried out his responsibilities, there was a growing unrest within him, a feeling that he was betraying his values and the memory of those who had suffered and died. Not for a moment had he ever suspected that his very own brother (Leon) could have been, and most probably was, killed in Katyń forests at the hands of the NKVD operatives.

As he sat at his desk, reviewing reports and issuing directives to further refine the censorship system, he could not shake the feeling that he was complicit in a great wrong. The power to control information, to dictate what could and could not be said, was a heavy burden, one that weighed on him more than he could ever have anticipated. And though he continued to do his job, the doubts gnawed at him, a constant reminder that the truth was being sacrificed on the altar of political expediency.

With a touch of weariness in his voice, my father once remarked that every word, every sentence, and each phrase in the proposed articles or book publications was dissected to ensure that the language used aligned perfectly with the ideological values of the ruling party, the PZPR. It was not enough for a piece of writing to be factual or informative; it had to echo the PZPR's rhetoric to reinforce the narrative that kept the nation's consciousness tightly bound to the principles of the State. In this way, my father became something of a gatekeeper for the gatekeepers, overseeing the minutiae of the

227

censorship process with a vigilance that, over time, began to erode his spirit.

But his tenure in this role was short-lived. After approximately nine months of what he described as tedious and uninspiring work, he came to a decision—this was not the life he had envisioned for himself. The task of sifting through endless pages of text and scrutinising them for the slightest deviation from the party line felt monotonous and painfully at odds with the ideals that had once driven him.

I can only imagine the toll this work took on him. The remnants of his Chronic Post-Traumatic Stress, combined with the weight of his Complicated Grief, would have made it difficult—if not impossible—for him to maintain the kind of focus and concentration required for such a role. Each day would have been an uphill battle, mentally exhausting, as the very nature of the work forced him to confront the memories he had tried to bury. The sterile environment of the censorship office, with its cold, calculating purpose, would have triggered flashbacks to a time when the underground KZMP activists were hunted, their movements shadowed by the relentless gaze of the undercover police and the Endecja informers.

In those pre-war days, he had been one of those activists, driven by a fierce desire for change, for justice, for a Poland that was free from the chains of oppression. Once a passionate advocate for change, he found himself caught in the machinery of a system that valued control over justice and silence over truth. As he sat behind his desk, redacting and revising, he must have felt a bitter irony of his role. He was no longer the hunted but the hunter, a man tasked with silencing the voices that had once spoken of revolution and freedom. The idealism that had burned so brightly in his youth was now dimmed by the realities of a system that demanded conformity and obedience above all else.

It became clear to him that neither his post in the Mokotów Prison nor his first civilian job at the Main Bureau of Control of Press and Publications aligned with the aspirations and values that had once defined him. These roles were a far cry from the future he had imagined when he fought in the war, when he had believed that Communism would bring about a new world of equality, freedom of thought, and justice. Instead, he found himself part of a system that was, in its own way, just as oppressive as the one he had fought to overthrow.

The decision to leave was not an easy one, but it was necessary. He could no longer continue in a role that felt so profoundly wrong, so disconnected from the principles that had once guided his life. The strain of suppressing his own beliefs, of forcing himself to participate in the very kind of oppression he had once fought against, was too much to bear. The work not only exhausted him, but drained him, leaving him with a sense of emptiness and a feeling that he had lost his way.

Ultimately, his departure from the Main Bureau of Control was an act of self-preservation, a necessary step to reclaim a part of himself that had been lost in the machinery of censorship. It was a quiet rebellion, a refusal to let the system take any more of his soul. And though he may not have known what would come next, he knew that he could not stay—not in a job that went against everything he had once believed in, not in a role that made him feel like a stranger to himself.

∞∞∞∞∞

In late April 1949, my father reached out to an old comrade from his army days, Major Marian Mazur—a decorated soldier who had earned his stripes in the brutal battle of Stalingrad. By that time, Mazur had risen to a prominent position as the Director of Staff Office within the Ministry of National Defence. Their bond, forged in the crucible of war, had remained strong, and it was through this connection that my father found a new path.

With Mazur's support, my father obtained the position of Chief of the Personnel Department within the Main Department of Physical Culture (Polish: Główny Urząd Kultury Fizycznej; GUKF). This role represented a significant change in his career, steering him away from the dark, oppressive environments that had weighed heavily on his conscience. It was a move that, on the surface, appeared like a breath of fresh air—a step towards a life much less burdened by the memories of war and its aftermath.

Yet, even in this new role, the shadows of his past continued to linger. The title, although prestigious, carried the weight of responsibility and tacit understanding that his work was still entangled in the fabric of the State's apparatus. The world of physical culture and sports, while seemingly benign, was not entirely free from the reach of political oversight. But in this new chapter, my father found a semblance of relief, a way to channel his energy into something that, at least on the surface, was life-affirming. It was a time when he could, perhaps, begin to imagine a different future— one where the past did not dictate every aspect of his existence. And yet, as with all things in his life, this new beginning was layered with complexities that only he could truly understand.

My father started his new role on the 1st of May, 1949, entering a world that was vastly different from his time at Mokotów Prison or the Main Bureau of Control of Press and Publications. The GUKF, where he now worked, was led by Lucjan Motyka, the Chief Director General. Motyka was not just a figurehead; he was a man with strong political connections; he was a close friend of Jozef Cyrankiewicz, who was then the Premier of the Polish People's Republic. Both Motyka and Cyrankiewicz were dedicated members of the Polish Socialist Party (PPS), a faction that, despite the sweeping tide of

Communism promoted by the Kremlin, remained committed to their own ideals.

My father often spoke of the peculiar atmosphere within the GUKF—a place where the old loyalties to the PPS ran deep, where the allegiance to the Socialist ideals was palpable and often at odds with the more hardline Communist doctrines of the PZPR, the party to which he was deeply committed. This tension was more than just ideological; it was personal, a quiet but persistent undercurrent that influenced every decision and every interaction.

It wasn't long before this ideological divide resulted in major clashes between my father and Lucjan Motyka. Three key events stand out, each a struggle of wills and a reflection of the larger power struggles unfolding across Poland's political landscape. These events weren't just about policy or procedure; they were about identity, loyalty, and the spirit of the new Poland shaped in the wake of the war, and something more extreme…the aftermath of the Holocaust.

In these moments of conflict, my father's resolve was tested in ways that went beyond physical or emotional. These were battles fought in the shadow of history, with the ghosts of the past whispering in his ear, reminding him of everything he had lost and everything he had gained through sacrifice. As the tensions mounted, it became clear that this new role, far from being a refuge, was yet another crucible in which his beliefs, his loyalty, and his very identity would be put to the test.

The first incident began innocuously enough, wrapped in the guise of a celebratory event—a soccer tournament organised by Warsaw University in honour of General Marian Spychalski. Spychalski was not just any figure in the political landscape; he was a revered architect and the Minister of Building and Construction, a man who had dedicated himself to the Herculean task of rebuilding Warsaw from the ashes of war. His efforts were nothing short of monumental.

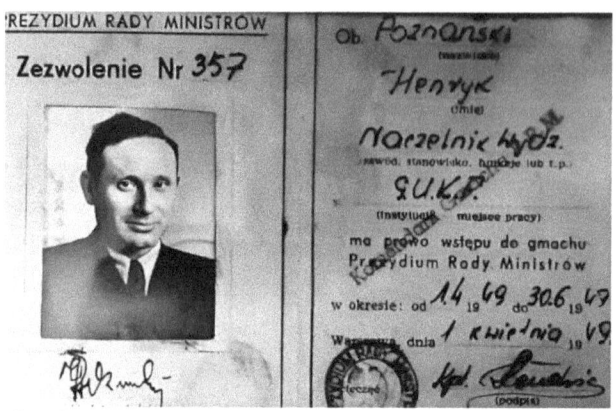

Authorisation for entry to the Presiding Council of Ministers for the specified period: 1 April 1949 – 30 June 1949.

He had overseen the restoration of some of the city's most significant landmarks: the Palace of Staszic, the Palace of Radziwiłs, the Church of St. Anne, and the Grave of the Unknown Soldier. These were not just buildings but symbols of the Polish nation's resilience, testaments to a culture that refused to be erased.

Like Motyka and Cyrankiewicz, Spychalski was strongly connected to the Polish Socialist Party (PPS). His political loyalties were clear and a key part of his identity, just as much as his architectural accomplishments. The tournament, therefore, was more than merely a sporting event; it was a tribute to a man who represented the spirit of post-war reconstruction, both physically and ideologically. [8]

But within the walls of the GUKF, this tribute took on a different significance. For my father, a staunch member of the PZPR, the event was a reminder of the ongoing tension between the old guard of the PPS and the rising tide of Communism he symbolised. While on the surface, the tournament was about soccer, beneath that surface lay the smouldering conflict between two visions of Poland's future—one rooted in the socialist ideals of the PPS and the other in the hardline

Communism of the PZPR. For my father, the tournament was not just an event to be logistically managed but a precursor to the power struggles that would soon unfold.

In the unpredictable political scene of post-war Poland, October 1949 brought about a tide of change that resembled a storm sweeping over one of Poland's leading figures, General Marian Spychalski. Once highly regarded for his achievements, he suddenly came under investigation by the feared "X" Department within the Ministry of Public Security (UB). The allegations against him were grave—he was accused of liaising with the right-wing nationalist intelligence, a heinous crime in the eyes of Bierut's communist regime. The accusations did not end there. Spychalski was also implicated in collaborating with the nationalist Home Army, and most damning of all, in being an accomplice to the betrayal of 48 underground movement members—communists of Jewish descent—whose lives were ended by the Gestapo in 1943.

As the investigation unfolded, Spychalski was unceremoniously removed from his government post, his once-bright future now clouded by the suspicion and paranoia that marked the era. By the beginning of 1950, he found himself imprisoned, a stark reminder of how quickly one could fall from grace in the ever-shifting sands of Communist Poland. The investigation sent shockwaves through the government, leading to a sweeping purge of all organisations tied to the PPS. The PPS, once a formidable force, was effectively banned by the Kremlin; its members faced a grim choice: join the ruling Polish United Workers' Party (PZPR) or lose their positions of power. It was a time of fear and uncertainty, where yesterday's heroes could become today's traitors and where even the most loyal party members could find themselves on the wrong side of history.

Amidst this political turmoil, my father made a decision with lasting effects. Recognising how fragile Spychalski's position was, he wrote to the Dean of the Faculty of Sport at the University of Warsaw,

233

advising against going ahead with plans for the soccer tournament in Spychalski's honour. My father, always cautious and aware of the shifting situation, warned that it would be unwise to celebrate a man under severe scrutiny and facing potential lengthy imprisonment.

The letter, intended as cautious advice, had the effect my father expected. It provoked a wave of anger from Lucjan Motyka, the Chief Director General of the GUKF. Motyka, who had been a close supporter of Spychalski, was furious about the tournament's cancellation. The tension between Motyka and my father, already simmering beneath the surface, now reached a breaking point. The letter had drawn a clear line between them, marking the start of a rift that would only widen over time.

Despite Motyka's fury, he found himself unable to dismiss my father. Perhaps Motyka understood all too well the precariousness of his position. Even those with the highest connections were not safe from the sweeping purges in the new political order. My father, ever astute, had navigated this treacherous situation with a careful hand, but the cost was the enmity of a powerful figure within the very organisation he served.

This was my father's reality at that time—a life lived in suspicion's shadow, where every action was weighed and every word scrutinised. The decision to speak out against the tournament wasn't just about duty; it reflected the tangled web of loyalty and fear shaping his life. In a world where the line between friend and foe often blurred, my father walked a narrow path, where the smallest mistake could lead to disaster. Despite the danger and tension, he held onto the ideals that had guided him through the war and into the uncertain peace that followed. He stayed true to his vision of a new Poland, even as that vision became more complicated and filled with contradictions. The conflict with Spychalski and Motyka was just one of many battles he fought—not with guns or grenades, but with words, strategy, and the quiet, unshakeable resolve that carried him through his darkest days.

My father's second conflict within the GUKF revolved around an Olympic Medalist named Jadwiga Wajs, whose life and career were as complex as the times she lived in. In late 1949, Motyka issued a directive that Wajs be appointed as the Head of the newly established Museum of Sport in Warsaw. Wajs, a Polish Jewish athlete, had earned a silver medal at the 1936 Berlin Olympics—a remarkable achievement under any circumstances, but particularly so given the dark clouds of anti-Semitism that loomed heavily over Germany at the time. [9]

Wajs's Jewish heritage, although not widely known due to her blond appearance, had not stopped her from competing in Berlin. My father, who had been in Berlin the year after the Olympics, was sharply aware of the Nazi regime's deeply rooted anti-Semitic policies. He had seen firsthand the widespread discrimination that prevented Jewish athletes from taking part in various sports and sporting clubs, where "Aryans only" signs were common. The vile doctrines of Nazi ideology stood in stark contrast to the fundamental Olympic ideals of unity and equality.

I remember my father reflecting on the heated debates leading up to the Berlin Games. Countries like the United States, Great Britain, France, Sweden, and the Netherlands wrestled with the moral question of whether to boycott the Olympics in protest against Germany's anti-Semitic policies. Individual athletes, too, felt conflicted, with some refusing to compete as a stand against the injustices unfolding before the world's eyes. The International Olympic Committee (IOC) was under significant pressure from various boycott campaigns, and there was a strong push to move the Games from Berlin to another city. One of the options was to hold the Games in Barcelona, turning them into a "People's Olympiad" that would sharply contrast with the Nazi spectacle. However, the outbreak of the Spanish Civil War dashed those plans, and the Games went ahead in Berlin, leaving many with a bitter taste.

For my father, the appointment of Wajs as the Head of the Museum of Sport wasn't simply an administrative decision—it carried the weight of history and unresolved tensions from the past. He understood what it meant to be a Jew in a world that often turned a blind eye to suffering. He was deeply aware of the symbolic importance of Wajs's role. However, the situation was complicated by the politics of the time. Some viewed Motyka's directive as a sign of recognition and inclusion. On the other hand, others, perhaps including my father, might have seen it with scepticism, questioning whether it was driven by genuine respect or simply a desire to align with the shifting political landscape.

The conflict between my father and Motyka over Wajs's appointment wasn't just about her qualifications or whether the position was suitable. It reflected deeper issues—how the past was remembered, how history was rewritten, and how the scars of anti-Semitism, though hidden, hadn't fully healed. My father's experiences in Berlin, along with his personal history and the loss of his family, coloured his views in more complex and conflicted ways than those of his peers. He bore the weight of memory, the burden of witnessing injustice, and the realisation that the world hadn't always stood up for what was right. Ultimately, this conflict was another layer in the complex web of my father's life—one that intertwined his personal history with his people's broader, often painful, history. It served as a reminder that even in the post-war world, where new governments and ideologies aimed to shape the future, the shadows of the past never truly faded, constantly influencing the 'present' in subtle and profound ways.

Two weeks before the 1936 Olympics, Hitler's government made a calculated decision to temporarily suspend its open anti-Semitic policies, removing many of the anti-Semitic signs that had become a hallmark of public life in Germany. Hitler used the Olympics as a platform to present Germany as a peaceful and culturally tolerant society. This superficial facade hid the true nature of the Nazi regime. To appease international opinion, the German authorities allowed Helen Mayer, considered a "non-Aryan" because of her Jewish father, to represent Germany at the Games. Mayer won a silver medal and, in a moment later remembered with a mixture of confusion and sorrow, she gave the Nazi salute on the Olympic podium. The gesture was loaded with tragic irony, representing the complex and often contradictory pressures faced by Jewish athletes under the Nazi regime.

The United States, despite the growing outcry against Nazi tyranny, failed to boycott the 1936 Olympics. Unlike the Soviet Union, which in a stance against the Nazi government, had refused to participate, Roosevelt's administration remained passive, choosing to engage rather than protest. This failure to act, to stand against the rising tide of fascism, was a bitter pill for many, including my father. My father viewed Poland's participation in the Berlin Olympics as deeply inappropriate, a tacit acceptance of a regime that sought to erase his people from existence. This moral and philosophical opposition to the Games, and by extension to any action that seemed to legitimise the Nazi regime, shaped his response to Lucjan Motyka's decision to appoint Jadwiga Wajs as the Head of the new Warsaw Museum of Sport.

For my father, Wajs's appointment was not just an administrative decision—it was a matter of integrity and memory. He could not reconcile honouring a participant in the Berlin Olympics, regardless of her achievements, with the horrific reality of what those Games had represented. To him, it was a stark reminder of a world that had chosen to look away and ignore the growing menace that would soon engulf Europe in flames. His opposition to Motyka's directive was not merely a professional disagreement; it was a deeply personal stand against what he saw as a betrayal of those who had suffered and died under the Nazi regime.

During a PZPR Party meeting, my father sought support for his objection to Motyka's decision. He spoke with a conviction born out of personal loss and moral clarity, arguing that the appointment of Wajs was an insult to the memory of those who had been oppressed and murdered by the very regime that had hosted the Berlin Olympics. His argument resonated with enough members of the Party that Wajs was ultimately denied the post. However, this victory came at a cost. Once again, my father found himself at odds with his superior, and the conflict with Motyka lingered, casting a shadow over his position within the GUKF.

This was not just a clash of personalities but a conflict between two visions of the future—one that aimed to move forward by selectively forgetting the past and another that insisted on remembering, on bearing witness to the atrocities that had shaped the present. My father's stance, rooted in his deep sense of justice and the scars of his own experiences, was emblematic of the broader struggles within post-war Poland, where the lines between right and wrong were often blurred by the harsh realities of political survival.

My father at the height of his career (in dark suit on far right) sitting in the Polish Government Tribune - 1949 during May Day Celebrations.

The third and most politically charged incident happened in January 1950 when my father received a phone call from Motyka. The message was direct but hinted at hidden motives: Premier Jozef Cyrankiewicz wanted a Polish General from the Piłsudski era to be included in the GUKF payroll. My father, always thorough in his approach, asked for specifics—what would this General's role be? What salary was suggested? Motyka's reply was disturbing: the position was entirely artificial, with no real responsibilities. My father saw this move as deeply inconsistent with the ideals of the Polish proletariat, a betrayal of the very principles he stood for.

The call sparked a fire within him, a familiar anger that had simmered since his youth in pre-war Poland's nationalist days. He felt an urgent need to oppose this decision, which he viewed as yet another sneaky move by those in charge—men who, in his eyes, were more motivated by personal gain and power grabs than by a sincere dedication to communist Poland. To my father, Cyrankiewicz and Motyka were cut from the same cloth as Spychalski, Moczar, and Gomułka—figures who claimed to champion socialism but whose hearts beat with the rhythm of nationalist right-wing beliefs.

In his acutely vigilant state, sharpened by years of survival and suspicion, my father took pride in his ability to sense the underlying motives of those around him. He could detect the hidden values and beliefs that fueled these political figures, even when they were carefully masked. To him, these men were not true communists but rather "PPS men" (Polish: "Pepesiacy"), who subtly conspired against the Marxist-Leninist government of Poland, with Bolesław Bierut at its vulnerable helm.

One might question the validity of my father's perspective, and indeed, history has shown that the lines between ideology and ambition were often blurred in those turbulent times. But for him, communist Poland represented the only possible future—a future where the horrors of the Holocaust and the tyranny of Nazism could

239

never again take hold. It was a vision born out of deep scars and hope that the world could be rebuilt on principles of equality, inclusion, and justice. Yet, as the years went by, this vision started to fall apart under the weight of reality. The figures he trusted to uphold these ideals appeared more interested in consolidating power than building the society he had dreamed of.

In the end, his hope for a truly communist Poland was short-lived. The betrayal he felt was not just personal but existential. The country he had fought for and the ideals he had cherished were slipping away, co-opted by those who still clung to the old ways. The disillusionment was profound, a slow erosion of the dreams that had sustained him through the darkest years of his life. And yet, in his heart, he continued to believe that somewhere, in some future, the world he had envisioned might still be possible, even if it would never be realised in his lifetime.

My father was once acquainted with a Polish General from the Piłsudski era—a man who may have even saved his life, General Szeptycki. He had shared an overcrowded cell with Szeptycki in the Kharkiv Prison in Ukraine, a memory etched deeply into his psyche. Yet, despite this connection, it did not sway his stance on the matter. In his eyes, the idea of creating a false 'full-time equivalent' position (Polish: 'pełny etat') on the payroll of the GUKF Personnel Department was 'not kosher'—a term he used with the total weight of its implications.

He could not stand by and let such a sneaky move go unchallenged. His resolve grew stronger, and he took action by writing his objections. But to whom would he send his protest? The answer came clearly: Edward Ochab. Ochab was not just another player in the complex world of Polish politics; he was someone my father could genuinely connect with. Like my father, Ochab had served as a soldier in Tadeusz Kościuszko's First Division. He was a committed communist, married to a Jewish woman named Rachel, and held a significant role as the Head of the Central Commission for PZPR Party Control. Most importantly, Ochab was not aligned with Poland's Premier, Josef Cyrankiewicz, or with the Chief Director General of the GUKF, Lucjan Motyka. In Ochab, my father saw an ally—someone who understood the stakes and shared his belief in the true ideals of Communism.

In his letter, my father did not mince words. He listed the members of the PZPR whom he viewed as adversaries, revisionists, and nationalistic supporters of the former London-based Polish Government-in-Exile. These were men who, in his view, were eroding the foundations of the very government they claimed to serve. Against this backdrop, he laid out the divisive actions of Cyrankiewicz and Motyka, focusing mainly on the proposed creation of the artificial 'pełny etat' (English. 'full-time employment') position. He argued that such a move was not only a breach of ethical governance but a threat to the integrity of the State itself.

For my father, this was not just about a job or a title but about protecting the ideals that had sustained him through years of struggle and sacrifice. It was about ensuring that the new Poland—his communist Poland—would not fall into the same traps that had led to the horrors of the past. To him, creating a fake position was a slippery slope toward the corruption and complacency he had fought against all his life. His objection was not just a bureaucratic manoeuvre; it was an act of defiance, a stand for his values, even if it meant placing himself in direct opposition to influential, powerful figures within the government.

In this act, you can see the echoes of a man who survived the horrors of war and the loss of his family, fighting not just for a country but for a vision of his society. It was a vision he refused to compromise, even when faced with the intimidating machinery of the State. In his letter to Ochab, he was not just defending the integrity of a government department; he was protecting the very spirit of the nation he believed he belonged to.

Soon after sending the letter, my father grappled with unease that grew heavier daily. The burden of his actions weighed upon him, and the chill of the Polish winter mirrored the cold tension that had settled within his soul. Seeking respite from the mounting pressure, he took his unused recreational leave, a rare chance to escape the confines of his official duties, even if just for a while. He composed a letter to Motyka requesting approval for his leave.

But Motyka's response was quick and direct, a brief handwritten note that left little room for discussion: "I do not support the request as it is essential to address the 'etat' (English: eft -employment full-time) issue first and foremost, for the WKKF and GKKF at this time" (Polish: "Nie popieram ze względu na konieczność obsadzenia WKKF and GKKF w tym terminie"). The acronyms—GKKF stands for the Main Committee for Physical Culture, and WKKF for the Provincial Committee for Physical Culture—represented the two bodies within the GUKF that were at the core of the issues my father had raised in his letter. Motyka's refusal felt like a tightening noose, a reminder that the fight my father had chosen to engage in was far from over.

Just a few days later, the weight of his actions hit him more clearly. The telephone rang; an authoritative voice spoke on behalf of the Party's Central Committee (KC). The message was straightforward: he was to report immediately to the Office of the KC PZPR. In the office's cold, sterile environment, my father was given a clear instruction. He was to sign a document agreeing not to reveal to any groups or individuals the content of the letter he had written to the Head of the Central Commission for PZPR Party Control, Edward Ochab. This declaration was not temporary; it was to stay in force indefinitely.

As he held the pen in his hand, ready to sign, the weight of the situation bore down on him. The act of signing wasn't just about silencing his voice — it was about suppressing part of his soul, locking away the truths he had endeavoured to defend. The words on the page blurred as his powerful emotions, 'feeling memories' from past traumas, clashed with the harsh realities of the present. He had fought against the oppression of one regime only to find himself caught up in the machinations of another. The ideals he once treasured now seemed distant, almost out of reach, as he was forced to navigate the treacherous waters of a system that demanded loyalty and silence in exchange for survival.

At that moment, he realised that the cost of dissent was steep, and speaking out could cost a man his position and sense of self. He signed the declaration, not out of fear but with a grim understanding of his world—a place where ideals could be as dangerous as weapons, and where silence, though painful, was sometimes the only way to survive.

Around that time, the tides were shifting for my father and Lucjan Motyka. Motyka's role as Chief Director General at the GUKF ended, marking a subtle yet significant change in the constantly fluctuating political landscape. The details of his departure were cloaked in the usual opacity that often accompanies such transitions in the Polish government. However, publicly available information suggested that Motyka still maintained his influence, holding onto his role as the Presiding Member of the GKKF (the Main Committee for Physical Culture) until 1951.

The end of Motyka's tenure as Chief Director General might have seemed like a minor footnote in the broader story of post-war Poland. Nonetheless, for my father, it signified the closing of a chapter filled with tension and political tactics. The conflict that had brewed between them, highlighted by the incidents involving the soccer tournament, Jadwiga Wajs, and the fake job position, had left a lasting impression on my father's mind. The shadow of these power struggles persisted, even as Motyka's direct influence over him diminished.

Yet, within the complex web of government machinery, where roles and titles often shifted, Motyka's ongoing presence in the GKKF indicated that his influence was not entirely erased. For my father, knowing that Motyka still held a position of power served as a reminder that the battles he faced were not merely against particular individuals but against an entire system that could replace one leader with another without changing the fundamental structure.

The transition period that followed his resignation was a time of introspection for my father, a moment to reckon with the forces that had shaped his journey. It was merely a change in the landscape that hinted at the impermanence of power and the relentless march of time, which left no position or person untouched. My father continued to navigate his path, aware that the faces might change, but the struggles remained. His experiences at the GUKF, marked by tension and ideological conflicts, became another layer in the complex tapestry of his life, a life shaped by the forces of history, the weight of loss, and the relentless pursuit of the "ideal" that seemed to slip further from his grasp with each passing day. [9]

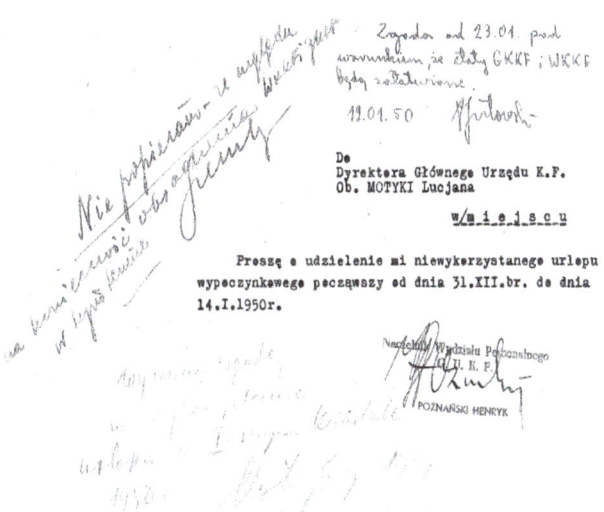

My father's letter to Lucjan Motyka, Chief Director General of GUKF, seeking approval of unused recreational leave; and Motyka's handwritten response: "I do not support the request as it is imperative to address the filling of new full-time positions."

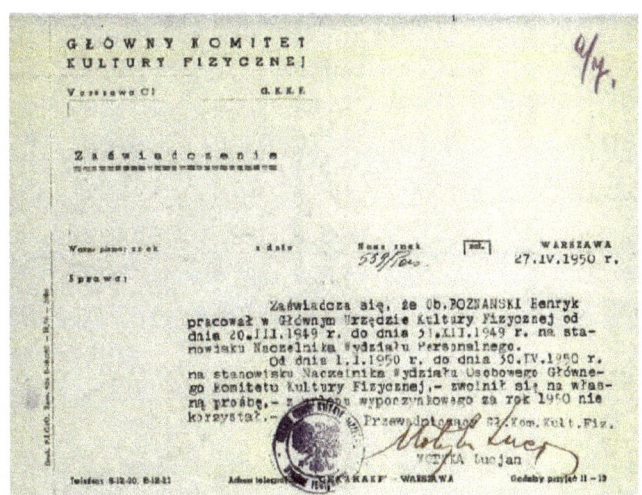

Motyka's final statement misrepresents my father's intentions. Motyka asserts that my father sought his dismissal and chose not to use the unused annual leave that was owed to him during the year 1950.

245

Notes

1. Tokarska-Bakir, Joanna (2017). The Polish Underground Organization Wolność i Niezawisłość and Anti-Jewish Pogroms 1945-1946. Patterns of Prejudice, 2017, Vol. 51, No 2, pp. 111-136. Polish Academy of Sciences, Routledge

2. https:////en.wikipedia.org/wiki/Taras_Bulba-Borovets

3. Historiography of the Volyn tragedy: https://en.wikipedia.org/wiki/Historiography_of_the_Volyn

4. Attack On Hrubieszow: May 26 - May 27, 1946 - Joint WiN & UPA Assault On Communist Held City of Hrubieszow, Part 2. see doomedsoldiers.com

5. https://en.wikipedia.org/wiki/mokotów_prison

6. justiceforpolishvictims.org

7. Fairweather, Jack (2019). Ochotnik: Prawdziwa Historia Tajnej Misji Witolda Pileckiego (Engl: Volunteer: True Story of the Secret Mission of Witold Pilecki). Instytut Pileckiego, Horyzont – Znak.

8. https://pl.wikipedia.org/wiki/Marian_Spychalski

9. https://en.wikipedia.org/wiki/Poland_at_the_1936_Summer_Olympics

11. The Psychology of Remembrance

In March 1950, my father was presented with an offer that could have shifted the course of his career—a redeployment to an administrative post as the Secretary to the Warsaw Commission for the PZPR Party Control. This offer, one that many would consider a significant step up the ladder of political influence, was uninspiring to him. He had his eyes set on something different that resonated more deeply with the aspirations he had nurtured despite the shadows of his past. He yearned to secure a position as the Chief of the Personnel Department within the Ministry of Art and Culture (Ministerstwo Kultury i Sztuki; MKiS). This was not just another bureaucratic role to him; it was a place where he believed he could make a meaningful contribution, away from the oppressive atmosphere that had marked much of his earlier service.

As he waited for this position to open, an unexpected opportunity arose—one that called to him with the quiet urgency of a higher purpose. Within the Board of Museums and Heritage Protection of the MKiS, there was a need for someone to oversee a task both delicate and profound. This role involved research and the meticulous oversight of the implementation of plans laid out by the Commission for the Protection of Places of Struggle and Suffering, a Commission whose work was enshrined by the Legislation of the Polish Parliament.

This task was a mission to preserve the very soul of a nation ravaged by unspeakable horrors. My father's heart, heavy with the memories of his own losses and the collective suffering of his people, found a deep meaning, a calling, in the idea of this work. It was about more than just overseeing projects—it was about ensuring that the sites of mass extermination, the graveyards of humanity's darkest chapter, would be protected as 'historical documents.' These places, where the very air still carried the echoes of unimaginable pain, needed to be preserved in their original form. They would stand as eternal witnesses to the atrocities of Nazism, transformed into museums and monuments that would speak to the world of human struggle and suffering.

For my father, this was not just a professional opportunity but a sacred duty. It was a chance to honour those who had perished, to ensure that their stories would not fade into the obscurity of forgotten history. This work aligned with the deepest parts of his soul, a labour that could perhaps offer him peace, knowing that he was contributing to the remembrance of those who could no longer speak for themselves. It was a role that resonated with the essence of who he was—a man shaped by loss, driven by a need to ensure that the horrors of the past would not be repeated or forgotten.

In accepting this task, my father understood he was stepping into a role that required not just his professional skills but his very heart and soul. He was tasked with ensuring that the suffering, the struggles, and the stories of those lost to the brutality of Nazism would be preserved in stone, in memory, and in the hearts of future generations. And in doing so, he hoped to find some small measure of redemption for himself, some way to honour the family he had lost and the ideals he had fought for. For my father, it was a way to bring some light into the darkness and ensure that the past would never be forgotten and that the suffering of so many would not have been in vain.

At the time of my father's application, the Board of Museums and Heritage Protection within the MKiS was led by the highly esteemed Professor Kazimierz Malinowski. A person of notable intellectual and moral character, Malinowski was deeply committed to preserving memories of a painful past, ensuring that the scars of war would not be forgotten. Malinowski inherited this grave duty from his predecessor, Professor Ludwig Rajewski, whose scholarly work laid the groundwork for understanding the systematic atrocities committed by the Nazi regime.

Rajewski's work, notably encapsulated in his book "RSHA At Work," was one of the earliest and most meticulous studies to reveal the chilling efficiency with which the Nazis orchestrated their campaign of mass extermination. His insights illuminated the strategic planning and deliberate nature of the atrocities that had scarred Europe and devastated millions of lives. Rajewski was not just a scholar; he was the President of the Commission for the Protection of Places of Struggle and Suffering, a body formed under the auspices of the Main Office of the Society of Fighters for Freedom and Democracy (Polish: Związek Bojowników o Wolność i Demokrację; ZBoWiD).

Before Rajewski, this role was held by another towering figure— Professor Romuald Gutt, an Auschwitz survivor whose very existence was a testament to the resilience of the human spirit. Gutt was not only a survivor but also a leader, serving as the Rector of the Warsaw Polytechnic and the Warsaw Institute of Fine Arts. His firsthand experience of the horrors of Auschwitz lent a profound weight to his work, and his unwavering commitment to preserving the memory of those who had perished.

These men, giants in their fields, weren't simply scholars or administrators; they were guardians of memory, keepers of the flame that would ensure the world never forgot the depths of cruelty to which humanity could sink. To my father, the chance to work under such leadership was an honour and a calling. It was an opportunity to contribute to a cause that was not just about preserving history but about honouring the dead and educating the living. It was a role that resonated with his deepest beliefs and allowed him to be part of an effort to make sure that the suffering of millions wouldn't be erased or overlooked, and that the sites of their struggle and death would be preserved as sacred spaces of remembrance. Under the guidance of men like Malinowski, Rajewski, and Gutt, my father saw a path forward—a way to reconcile his grief and loss with a mission that was both personal and universal.

These leaders' influence, passion, and unwavering dedication to preserving history no doubt left an indelible mark on my father. They were men who had seen the worst of humanity and yet remained committed to the best of what it could be—a commitment that my father, with all his scars and memories, embraced with all his heart. In this new role, he found a sense of belonging, a community of like-minded individuals who understood the importance of their work, not just as a duty to the past but as a responsibility to the future. It was a chance to contribute to something that mattered deeply, to ensure that the legacy of suffering and the lessons of history would not be lost to time.

Before my father could secure his new position, he was required to undergo a rigorous process that went beyond the usual formalities. The role demanded not only administrative skill but also a deep understanding of the socio-political landscape shaped by the horrors of the Nazi occupation. To demonstrate his readiness for this significant responsibility, he was asked to prepare and present a detailed socio-political study on a topic closely linked to this dark chapter of history. His chosen subject, "General Plan of Reichsführer SS Himmler to Resettle 50 million Slavs," explored the chilling ambitions of Nazi Germany to reshape the population of Eastern Europe, a plan that was as ruthless as it was expansive.

The submission was more than just an academic task; it was a reflection of my father's intellectual abilities and understanding of the harsh realities that scarred his homeland. His research was carefully detailed and delivered with the seriousness the topic deserved. When he faced the MKiS Interview Selection Panel, chaired by the respected Professor Jan Zachwatowicz, his work received approval.

The panel, made up of experts in history and cultural preservation, reviewed his presentation with great interest, recognising his knowledge and passion for the subject.

The panel's favourable assessment led to his acceptance of the position he had long sought. On May 30, 1950, my father formalised his commitment to this new role by signing a Memorandum of Understanding with the Vice-Minister, Dr. Włodzimierz Sokorski. His formal title was Senior Inspector within the Central Office of the MKiS, specifically at the Board of Museums and Heritage Protection.

Besides his role as Senior Inspector, his new job also involved joining the Polish Council for the Protection of Monuments of Struggle and Suffering, a body dedicated to protecting the sites of history's most painful marks. He also became an active member of the Commission for the Protection of Places of Struggle and Suffering, strengthening his involvement in efforts to keep alive the memories of those who endured under Nazi rule. His dedication to these roles was highlighted by his membership in ZBoWiD, an organisation uniting veterans and survivors who fought and suffered under foreign oppression. He had been a member of ZBoWiD since it was established on September 2, 1949, a detail that only deepened his connection to the work ahead.

This new chapter in his life marked a convergence of his personal history, intellectual pursuits, and dedication to preserving the truth. My father's work in this unique field was about ensuring that the lessons learned would resonate with future generations. In this role, he found a way to channel his grief, memories, and his pursuit of justice into something that could influence the collective memory of a nation. When my father started his work at the MKiS, Poland was still confronting the heavy burden of the genocide that had scarred its land. The tragedy, now widely recognised as the Holocaust, claimed the lives of six million Jews—a horrific atrocity committed by the German Nazis during their brutal occupation of Poland. The scale of this crime defies understanding, and its shadows still cast a heavy weight over every corner of the country.

At the heart of this horror was Auschwitz-Birkenau (Polish: Oświęcim-Brzezinka), where approximately 1.5 million Jewish souls were lost in the gas chambers of Birkenau. This site stood only three kilometres from the main Auschwitz Concentration Camp. The name Auschwitz-Birkenau has since become synonymous with the very essence of evil, a place where the machinery of death operated with a chilling efficiency. Yet, this was not an isolated horror. Scattered across Poland were other extermination camps—Treblinka, Bełżec, Majdanek, Sztutowo, Sobibór—each a cog in the monstrous wheel of Hitler's 'Final Solution.' These camps were not merely places of death; they were meticulously designed instruments of destruction, where Jewish men, women, children, and the elderly were systematically murdered upon arrival, their lives extinguished in the most brutal of fashions. The Germans had established these places with deliberate intent, creating an industrial-scale genocide that sought to erase the Jewish people from the face of Europe. The trains, laden with despair and terror, brought their human cargo to these destinations of doom from all parts of the European continent. There was no escape, no reprieve—only the inevitability of death awaited those who arrived.

In the years after the war, as Poland aimed to rebuild and recover, these sites of mass murder assumed a deep and complex significance within Polish society. For many Poles, they became symbols of the broader Polish experience under Nazi occupation. They were regarded as places of Polish martyrology, where the nation's suffering and sacrifice were honoured. The memory of these sites was woven into the story of Polish resistance and struggle.

These places became sacred grounds where the memory of suffering intertwined with the story of a nation's resilience. In the late 1940s and throughout the 1950s, as Poland emerged from the rubble of war, the camps were remembered not only as Jewish gravesites, but primarily, as monuments to Polish endurance. They were sites where the blood of the oppressed had soaked into the earth, places where the fight against Nazi brutality had been fought with courage and desperation.

Identification (Polish: Legitymacja) indicating my father's active membership of the Union of Fighters for Freedom and Democracy (Polish: Związek Bojowników o Wolność i Demokrację - Society of Fighters for Freedom and Democracy ZBoWiD). ZBoWiD was an official Polish state-controlled veterans association in the People's Republic of Poland. During the 1950s, it mainly consisted of former Soviet-sponsored Polish People's Army veterans, communist partisans, and former concentration camp inmates. However, with the emergence of Gomulka's 1956 'political thaw' ZBoWiD began to include the veterans of other Polish formations that had fought in World War II. These included former members of the Polish Socialist Party (PPS). In the 1970s, ZBoWiD's membership grew to 330,000 members. The leadership of ZBoWiD gradually changed from staunch communists like Franciszek Jóźwiak or Roman Zambrowski in the early 1950s, to members of the PPS like Mieczysław Moczar and Kazimierz Rusinek. In April 1990, ZBoWiD was reformed into the Society of Veterans of the Republic of Poland and Former Political Prisoners (Polish: Związek Kombatantów RP i Byłych Więźniów Politycznych; ZKRPiBWP) to include members of all Polish military formations, such as National Home Army, partisans, self-defence units, and the Polish Underground State. [1]

Identification indicating that my father is an employee of the Ministry of Culture and Art within the Board of Museums and Heritage Protection, Co-signed by Prof. Malinowski.

My father, working at the MKiS, understood the importance of these places as historical documents, as eternal witnesses to the crimes that had been committed. They were to be preserved in their original form, untouched by time, so the world would never forget the depths of human cruelty and the need for eternal vigilance. These sites were warnings for the future; reminders of what humanity must never allow to happen again. As my father worked to ensure their preservation, he was driven by the belief that these places must stand as lasting testaments to the suffering endured and the strength shown in the face of evil.

During his initial stages of work at the MKiS, my father became aware that in the early months of 1947, Professor Ludwig Rajewski, then Director of the Board of Museums and Heritage Protection within the MKiS, took a monumental step in preserving history. He conceived and presented a plan to establish the Auschwitz-Birkenau State Museum as a "historical document," a site that would bear

254

witness to the atrocities committed during the Nazi occupation. Understanding the importance of inclusivity and accuracy, Rajewski involved the Central Committee of Jews in Poland (CKŻP). The Committee's role was crucial in establishing the approximate number of Jewish victims who had perished in the Auschwitz-Birkenau Konzentrationslager (KL). The annihilation of the Jewish people, though unique in its scope and brutality, was officially named "The Extermination of Millions." This broader term was chosen to acknowledge the other victims of Nazi terror as well—Romani people, political prisoners, Soviet prisoners of war, and Poles, many of whom were targeted for their resistance against the occupation.

On the 25th of April 1947, a pivotal meeting took place. Delegates from the CKŻP, alongside Natan Blumental, the Head of the Central Jewish Historical Commission (CŻKH), met with Rajewski and Kazimierz Wąsowicz, the newly appointed head of the Auschwitz State Museum. The purpose of this meeting was profound: the Jewish representatives sought a direct role in shaping the museum's narrative, particularly in the memorialisation of the tragic suffering endured by the Jewish community. Their request was not only reasonable but essential, and it was approved. [2]

Yet, despite this approval, the representation of Jewish suffering within the museum was constrained. The exhibits that focused on the Holocaust were relegated to a modest segment, housed in what was known as the "Jewish Hall," identified as Block No. 4. This allocation, though significant, was far from sufficient to encompass the magnitude of the Jewish tragedy. The broader narrative of Auschwitz-Birkenau, while inclusive of various groups, did not fully capture the unique horror of the Holocaust—a genocide that sought to erase an entire people from existence—the Jewish people.

My father understood the weight of history and the importance of bearing witness to the truth. He knew that the museum had to serve as a living memorial where the voices of the lost could be heard, and their stories told with the gravity they deserved. However, he quickly realised the complexities and challenges involved in preserving history within a politically driven context. There was a palpable tension between universalising suffering and genuinely recognising the specificity of the Jewish experience at Auschwitz-Birkenau. This tension reflected the broader struggle within Polish society to come to terms with its history. This was not simply about creating a museum; it was about shaping collective memory, about deciding whose stories would be told and how they would be remembered. [3]

Around that time, the importance of conserving the sites of mass extermination carried out by the German Nazis was highlighted by the legislative acts of the Polish Parliament, announced on 2nd July 1947. These acts (DURP 1947, No. 51, Pos. 264 & DURP 1947, No. 63, Pos. 372) mandated that the grounds of these former death camps remain untouched and preserved as eternal monuments. These locations were to serve as solemn memorials to the victims' memory, bearing witness to an unparalleled crime against humanity. [4]

These laws were a collective vow—a promise to ensure that the horrors of the Holocaust would not fade into the obscurity of forgotten history. Each preserved site was a silent cry, a plea to the world to remember, never to let such darkness envelop humanity again. The fields, the ruins, and the gas chambers were sacred grounds where the echoes of pain and suffering still lingered in the air, where the silence spoke louder than words.

For my father and many others, these sites symbolised the very essence of loss and grief, too profound for tears, and sorrow that no passing of time could ever mend. Preserving these places was an act of reverence, acknowledging the unimaginable pain endured by so many, and pledging to ensure the memory of their suffering would never be forgotten.

Approximately two weeks before this legislation was introduced, the deep acknowledgment of the human suffering at Auschwitz-Birkenau KL was solemnly observed during the first commemoration ceremony on 14 June 1947. At this moving gathering, the Minister of the MKiS, Stanislaw Dybowski, announced a crucial new initiative: the creation of the Polish Council for the Protection of Monuments of Struggle. This council was to act as the guardian of memory, responsible for ensuring that all sites where the mass killing of innocent civilians took place are preserved as living monuments to a tragedy beyond understanding. [5]

The announcement came at a time when the raw wounds of the Holocaust were still fresh in the hearts of survivors and the wider community. The establishment of the Council was an affirmation that the horrors of the past would not be allowed to fade into the shadows. The Council's mandate was clear: to protect these grounds as places of reflection, where the agony and resilience of those who perished could be honoured and remembered for generations to come.

This initiative was a response to the overwhelming need to confront the atrocities committed by the Nazis and to offer a place for collective mourning. It was also a powerful statement of the nation's commitment to remember, educate, and ensure that such a dark chapter in human history would never be repeated. The Council's work would ensure that these sites remained untouched, their grim reality preserved as a testament to the unimaginable suffering endured by millions. Through these efforts, the memory of the Holocaust would remain indelibly etched into the fabric of history, a constant reminder of the depths of human cruelty and the enduring spirit of those who suffered.

During the commemoration, attended by a crowd of 30,000 Poles, the atmosphere was heavy with history and memory. The Polish Prime Minister and Leader of the Polish Socialist Party, Jozef Cyrankiewicz—himself a survivor of Auschwitz—stood before the gathering to deliver a speech that would resonate through time. With a voice reflecting the weight of personal and collective suffering, Cyrankiewicz declared that survivors of the extermination camps were themselves living "documents" of the horror that must never be allowed to happen again.

As he spoke, Cyrankiewicz's words carried the weight of a man who had firsthand experience of human cruelty. He solemnly observed that the Auschwitz State Museum, now officially established on the grounds of the Auschwitz Base Concentration Camp, would act as an everlasting warning, a "document of unbound German bestiality," preserving the evidence of darkness so profound in the history of humanity that it defied understanding.

But Cyrankiewicz went further, emphasising that this museum would also serve as "an evidentiary symbol about man and his struggle for freedom." [6] In this place of immense suffering, where the limits of human endurance were tested, the resilience of the human spirit would be preserved. The museum would not only commemorate the atrocities but also honour the unbreakable will to survive, the courage to resist, and the hope that shone through even in the darkest times.

In his closing words, Cyrankiewicz emphasised the grave responsibility that lay ahead. The Auschwitz State Museum, he stated, would forever serve as a monument to remind future generations to stay alert. It would be a stronghold against the resurgence of those seeking genocidal power, a lasting testament that the world must never again permit such heinous goals to be realised. His speech, both a call to remember and a plea for vigilance, deeply resonated with those gathered—survivors, mourners, and witnesses—ensuring the lessons of Auschwitz would endure long after the voices of those who experienced it had fallen silent.

For my father, his role in the deliberations of the Commission for the Protection of Monuments of Struggle and Suffering was a mission that resonated with the deepest levels of his soul. The knowledge that his entire family had perished in the German Nazi extermination camps weighed heavily on his heart, infusing his work with a profound sense of responsibility and personal grief. Each meeting and discussion was a step in a journey to preserve history and the memory of those torn from the world without a trace.

His work at the Board of Museums and Monuments Protection became the cornerstone of his life. It was a way to connect with the memories of his parents, brothers, and the many others who had shared their fate. Every day he spent in this role was a day fighting to prevent their existence from being erased, to stop their stories from fading into the oblivion of history. It was his way of making sure that their suffering was not in vain and that the world would remember long after he was gone.

The bookshelves in my father's office stood as silent witnesses to his unwavering pursuit of understanding. Positioned on the first floor overlooking the lively Krakowskie Przedmieście Street, the office was a place where the external noise sharply contrasted with the heavy silence of the past that filled the room. The shelves were lined with books, each offering a glimpse into the darkest chapters of human history. Written in German, these volumes explored the complexities of Nazism, the rise of the National Socialist movements across Europe, and the sinister goals Hitler had set for the Third Reich. They discussed Lebensraum, the twisted ideology justifying expansion at the expense of millions of lives—an idea that had been at the heart of my father's initial submission to the MKiS interview selection panel.

My father immersed himself in these texts, motivated by a need to understand the unexplainable. What had caused Germany—once hailed for its culture, philosophy, and artistic and scientific

259

achievements—to succumb to such a powerful and destructive dictatorship? How was this machinery of genocide built right in the centre of old Europe, a continent proud of its civilisation and enlightenment?

These questions haunted him, fueling his relentless study of the forces that had unleashed such unprecedented horror upon the world. The more he read, the more he sought answers, as if understanding the roots of this madness might offer some solace or sense of closure. But it was also a way to wrestle with his demons, to confront the pain of his loss by confronting the ideology that had taken his family from him. In those books, he looked for explanations, for reasons that could make sense of the meaningless. But even as he dug deeper, he realised some questions might never be answered. The books, with their detailed accounts of policies and strategies, gave insights, but they couldn't explain the human cost—the mothers, fathers, children, and siblings lost to the chasm of hate. Still, he kept going, driven by a need to understand and connect the dots between ideology and atrocity, between words on a page and the blood spilled.

His office, with its shelves filled with history's darkest chapters, became a sanctuary for his grief and his quest for meaning. Here, he could immerse himself in the past, dissecting and analysing it, trying to piece together how a nation could be led so far astray. In this way, his work was both an intellectual pursuit and a deeply emotional journey, a way of grappling with the past to find some measure of peace in the present.

As time passed, my father became wholly consumed by his work, each day drawing him deeper into the weighty responsibility that now defined his life. As a Senior Inspector, he wielded considerable influence over the emerging practical processes designed to protect and preserve the sites that had witnessed the systematic genocide of millions during the Nazi occupation of Poland. These sites, now silent, bore the echoes of horror too immense to grasp fully, and it was his duty to ensure they would forever stand as grim reminders of the past, lest the world forget.

But even as he dedicated himself to this sacred task, a disquieting realisation gnawed at him. While it was undeniable that the German Nazis had established these places of terror to carry out Hitler's 'Final Solution,' there was a subtle, insidious resistance he could not ignore—a reluctance, both within the public sphere and the government, to acknowledge this fact entirely. It was as if an unspoken agenda hovered in the air, a collective discomfort that sought to obscure the truth, to downplay the singular horror these camps had been designed to perpetrate: the murder of the Jewish people.

Entrance to the MKiS; 15 Krakowskie Przedmieście Street, Warsaw. The two windows above the entrance offered a view from my father's office.

This resistance was subtle, but my father felt it sharply, like a whisper beneath the surface of official rhetoric and public chatter. Whether aware or not, this reluctance to face the truth seemed to run through the society around him. It was as if recognising the full extent of the atrocity—calling it by its right name—the Holocaust (Polish: Zagłada Żydów), threatened some deeply embedded narrative or national identity.

In his role, my father often found himself navigating this uncomfortable terrain, where memory preservation clashed with the forces of denial or minimisation. The death camps, though undeniably places of immense human suffering, were frequently framed in a broader context of Polish martyrdom and resistance against the Nazi occupation. This narrative, while not untrue, often overshadowed the specific and targeted genocide of the Jewish people.

He understood the importance of these sites, not only as symbols of resistance or widespread suffering but as the final resting places of millions of Jewish men, women, and children—who had been systematically hunted, dehumanised, and exterminated. However, he sensed that this part of the camps' history was often pushed aside, perhaps because it was too complex or uncomfortable to fully acknowledge. It was a subtle yet deep form of erasure that threatened to undermine the very purpose of his work. How can these sites serve as memorials to the past if the truth they hold is not fully highlighted? How can the memory of the millions murdered be properly honoured if the very reason for their deaths is minimised or obscured?

These were the questions that haunted my father as he continued his work—questions that added another layer of complexity to an already arduous task. He was fighting against the forces that would see it rewritten or forgotten. And in this fight, he felt the weight of responsibility not only to the dead but to the living—to those who would come after, who needed to know the truth, unvarnished and whole. It was a lonely battle, one that took its toll on him, but he pressed on, driven by the memory of his family and the countless others who had perished. This was his purpose; although fraught with challenges, it gave his life a sense of meaning amidst the lingering shadows of grief and loss.

The Nazi death camps were not places where the struggle for freedom held any vital meaning, despite what leaders like Cyrankiewicz might have suggested in their speeches. These were not sanctuaries of heroic sacrifice or battlegrounds where the fight for survival or democracy played out. They did not represent any political framework or ideological battleground that could be neatly packaged into a narrative of resistance or defiance. The Nazi death camps were, above all else, places of cold, calculated extermination designed for one purpose alone: the annihilation of the Jewish people.

The unspoken resistance of post-war political forces in Poland, this subtle yet widespread reluctance to face the full truth, reflected a deeper, more uncomfortable reality. Polish Catholic society struggled with the unspeakable guilt over what had happened to their Jewish neighbours. It was as if recognising that these death camps were not just places of suffering but of systematic genocide—where innocent, defenceless women, men, and children were murdered, simply because they were Jewish—was too overwhelming to accept.

These victims were not chosen for their political beliefs or for any actions they had taken. They were not murdered because they were communists, socialists, or capitalists, nor because they had aligned themselves with any particular socio-political identity. They were murdered because of who they were, because of the blood that ran in their veins, because they were Jewish.

Millions of innocent civilians were herded like cattle, under the threat of German submachine guns, into cramped and suffocating freight wagons that traversed across Europe to Poland. These were not journeys of hope but of unimaginable despair, transporting people to mysterious places of unspeakable horror. Most were not granted the grim "privilege" of being tattooed, of becoming a numbered prisoner within the camp's system. For most, within an hour of their arrival, their fate was sealed as they were forced into gas chambers, where life was extinguished in the most brutal and inhumane of ways. Within the next twelve hours, their bodies, once vessels of life and spirit, were reduced to ash in the crematoria or on open pyres, leaving behind nothing but memories and a deep, enduring silence.

My father grappled with this reality as he carried out his work, a reality that refused to be simplified or wrapped in comforting stories. The death camps weren't just places of death; they marked the end for countless souls, erased not for what they believed or did, but simply because of who they were. This harsh truth, this unbending reality, cast a long shadow over everything else, making any effort to frame these places in terms of struggle, resistance, or heroism seem empty, even obscene. For my father, there was no making peace with these horrors through grander stories; there was only the stark, brutal truth—a truth he felt deeply compelled to hold onto despite the resistance and political maneuvring around him.

It was both morally and emotionally agonising for my father to navigate the unspoken, subtle resistance from the Polish government and the broader Polish society to openly acknowledge the Jewish tragedy inflicted by German Nazi murderers. Though every Pole knew what had happened to the Jews of Poland, there was a widespread, almost tangible difficulty in reaching a point of collective recognition, of voicing a reverent acknowledgment. It was as if the nation, already immersed in its suffering, could not bear the burden of another's grief, especially when that grief was so immense and unfathomable.

This resistance was not born of ignorance or denial but rather from a complex, deep-seated discomfort—a struggle to reconcile the shared pain of a nation with the singular, unparalleled tragedy of the

Holocaust. The Polish people themselves had endured unimaginable suffering under Nazi occupation. When one is submerged in pain, it is often difficult to summon the strength to step into the suffering of others. Perhaps this is a reasonable argument or a natural human response. Yet, the difficulty in embracing a collective acknowledgment of the Jewish tragedy goes far deeper than mere emotional exhaustion. It speaks to something more profound and troubling within the fabric of post-war Polish society.

The Holocaust was a crime of such staggering magnitude that it dwarfs even the most brutal atrocities of the past. When we contemplate the Holocaust today, we must picture not just six million lives lost but six million burning crosses upon which Jewish mothers, fathers, and their children were metaphorically crucified. In Auschwitz-Birkenau alone, 1,500,000 Jewish souls were extinguished—each life a flame snuffed out in a storm of hatred, each voice crying out in pain and horror, unheard by the world.

This silence, this failure to hear and respond to the cries of suffering, was not just a failure of individuals; it was a failure of humanity itself. The scale of the Holocaust—its cold, calculated execution—was unlike anything the world had seen before. It was not a mere act of war nor a consequence of political strife; it was a systematic, industrialised extermination of a people, rooted in an ideology of pure, unadulterated evil. And yet, for all its horror, Catholic Poland had a quiet difficulty in facing this reality head-on to offer the reverence and acknowledgment that the magnitude of this tragedy demanded.

The Polish society's unconscious resistance to openly discuss the Holocaust as a uniquely Jewish tragedy in the aftermath of World War II was not merely a result of ignorance or indifference; it was a deeply rooted legacy of centuries-old doctrinal teachings. These teachings had woven themselves into the very fabric of the collective conscience, instilling in the faithful the belief that the Jews were forever marked by the sin of deicide—the murder of Christ. This belief, propagated relentlessly by the Polish Catholic Church across the ages, cast a long and oppressive shadow over the nation's soul.

The Constantinian doctrine, which held that Jews bore the eternal guilt of Christ's crucifixion, was not merely a historical footnote; it was a living, breathing element of the religious and cultural landscape. In grand cathedrals of major Polish cities and across the countryside's humble parish churches, this doctrine was preached with quiet certainty, shaping the hearts and minds of generations. It was a teaching that subtly, yet profoundly, influenced how the Polish Catholics viewed their Polish Jewish neighbours—not as fellow sufferers under Nazi oppression, but as a people whose pain was, in some indefinable way, deserved.

In this context, the Holocaust was not perceived as a uniquely Jewish tragedy. The murder of six million Jews, the systematic annihilation of an entire people, was not fully acknowledged in its dreadful singularity. Instead, it was often subsumed under the broader narrative of wartime suffering, where the lines between victims blurred, and the specificity of Jewish suffering was lost. The shadow of the Constantinian doctrine lingered in the background, unspoken yet pervasive, colouring the nation's collective memory.

This belief, though rarely voiced outright, influenced how the Holocaust was understood and remembered in Poland. It was not a conscious malice but rather a deeply ingrained perspective, an unexamined assumption that shaped attitudes and muted the response to the horrors that had unfolded. The reluctance to fully acknowledge the Holocaust as the Jewish catastrophe came from a place of profound discomfort, a place where traditional religious teachings clashed with the brutal reality of what had occurred on Polish soil.

For many, the suffering of the Jews during the Holocaust was seen as a result of a supposed ancient crime passed down through generations over centuries. This view, rooted in the very core of Polish Catholicism, made it difficult for the nation to face the Holocaust in all its harrowing details. The unspoken reluctance to do so wasn't just about the past but also a testament to the lasting influence of those old doctrines, shaping the present and casting a long shadow over the future. The Polish Catholic Church, with its teachings and silence, had unknowingly laid the groundwork for the conditions that made the Holocaust possible. In the shadows of its doctrines, a seed was sown, growing into a distorted perception of the Jewish people—a perception that fueled one of the darkest chapters in human history. As the shattered nation struggled to rebuild from the ruins, in the aftermath, the Church and the society it profoundly influenced found it difficult, if not impossible, to fully face the enormity of what had happened.

The reluctance to speak openly about the Holocaust as a uniquely Jewish tragedy was a reflection of the deep-seated beliefs that had been instilled over centuries. These beliefs, rooted in the ancient charge of deicide, had long cast the Jewish people as the eternal 'other'—a community set apart by an inherited and unshakable guilt. This narrative had been woven so tightly into the fabric of religious life that it became almost invisible, a silent undercurrent that influenced thoughts and actions without ever needing to be explicitly stated.

When the Holocaust tore through Europe, the shockwaves were felt by all, but the response was not uniform. For many, the suffering of the Jews was filtered through the lens of these old religious and cultural beliefs, reducing the horror of genocide to something that could be rationalised or even dismissed. The silence and reluctance of the Polish Catholic Church, and by extension, the society it influenced, were not born out of ignorance alone. They were the manifestations of an entrenched ideology in a society that found it difficult to reconcile the doctrine of Jewish culpability (i.e. killing of

Christ) with the undeniable innocence of six million lives extinguished in the gas chambers. This cognitive dissonance, this profound inability to fully accept the truth, reflected the long, dark shadow that centuries of clerical indoctrination had cast over the national conscience.

To fully confront the Holocaust would have required not only a reckoning with the facts of history but also a fundamental re-examination of the beliefs that had underpinned Polish society for generations. For many, such a task would be too painful and too challenging to undertake. And so, the memory of the Holocaust remained clouded, its true nature obscured by the remnants of ancient prejudices that are unlikely to be entirely discarded in the future.

In every nation and culture, there exists a hidden collective "shadow"—a dark undercurrent of prejudice, fear, and mistrust that rarely is ever openly acknowledged; nevertheless, this unconscious shadow subtly supports the culture, its social mores and the attitudes of its people. In Poland, this shadow was shaped by centuries of religious doctrine that dominated society's cultural identity. One could argue that the Polish Catholic society, in its fervent nationalism, clung to the belief that Poland was for Poles and that it was the faith of Catholicism that fundamentally defined what it meant to be truly Polish. In this view, the Polish Jews, despite having lived in Poland for eight centuries, were always seen as somewhat apart, and thus, not entirely Polish, because they spoke a different language, practiced a different faith, and followed different customs. In contrast to Poland, however, Jews who live in the USA, and speak Yiddish and practice Judaism are treated as Americans, and see themselves as Americans, rather than unwanted strangers who refuse to accept the American way of life.

To many, especially those with deep religious adherence to the Catholic faith, the Jews and their communities were viewed with suspicion, seen as an untrustworthy entity that refused to assimilate into the Polish way of living. This mistrust was deeply rooted in religious differences, with the Jews seen as a people who had rejected Poland's true saviour, Jesus Christ. This religious divergence was not just a matter of theological disagreement; it was perceived as a refusal to accept the very cultural and spiritual foundation upon which Polish identity was built on. Thus, the Jews, with their adherence to Judaism, stood as a constant reminder of a different path, one that diverged from the nation's Christian narrative.

Yet, the story of the Polish Jews is not one of complete estrangement. For nearly eight centuries, they lived in Poland, which, in its initial stages, was considered by many Jewish newcomers as a haven that they fondly called 'Polin.' In the vast expanse of the Jewish Diaspora, Poland was often seen as a place of relative safety, where Jews could live in peace, if not always in perfect harmony, with their Polish Catholic neighbours. The Jewish communities' cultural heartstrings spread across Poland's shtetls and cities, and they were deeply intertwined with the nation's life, even if they remained distinct.

Polish Jews historically found a sense of belonging and shared purpose with the Polish intelligentsia, comprising poets, writers, educators, and thinkers who shaped the nation's intellectual and cultural life: a robust dialogue and mutual respect allowed for a flourishing of ideas and creativity. The contributions of Polish Jews to the sciences, literature, and arts were not just additions to Polish culture; they were integral to it, enriching the national identity in profound and enduring ways. In turn, Polish Jews found in Poland a space where they could express themselves, where their voices could be heard and appreciated within the broader tapestry of the society they were a part of.

But this relationship, complex and multifaceted, was also fragile. The shadow of suspicion, stemming from religious and cultural differences, always loomed, ready to be cast over any interaction. The coexistence, while often peaceful, was never entirely free of tension. The Jewish communities, despite their deep roots in Polish soil, were never fully integrated into the Polish national identity. They were, at best, respected contributors to Polish culture; at worst, they were seen as outsiders, forever separate, their allegiance questioned, their presence tolerated but never wholly accepted.

This duality—of connection and separation, of contribution and exclusion—defined the experience of Polish Jews for centuries. It was a dynamic that allowed for periods of flourishing, of shared achievements, but also one that harboured the seeds of discord and distrust. When the dark tide of Nazi ideology swept over Poland, these latent suspicions and divisions were brutally exploited, leading to a rupture that would forever alter the course of history. Yet, the legacy of that hidden collective shadow continues to influence how the Holocaust is remembered and understood in Poland today. The contributions of the Jewish community to Polish culture, their deep connection to the land, and the horror of their destruction, all form part of a complex narrative that is still being grappled with—a narrative that is as much about the light of shared achievements as it is about the darkness of prejudice and loss.

The history of Jewish life in Poland is one of resilience forged in the crucible of adversity. For eight centuries, the Jewish communities in Poland navigated a landscape constantly shifting beneath their feet, where sovereign borders were redrawn, and Poland's very existence as a nation was repeatedly threatened and erased. These upheavals, coupled with the economic and social discontents, often strained the fragile ties between the diverse communities that called Poland home, particularly between Polish Catholics and Polish Jews. It is an undeniable truth that the Jewish people, scattered across the world in their long Diaspora, developed a unique ability to adapt and endure. Over two millennia, they became seasoned in the art of survival, their resilience refined by waves of persecution, pogroms, and socio-political crises. With each new wave of hardship, whether it was economic boycotts or violent pogroms, the Jewish communities grew more resilient, their collective spirit fortified by the trials they faced. It was as if, with every attempt to extinguish their flame, they drew closer to some 'good and divine' force that sustained them through the darkest of times. In Poland, this resilience was both a blessing and a burden. The Jewish communities managed to thrive in a country that, at times, offered them refuge and, at other times, subjected them to suspicion and hostility. The delicate balance between coexistence and tension reflected Poland's turbulent history—a nation often at the mercy of powerful neighbours, its sovereignty contested, and its identity threatened. In such an environment, the Jewish communities learned to navigate the complexities of Polish society, contributing to its cultural and intellectual life while remaining acutely aware of their precarious position.

But this resilience came at a cost. The ability to adapt and survive often meant living with the constant undercurrent of mistrust and the knowledge that acceptance could be as fleeting as the political winds that swept across Europe. The shared history between Polish Catholics and Polish Jews was marked by periods of collaboration and mutual enrichment, but also by episodes of deep-seated animosity fueled by socioeconomic tensions and religious dogma. Yet, through it all, the Jewish spirit remained unbroken. Each crisis, each act of persecution, was met with an indomitable will to survive, rebuild, and find meaning in the face of suffering. This ability to extract something 'good and divine' from the depths of despair became a defining characteristic of the Jewish experience in Poland—a testament to the enduring faith and unyielding hope for a better future.

In this way, the Jewish communities of Poland became living paradoxes: deeply rooted in a land where they had lived for centuries, yet always prepared to face the next wave of adversity with a quiet, steadfast determination. Their history is a chronicle of suffering and a powerful narrative of survival and the relentless pursuit of life, even in the most trying of circumstances. It is a story of a people who, no matter how many times they were attacked and knocked down, found within themselves the strength to rise again, carrying with them the hope that something good and divine would always follow. This is the story of the contemporary State of Israel in many respects, but that is another subject altogether.

With the rise of Marxist thought and the publication of The Communist Manifesto, a significant shift began to take hold among young Polish Jews. Many viewed Communism as a new vision—a way to bridge the growing gap between their Jewish cultural heritage and Polish society. They started shedding the traditions that had defined their ancestors for generations. This push towards assimilation, to fully integrate into Polish society, was a powerful force during Józef Piłsudski's era, when the promise of a united, secular Poland seemed within reach.

For many young Jews, embracing secularism and Marxist ideals offered a path to belonging in a country where their religious identity had often set them apart. The dream was to become not merely residents of Poland, but Poles in the fullest sense—active participants in the nation's social, cultural, and political life, free from the stigma that had long accompanied their Jewishness and "otherness". The hope was that in shedding the outward signs of their faith, they could also shed the prejudice and isolation that came with it.

However, as history would tragically reveal, this drive towards assimilation met an abrupt and horrific end. By the time Communist movement began to take shape in Poland, the momentum for integration had faltered. The Jewish communities of Poland were obliterated in the Holocaust. What had once been a vibrant, complex mosaic of Jewish life across Poland's cities, country towns, and shtetls, was reduced to ashes, replacing the hum of life with an eerie silence, in place where once there had been the hum of life.

In this new Poland, devoid of its Jewish folk, a strange and unsettling vacuum emerged. The historical, often uneasy bond between Polish Catholics and Polish Jews was severed, not by the gradual process of assimilation but by the brutality of genocide. Suddenly, the Polish society found itself free from what many had perceived as the uncomfortable 'bondage' to the Jewish 'inhabitants of their land.'

This freedom, however, was a hollow victory. The disappearance of Jewish communities from the socio-topographical landscape of Poland left a void that could never be filled. The richness of Polish-Jewish culture, with its unique blend of traditions, languages, and ideas, was gone, leaving a nation grappling with the ghosts of those who had been erased. The land was the same, the cities and towns unchanged in their physical geography, yet something vital had been lost—a connection, a dialogue, a shared history that could never be fully reclaimed.

The drive for assimilation had been born of hope, of a desire to bridge the gap between two worlds. But in the end, that hope was extinguished not by failure but by an atrocity so profound that it defied comprehension. What remained was a nation free from its historical ties to its Jewish neighbours but also deeply impoverished by their absence, haunted by the memory of what had been and what had been lost forever.

Within the Polish community, the remembrance and commemoration of places like Auschwitz-Birkenau often took on a distinctly nationalistic tone, one that emphasised the Polish experience of suffering and resistance. The narrative that emerged focused on the heroic struggle of the Polish people against the German oppressors, highlighting the national sacrifice and the resilience of the Polish spirit in the face of unimaginable cruelty. This perspective, deeply embedded in the collective consciousness of the Polish society, served as a way to process the trauma of the war.

However, it also operated as a subtle yet pervasive means of displacing the Jewish tragedy that had unfolded on Polish soil.

The unconscious motive behind this response was complex. On one level, it was about preserving a sense of national pride, of seeing Poland not just as a victim of Nazi aggression but as a nation that had fought valiantly for its survival. On another level, it was about avoiding the painful necessity of fully acknowledging the scale and specificity of Jewish suffering. The Holocaust, in which millions of Jews were systematically exterminated, was a tragedy of such magnitude that it threatened to overshadow the Polish narrative. And so, by framing the events within a broader context of "international suffering," the unique horror of the Jewish experience could be somewhat subsumed into a more generalised narrative of oppression.

This approach was not unique to Poland, but in the context of a society that had been steeped in centuries of Catholic doctrinal teachings—teachings that often portrayed Jews in a negative light—it became particularly potent. The speeches of political figures, such as Cyrankiewicz in 1947 and later Kazimierz Rusinek, Minister of Culture and Art, exemplified this ideological perspective. Both men, in their public addresses, highlighted Poland's national sacrifice and struggle against German Nazi oppression, while simultaneously framing the Holocaust within the Communist ideological framework of the "international suffering of nations oppressed by forces of Nazism and Fascism." By doing so, they effectively diluted the specificity of Jewish suffering, placing it within a broader context that, while not denying the horror of what had occurred, also did not fully confront it. This allowed the Polish Catholic society to engage in a form of collective amnesia, where the painful reality of the Jewish genocide could be acknowledged, but only in a way that did not threaten the primacy of the Polish narrative. The result was a remembrance that, in many ways, was an incomplete commemoration—a commemoration that honoured the victims, but did so in a manner that reflected the ideological needs of the time. The Jewish tragedy was recognised, but it was also reframed and, to some extent, distorted to fit within a narrative that was more comfortable and more aligned with the national identity that post-war Poland sought to construct.

This approach to memory and history, driven by an unconscious need to protect the Polish self-image, had long-lasting implications. The whole, unvarnished truth of the Jewish experience during the war—the scale of the atrocity, the specific systematic targeting of Jews for extermination—was something that, for many years, remained at the edges of the national consciousness, acknowledged, but not fully integrated into the collective memory of the nation. Even today, one may hear on some occasions the words, "My grandfather was in Auschwitz camp too," expressed by a Polish national who equated entrapment and slavery within the Auschwitz complex, on the par with the brutal murder of 1.5 million people who arrived in cattle freight trains, and were sent directly to the gas chambers.

In the end, this displacement and distortion of memory served to distance the Polish society from the complete moral reckoning that the Holocaust demanded. It allowed the wounds of the past to remain half-healed, festering beneath the surface of a nation that had yet to fully come to terms with the darkest chapter in its history. And in that space of unresolved grief and unspoken truths, the ghosts of those who perished still continue to linger, their voices were muted but never entirely silenced. [7]

In his quiet moments, I imagine my father grappling with this issue, seeking resolution. Perhaps he justified the political stance of the MKiS and the broader Polish government by telling himself that, at the very least, these places of horrific genocide were being preserved and protected. The communist government, for all its flaws, was committed to ensuring that these sites of atrocity and human suffering would not be erased from memory. To him, this preservation was a vital acknowledgment—not just of the Jewish victims but of the shared humanity that bound all human beings together in death. It was this recognition that allowed him to hold on to his ideological belief that in the communist Poland of the future, Jews and Poles could finally be seen as equals.

This hope, fragile as it was, might have been what allowed him to reconcile himself with the government's reluctance to fully acknowledge the Jewish tragedy. It was a hope rooted in the belief that the horrors of the past could give rise to a fairer, more just society. Yet, deep down, he knew that the Holocaust was not solely a result of German Nazism but also of the deep-seated racism that had long festered in Europe, largely fueled by the ideological complicity of the Roman Catholic Church. This devout institution, which had shaped the minds and souls of its followers for centuries, had played a part in planting the seeds of hatred by perpetuating the idea that the Jews were Christ-killers—a belief that stained Europe's conscience and, in its darkest moments, helped bring about the atrocities of the Holocaust.

In communist Poland, my father found himself navigating a delicate balance, caught between his atheistic ideals and the tough realities of the society around him. He held onto hope that in this new Poland, there might be a place where old hatred could finally be put to rest. But he was not blind to the complexities of the situation. He understood that resistance to fully acknowledging the Jewish Gehenna was not just about politics — it was rooted in centuries of prejudice, a cultural and religious legacy that could not be easily undone. Still, despite this, he kept working with quiet resolve. For him, preserving these sites of genocide was not just about memory — it was about justice. It was about ensuring the suffering of millions would not be forgotten and that the lessons of the Holocaust would remain alive in history. In doing so, he found a purpose, a way to honour the memory of his family and the millions who had perished.

It was his way of confronting the darkness, standing against silence and resistance, and keeping alive the hope that, one day, in this brave new world, true equality and proper recognition of our shared humanity — regardless of race, religion, or creed — might be achieved.

Notes

1. Society of Fighters for Freedom and Democracy see: https://en.wikipedia.org/wiki/Society_of_Fighters_for_Freedom_and_Democracy

2. The first years of the Memorial. Memorial and Museum Auschwitz-Birkenau. See:www.auschwitz.org/en/museum/history-of-the-memorial/the-first-years-of-the-memorial/

3. Huener, Jonathan (2003). Auschwitz, Poland, and the Politics of Commemoration, 1945-1979. Ohio University Press. Athens p.75

4. https://isap.sejm.gov.pl/isap.nsf/search.xsp

5. Huener, Jonathan (2003). Auschwitz, Poland, and the Politics of Commemoration, 1945-1979. Ohio University Press. Athens p.32

6. Ibid., p. 32

7. Ibid., p. 166

12. Disillusion

"The truth of history is never as simple as the narratives we construct around it. It is rather a complex tapestry of experiences, perspectives, and emotions that cannot be easily untangled or neatly categorised." - Janusz

The amendment to the Act on April 7th, 1949, marked a significant shift in how the Polish government sought to memorialise the sites of unimaginable horror that had scarred the nation's landscape. The Sejm's decision to rename the Council for the Protection of Monuments of Suffering to the Council for the Protection of Monuments of Struggle and Suffering might, on the surface, seem like an inclusive gesture—a recognition that the tragedy of the Holocaust and the atrocities committed in concentration camps were not confined to Polish borders but extended to victims from various parts of Europe. Yet, as with many official acts of recognition, what is left unsaid often speaks louder than what is explicitly stated.

The new name suggested a broader scope, commemorating the shared suffering of all nations ravaged by war. However, this shift also obscured the particularity of the Jewish experience, diluting the acknowledgment of the fact that the vast majority of those who perished in these camps were Jewish. It was as if, in the effort to universalise the suffering, the unique identity of the victims was being quietly erased. The amended Act did not mention the Central Committee of Jews in Poland (CKŻP), an organisation explicitly included in the original Act. This omission was telling—a subtle but profound erasure of the Jewish voice in the ongoing memorialisation process.

For my father, who had devoted himself to preserving these sites as sacred spaces of memory, this change must have been both perplexing and disconcerting. He understood the importance of recognising the diverse origins of the victims. Still, he also knew, deep in his heart, that the Holocaust was a tragedy that had uniquely targeted the Jewish people. The horror of what had been done could not be fully comprehended without acknowledging the anti-Semitic hatred that had fuelled the Nazi machinery of death.

The amended Act's insistence on protecting all war crime sites in Poland for commemorative purposes alone seemed, on the surface, a noble endeavour. Yet, the very language used in the amendment hinted at a broader reluctance to confront the specificity of horrors faced by the Jews. By reframing the narrative around a more generalised notion of "struggle and suffering," the amended Act risked obscuring the true nature of the atrocities committed on Polish soil. It was as though the struggle to preserve these sites as monuments to human suffering was being waged against the very forces that sought to blur the lines between the victims, to wash away the specificity of their identities in a sea of generalised grief.

In this atmosphere of quiet resistance, my father grappled with the conflicting emotions that such decisions provoked. He was a man committed to the ideals of equality and human dignity, who believed that in death, all people were equal—Poles and Jews, Christians and atheists, all victims of the same inhuman system. But he was also a man who could not ignore the reality of what had happened, who could not turn away from the fact that his family, like millions of others, had been targeted not because of their political adherences or their actions, but simply because they were Jews.

The erasure of the Jewish identity from the official narrative of these sites of memory must have weighed heavily on him. He knew that the fight to preserve these places was not just about bricks and mortar, about ensuring that the physical remnants of the camps remained intact. It was about preserving the truth of what had happened there, about ensuring that the world would never forget the specific, targeted cruelty that had been inflicted on the Jewish people.

It was about fighting against the silent, insidious forces that sought to rewrite history, to downplay the role that centuries of anti-Semitic hatred had played in leading to the Holocaust.

For my father, this battle could not be won by force of arms or political manoeuvring. It was a battle fought in the quiet halls of memory, in how history was told and retold and how the dead were remembered. And in that battle, as the only employee of the Ministry of Culture and Art (MKiS) with a Jewish heritage, he must have felt, at times, both deeply committed, vulnerable to rejection, and profoundly alone. As he continued his work, he knew that the struggle to preserve these sites as monuments to the Jewish tragedy was as much a fight against the forces of oblivion, as it was against the passage of time. He knew that the true horror of the Holocaust could never be fully grasped if it was allowed to be diluted into a general narrative of suffering. And he must have hoped that, in some small way, his efforts would help to keep the memory alive, so that the Jewish voices that the gas chambers had silenced would continue to be heard, even in the face of official silence. [1]

The past is never just the past; it is constantly reshaped and reinterpreted through the lens of the present, influenced by the prevailing Zeitgeist of the time. When my father began his work at MKiS, the Cold War had already cast its long shadow over Europe. The ideological battle between East and West was not just a clash of military might, but a clash of narratives—each side seeking to define history in a manner that justified its past, present, and future actions and ambitions. In this climate, my father found himself deeply involved in the creation of a new exhibition within the grounds of Auschwitz-Birkenau, a place that had become synonymous with the horrors of the Holocaust.

The exhibition, titled "Imperialism Unmasked," was a carefully crafted narrative that sought to link the atrocities of the Nazi regime with the dangers of Western imperialism. The message was clear: if all of Europe had embraced Communism, the genocide that took place on Polish soil would have been an impossibility. The underlying implication was that the capitalist West, with its imperialistic ambitions, which were often hidden beneath the veneer of democracy, bore a share of the blame for the horrors that had occurred.

My father spent hours on the grounds of Auschwitz-Birkenau, where the echoes of the past seemed to reverberate through the air. The exhibition's focus was not on the millions of innocent lives lost, nor on the uniquely Jewish tragedy that the Holocaust represented, but on a political message that sought to serve the current regime's goals. This instrumentalisation of history was glaringly apparent, yet it was an issue that remained unspoken, buried beneath layers of ideological rhetoric.

My father, a man who had lost everything to the very forces that Auschwitz-Birkenau symbolised, must have felt a profound conflict. On the one hand, he believed in the ideals of Communism, hoping that they would bring about a world where such atrocities could never happen again; on the other, he could not ignore how the memories of those who perished were being reshaped to fit a narrative that suited the needs of the State.

The exhibition was part of a broader effort to ensure that the memory of the Holocaust was aligned with the ideological framework of communist Poland. It was a subtle but powerful form of control, one that dictated not just how people lived but how they were remembered. The victims of Auschwitz-Birkenau were no longer just individuals; they were symbols, their suffering co-opted into a story that was not entirely their own. For my father, this reality must have been a heavy burden. He had dedicated his life to preserving the memory of the Holocaust, to ensuring that the horrors of the past would never be forgotten. Yet, he found himself in a world where that memory was being manipulated, where the demands of the present were overshadowing the true nature of the tragedy.

Even as he worked to protect and preserve the sites of these atrocities, he must have struggled with the knowledge that the whole truth was not being told. The emphasis on Polish suffering and resistance, while important, was also a way of avoiding the uncomfortable reality of the Holocaust as a uniquely Jewish tragedy. It was a way of displacing the responsibility for what had happened, of creating a narrative that was more palatable to a society that had been shaped by centuries of anti-Semitic doctrine, and now it was shaped by additional layer of communist dogma.

My father's work at Auschwitz-Birkenau was a mission, a way of making sense of the loss and trauma that had defined his life. But it was also a reminder of the power of history, of how it can be used to shape the present and the future. The exhibition he helped create was a testament to this power, but it also reflected his limitations and the compromises he had to make to serve a cause he believed in.

Ultimately, my father's work was a complex and often painful journey, forcing him to confront how history can be both a weapon and a shield. It was a journey that required him to navigate the treacherous waters of memory and ideology, to find a way to honour the past even as it was being reshaped by the forces of the present. And it was a journey that left him with the knowledge that the truth, however elusive, was worth fighting for—even when it seemed that the world was determined to forget.

From my father's perspective, the Western powers, particularly Great Britain and the USA, bore some moral responsibility for the horrors that unfolded in places like Auschwitz-Birkenau. They had been aware of the atrocities of the systematic extermination of European Jewry, and yet they did nothing to intervene. The USA, in his eyes, had entered the war far too late; their delayed intervention did not prevent the flames of the Holocaust from consuming millions of lives. For my father, this delay was unforgivable. He often pondered how many more might have been saved if the Western powers had acted with the urgency that the situation demanded. The images of the gas chambers and the crematoria belching black smoke into the sky were seared into his memory. He believed that these instruments of death could have been stopped sooner if only there had been the will to do so.

But it wasn't just about the timing of the American intervention. My father saw the West's inaction as a profound failure of humanity. Despite their knowledge, despite the reports that had trickled out of occupied Europe, the Western powers had chosen to turn a blind eye. The reports of mass extermination, of entire communities being erased, were met with bureaucratic indifference and a reluctance to divert resources from the larger war effort. In this, my father saw a chilling parallel to the indifference that had allowed the Holocaust to unfold in the first place—a world that was willing to stand by and do nothing as millions were led to their deaths.

In contrast, it was the Soviet advance, the relentless push of the Belorussian front, that ultimately brought an end to the operation of the gas chambers and crematoria. The Red Army took decisive action. They liberated Auschwitz-Birkenau and stopped the killing. For my father, this was a stark reminder of the realities of power: that it was not the high-minded ideals of the West but the grim determination of the Soviets that had finally ended the horror.

To my father, the Holocaust was not just a crime of the Nazis; it was also a crime of omission by those who could have done more and who should have done more. It was a failure of the entire world, including the Western allies who had the power to intervene but chose not to. This belief was a bitter truth he carried with him, a reminder that the moral high ground claimed by the West was built on a foundation of inaction and indifference.

The Soviet soldiers marching through the gates of Auschwitz-Birkenau on the 27th of January 1945 were not regarded by my father as mere liberators; they were, in a sense, avengers, the ones who had done what the West could not—or would not—do. He believed that the gas chambers and crematoria might have continued operating throughout 1945 and perhaps even longer if not for the Soviet advance. This knowledge, this deeply held belief, shaped his view of the world in the years that followed.

Poland suffered greatly under the German Nazi occupation, enduring brutal repression, mass executions, and the destruction of its cities and cultural sites. The hardships faced by the Polish people were real and significant, a collective trauma that warranted recognition and remembrance. However, within this story of Polish martyrdom, there was a quiet tension—a reluctance to fully acknowledge the parallel, even more devastating suffering of the Jewish people. My father noticed this tension, like an unspoken undertone in every discussion about the war and its aftermath. Polish society found it difficult to integrate the horrors experienced by the Jews into its national narrative. The Holocaust, in all its brutality, was an enormous tragedy—an unfathomable wound so deep it risked overshadowing the suffering of the Polish nation itself.

There was an unconscious impulse within Polish society to avoid or minimise the reality of the Jewish tragedy to ensure that the narrative of Polish martyrdom remained at the forefront of the nation's collective memory. This was not necessarily born of malice but of a deep-rooted need to find meaning and identity in the face of overwhelming loss. The Polish people had endured unspeakable hardships, and in the aftermath, there was a natural desire to assert their own suffering as central, as the most salient element in the memorialisation of World War II.

One of the political exhibits that was presented in Auschwitz State Museum in 1955: "And in West Germany, Anglo-Saxon imperialists again are arming my murderers" [2]

The memory of the Holocaust had to be shaped, moulded, and, in some ways, manipulated to serve the ideological needs of the State. The narrative of Jewish suffering was subsumed under the broader story of the fight against fascism, of the victory of the proletariat over the forces of evil. The Jewish tragedy was acknowledged in this story, but it was often relegated to a secondary role, overshadowed by the tale of Polish resilience and communist victory.

In the end, my father's work reflected this inner conflict. He was a man caught between two worlds: the world of political ideology—where the Holocaust was a tool to highlight the dangers of Fascism and Imperialism; and the world of personal memory, where the Holocaust was a profound, inescapable tragedy that demanded full acknowledgment. His efforts to preserve the memory of the Holocaust were driven by both a sense of duty and a deep, personal need to honour the victims—his own family among them. But he was also

286

haunted by the knowledge that the society he lived in and the political system he was committed to might never fully come to terms with the true magnitude of what had happened.

For my father, the early 1950s were a time of intense emotional struggle, a period when the lines between memory, ideology, and reality were blurred. He carried the weight of the Holocaust with him every day, even as he worked within a system that sought to shape and control that memory for its own purposes. In that struggle, he found himself confronting the deepest questions of his identity, beliefs, and place in a world—forever scarred by the horrors of the past.

For Christian Poles, the 135,000 Polish prisoners who perished in Auschwitz-Birkenau KL were revered as heroes—martyrs who died for their Roman Catholic faith, their unwavering national values, and their deep love for Poland, their homeland. They were seen as the righteous, the first victims of German Nazism, who, despite the horrors they faced—being rounded up, incarcerated, tortured, and shot—rose valiantly against the oppressive forces. This narrative, deeply embedded in the Polish collective memory, was embraced as a profound truth, a testament to the resilience and courage of the Polish people. Indeed, it is also a fact that a larger section of Polish political prisoners survived the war, their survival stories adding layers to the fabric of national pride and remembrance.

In this landscape of Polish suffering and heroism, there was a widespread, unspoken understanding that the Jews—and the Gypsies—did not die for the same heroic ideals. They were not martyrs of faith or the nation; they were simply victims, casualties of genocide. They were taken to places of unspeakable horror, where they vanished into thin air, their bodies consumed by the relentless flames of Auschwitz-Birkenau or Treblinka's crematoria.

287

Among many Christian Poles, Jews were often seen as 'God's unfaithful lost souls,' their suffering viewed with detachment, if not outright indifference. Beyond this, there was little more to acknowledge. Their mass murder was not regarded as a national tragedy but as a harsh reality separate from the Polish experience of the war. This marginalisation of the Jewish tragedy, this quiet dismissal, was not just a passing oversight; it was a deeply rooted attitude that persisted in post-war Poland.

In the shadow of this national narrative, the Jews of Poland were rendered almost invisible, their suffering acknowledged only in the most cursory of ways. Their deaths were not woven into the tapestry of Polish heroism; instead, they were left on the fringes, a sad footnote to a story that centred on Polish heroic resistance, suffering and martyrdom. This marginalisation speaks to a broader issue within Polish society—the Jewish victims were not seen as part of the same struggle; they were viewed as the 'other,' their deaths a separate chapter, distant from the narrative of Polish resilience. The tragedy of this perspective is profound. It reflects a collective reluctance to grapple with the full implications of the Holocaust and resistance to acknowledge the stark truth that the extermination of six million Jews was not just another atrocity of the war, but a unique and unparalleled crime against humanity. For my father, this marginalisation was not just an intellectual frustration; it was a source of deep emotional pain, a wound that cut to the heart of his own identity and his place in the world. He knew that the Jewish victims of the Holocaust were not just numbers or faceless casualties—they were individuals, families, and entire communities who had been annihilated simply because they were Jews. And he understood, perhaps more acutely than most, that this truth needed to be spoken, remembered, and honoured, not pushed to the margins of history.

Above is the 195-page declassified document of the British-American 'G-2 Counter-Intelligence Sub-Division' which gathered intelligence on the Operation of German Nazi concentration camps throughout Europe in 1943-1944. [3]

In the end, the marginalisation of the Jewish tragedy in post-war Poland was a failure of empathy, a reluctance to see the full humanity of those who had perished. It is a painful reminder that even in the aftermath of unimaginable horror, the boundaries of 'us' and 'them' can persist, shaping how we remember, how we mourn, and how we understand the past. [4]

It is an undeniable truth that Polish society endured unspeakable suffering during the years of World War II, under the brutal Nazi Germany's occupation of their homeland. The scars left by the war were deep and widespread, touching every corner of the nation. In the aftermath, the collective longing among Poles was to move forward, to distance themselves from the relentless reminders of the tragedy that had unfolded not only within their borders but also within their own communities. The sheer magnitude of the destruction and oppression had left the people of Poland with a profound psychological numbness, a weariness born from years of witnessing and enduring unimaginable human trauma.

In this post-war landscape, the overwhelming desire was to shed the heavy cloak of despair, to find a way to rebuild and restore some semblance of normal life. The government, through the MKiS, found itself in a delicate position of balancing this collective need for healing with the responsibility of documenting and commemorating the atrocities that had occurred on Polish soil. The strategy was to contain these commemorations, limiting them to the actual sites where the mass exterminations happened. There was a conscious effort to craft a narrative that would heal the nation's wounds. This narrative depicted Jews and Poles as brothers in suffering, as comrades who had faced the stormy seas together, fighting side by side in the uprisings for freedom and democracy.

Yet, beneath this constructed myth lay a painful distortion of the truth. The harsh reality was that the experiences of Jews and Poles during the Nazi occupation were not the same. While both communities suffered, their fates were not entwined as the myth suggested. The systematic, genocidal extermination carried out by the Nazis was directed at the Jewish population with a singular, chilling focus. The Jews were hunted, rounded up, and transported to death camps with the explicit intent of annihilation—a fate that the

Christian Poles did not share in the same systematic, calculated manner.

The narrative that sought to unite Jews and Poles in a common struggle against the Nazis was, at its core, a comforting fiction, one that allowed Polish society to believe they had stood together, shoulder to shoulder, against a common enemy. But in reality, they were not "in the same boat." The Jews were targeted for complete eradication, a fact that was difficult for post-war Polish society to acknowledge and incorporate into its national consciousness. The myth, though well-intentioned, served to blur the lines between two distinct experiences of suffering, leaving the Jewish tragedy inadequately recognised and poorly understood.

For my father, this was a source of inner conflict, a struggle that played out in the quiet recesses of his mind. As someone who worked within the government apparatus responsible for shaping this narrative, he was acutely aware of the disparity between the myth and the reality. He knew the truth, yet he also understood the powerful need for a collective narrative that could help a broken nation heal. It was a delicate balancing act—one that demanded a sacrifice of truth for the sake of national unity, a sacrifice that left the memory of the Jewish suffering overshadowed, if not outright obscured, by the broader narrative of Polish martyrdom.

In this way, the past was both remembered and forgotten—commemorated in stone and monument, yet quietly altered in the telling, as the truth of the Holocaust was woven into a broader tapestry of national suffering that, while inclusive, did not fully honour the unique horror endured by the Jewish people. This uneasy compromise, this selective remembrance, reflected the deep and unresolved tensions within Polish society—a society still reeling from the war, still struggling to make sense of a tragedy that had shattered not only lives but also the very fabric of its national identity.[5]

It is vital to recognise that, amidst the horrors of the Holocaust, many Poles risked their lives and the safety of their own families to hide their Jewish neighbours and friends or to shelter the Jewish children who had miraculously escaped or avoided the Nazi death trains. These brave individuals, driven by a deep sense of humanity and moral courage, defied the terror gripping their country, standing against the tide of hatred and fear, to provide sanctuary to those most in need. Their actions were not simply acts of kindness, but extraordinary heroism undertaken in the face of unimaginable danger. Poles make up an overwhelming proportion of Righteous Among the Nations. In reality, most of these heroes were unsung, as they did not seek recognition.

Yet, alongside this valour and bravery, it is also essential to confront the darker, more complex realities of human behaviour in such extreme circumstances. When a society is gripped by fear and a threat of violence looms over every household, the instinct for self-preservation can lead to devastating consequences. In situations where individuals or groups are targeted for victimisation, those around them may dissociate themselves from the 'targets' in a desperate bid to ensure their safety. This distancing, while understandable in its raw human desperation, can result in a troubling phenomenon where some individuals, in their quest for self-preservation, become supporters of the perpetrators or even collaborators in the very atrocities they fear. This dynamic is not unique to any one society or historical moment; it is a well-documented phenomenon in social psychology, often referred to as Stockholm Syndrome. This term describes the complex psychological response seen in some hostage situations, where victims, feeling utterly powerless and desperate to regain some sense of control over their fate, begin to identify with their captors. In these cases, the very people who threaten their lives become, paradoxically, figures of trust and even affection as the victims seek to alleviate their sense of helplessness and vulnerability.

In the context of wartime Poland, this psychological mechanism played out in tragic ways. There were indeed those who, out of a deeply ingrained anti-Semitism, or perhaps more commonly, out of sheer terror, became informers for the German Gestapo. These were not just the Nazi sympathisers who had existed in Poland before the war; they were also ordinary Poles, people who might otherwise have lived quiet, unremarkable lives, but who, under the immense pressure of the Nazi occupation, turned against their Jewish neighbours. They pointed fingers, not out of any deep-seated ideology, but out of a desperate belief that by betraying the Jews hiding among them, they could protect themselves and their communities from the all-consuming wrath of the German Nazi occupiers.

This betrayal is one of the most painful aspects of the Holocaust—how fear and the survival instinct could drive people to commit acts that, in any other context, they might have found unthinkable. The choice to collaborate, inform, or simply turn a blind eye was often made under unimaginable pressure, where the line between victim and perpetrator could become dangerously blurred. Yet, this reality does not absolve those who chose this path; instead, it deepens the tragedy of the Holocaust, showing how fear can twist the moral compass and lead people down the path of darkness.

The story of Poland during the Holocaust is, therefore, a story of extremes. It is a story of extraordinary courage, in which individuals risked everything to save others' lives. But it is also a story of the terrible choices made in the shadow of fear, where the instinct for self-preservation led many to acts of betrayal that, even today, remain complex to acknowledge. Both aspects of this story must be told, for it is only by recognising and validating the full complexity of human behaviour in these extreme circumstances that we can hope to understand the true impact of the Holocaust on Poland and its people.

For my father, the events that transpired in Poland during the Nazi occupation could never be consigned to the shadows of oblivion. His work, deeply connected to his beliefs, was a battleground of conflicting paradigms. On one side was the prevailing view that Auschwitz-Birkenau and similar sites were "Golgothas of Polish martyrdom," symbols of the nation's suffering under Nazi oppression. On the other side, these same places stood as "remaining documents" of the mass genocide perpetrated against Polish and European Jewry. This latter paradigm was not just an intellectual or academic stance for my father—it was personal, tied irrevocably to the loss of his family. It confronted his very sense of identity and purpose, and it was this truth he wished to highlight the most in his work. Yet, he knew this was a battle he might never win. Despite the legislative acts passed by the Sejm in 1947 and 1949 to preserve these sites, powerful external forces were working towards their closure or repurposing.

For example, two years before my father commenced working at MKiS, in June 1948, Jerzy Putrament, a government official and columnist for the Polish Daily, launched a scathing critique of the Auschwitz State Museum. Putrament accused the museum of distorting reality, suggesting that the land on which Auschwitz-Birkenau stood could be put to better use as part of Poland's economic Three-Year-Plan. His words were like a knife twisting in my father's heart, cutting at the very core of what he believed in. Similarly, Kazimierz Koźniewski, a well-known journalist, penned an article titled "A Delicate Problem," in which he criticised the preservation of extermination sites as a strategy to "sensationalise history". He argued that such sites if maintained with a "tourist-oriented approach," did "more harm than good" to the memory of the horrors that had occurred there.

These critiques struck at the very essence of my father's work. He was caught in a painful paradox. On the one hand, he recognised the necessity of maintaining these sites as solemn reminders of the atrocities committed. On the other hand, he was forced to confront the harsh reality that even within the Polish government, some sought to diminish or repurpose these sacred grounds. The idea that these sites could be closed or their significance diluted was an insult to everything my father held dear, a betrayal of the countless families who perished —like his own—and who were mourned in silence.

In his mind, the Holocaust was a wound that continued to bleed, a horror that should never be forgotten or downplayed. His work at the MKiS was a mission to ensure that the memory of his family and millions of others would not be erased or misrepresented by those who wished to rewrite history to suit economic or political ends. This internal struggle was a source of deep anguish for my father. How could he reconcile his role in a government that seemed indifferent to the very tragedy that had shaped his life? How could he honour the memory of his family when powerful voices were pushing to silence or distort that memory? The task before him was fraught with obstacles that were as much about the 'politics of the present' as they were about the 'ghosts of the past'. And yet, he persisted, driven by a need that was both personal and universal—a need to ensure that what happened in Auschwitz-Birkenau and other death camps would be remembered with the solemnity and truth it deserved. His struggle was not just against the forces of the past but also against the forces of the present—against those who would forget, those who would distort, and those who would erase the memory of what had been. [6]

With these widely publicised words that seemed to have easily slipped through the machinery of press censorship, a troubling undercurrent began to surface in Poland. There were emerging government forces intent on closing the commemorated places of extermination or repurposing the land for economic productivity. This was not merely a logistical or economic concern; it was emblematic of a deeper, more insidious issue—the growing unrest within Poland's political landscape. To keep the memory of German Nazi crimes alive, to continue commemorating these places of unimaginable horror, was to risk pulling back the curtain on another chapter of suffering, one that the Polish government was not eager to confront. To memorialise the atrocities committed by the Nazis was to invite a closer examination of Polish suffering—suffering not just under the German occupation but under the Soviets as well. The spectre of the Soviet labour camps loomed large, a dark shadow over the nation's collective memory. For to acknowledge the full extent of the horrors inflicted by the Nazis would inevitably lead to questions about the Soviet crimes that had been swept under the rug. It would force a reckoning with the unacknowledged massacre of 22,000 Polish elite officers and intelligentsia in the forests of Katyn, near Smolensk. This crime had been buried under layers of propaganda and denial.

Various Polish government officials were acutely aware of this delicate balance. The intense memorialisation of Nazi brutality risked blurring the carefully maintained distinction between the "German perpetrators" and the "Soviet liberators." To emphasise the crimes of one side could inadvertently shine a light on the crimes of the other, a prospect that was politically and ideologically unacceptable in post-war Poland. The official narrative, shaped by Soviet influence, needed to present the USSR as the great liberator, the force that had rescued Poland from the clutches of Nazi terror. But to fully engage with the history of Nazi atrocities was to remind the world, and the Polish people themselves, of the Soviet atrocities that had been committed in the very same land.

My father was aware that, in his role, he had to navigate a minefield of political sensitivities in which the memory of suffering was being manipulated, sanitised, and, in some cases, erased to serve the State's needs. Had he known that his brother, Leon, was a likely victim of the Katyn massacre, his struggle to achieve his goals of preserving the memory of the Holocaust would have been even more painful and problematic. How could he work within a system that sought to erase or distort the truth to maintain a political fiction? These questions weighed heavily on him, complicating his work and gnawing at his conscience. His role was indeed precarious in this growing unrest and political manipulation. He was preserving history and fighting those who sought to rewrite or erase it. The commemoration of Nazi crimes was a double-edged sword, one that could cut through the lies and half-truths, and also one that could expose wounds that had never healed. And in a country still reeling from the devastation of war, where the lines between victim and perpetrator, or liberator and invader, were not always clear, this was a risk that many were unwilling to take.

The work of memorialisation was a sacred duty for my father, a constant struggle against the tides of political expediency and historical revisionism. He knew that the memory of the Holocaust could not be separated from the broader context of suffering in Poland. Yet, he also knew that the truth about the Holocaust was one that many were unwilling to confront. In the end, his work was as much about fighting for the integrity of memory as it was about preserving the physical sites of atrocity. It was about ensuring that past horrors would not be twisted or erased in the service of present-day politics. And it was about bearing witness, not just to the suffering of the Jews, but to the complex and painful history of a nation that had been torn apart by forces beyond its control. [7]

In 1950, as my father embarked on his work at the Auschwitz State Museum, a significant shift in the narrative surrounding the Holocaust was underway. A Soviet delegation had visited Auschwitz and sharply criticised the museum's "un-Marxist exhibition," arguing that it placed too much emphasis on "Polish Nationalism" and portrayed the German nation as inherently "cannibalistic." The delegation's critique struck a chord with the ruling powers, triggering a re-evaluation of how the atrocities of Auschwitz—and, by extension, the Holocaust—were to be memorialised within the broader context of communist ideology.

In response to these criticisms, the Society of Fighters for Freedom and Democracy (ZBoWiD) submitted a report to the Central Committee of the Polish United Workers' Party (PZPR), advocating for a drastic overhaul of the existing exhibitions. The new directive shifted the focus away from Polish martyrdom and the German nation as a singular villain. Instead, it emphasised that the true enemy was not the German people but the fascists and Anglo-Saxon imperialists—particularly the United States and the United Kingdom—who were portrayed as having funded and supported Hitlerite fascism as part of a broader imperialistic agenda.

This pivot in the new narrative required a complete reimagining of the Auschwitz exhibitions, and my father found himself at the heart of this transformation. His involvement in creating the new exhibition, "Imperialism Unmasked," was both intense and deeply personal. For weeks, he travelled regularly between Warsaw and Auschwitz, overseeing the development and installation of the new displays. This task demanded meticulous attention to detail, as every aspect of the exhibition was scrutinised and sanitised to align with the new Marxist interpretation.

Gone were the exhibits that highlighted the Polish struggle and heroism, which had been central to the original narrative. In their place were displays that framed the Holocaust within the context of a broader ideological battle against imperialism. The new exhibition sought to expose the supposed complicity of the American and Anglo-Saxon powers in the rise of fascism, casting them as the true architects of the horrors that had unfolded in Europe.

For my father, this project became a test of his ideological commitment and personal resolve. The work was gruelling emotionally as he wrestled with the need to honour the memory of the victims, while adhering to the demands of the State, which he believed in. The task was further complicated by the knowledge that his efforts were part of a broader campaign to reshape historical memory, to mould it into a tool for political propaganda.

The revamped exhibition was completed by 6 November 1950, the anniversary of the Bolshevik Revolution. Its aim was not to emphasise the Jewish tragedy or a chapter of Polish suffering but the horrific consequences of the global struggle between oppressive imperialist forces and the liberating power of Communism.

Yet, despite the official story, my father remained sharply aware of the deeper truths beneath the surface. He understood that the history of Auschwitz could not be fully contained within the limits of political ideology. The gas chambers and crematoria, the barbed wires and watchtowers stood as clear reminders of a reality that went beyond any attempt at historical revisionism. And while the new exhibition might have aimed to present a sanitised version of events, the memory of the millions who had perished could not be so easily rewritten.

For my father, the work at Auschwitz was a constant balancing act—between the demands of the State and the need to preserve the truth, between the official narrative and the unspoken realities that lingered in the shadows. It was a struggle that mirrored the broader tensions within Polish society, where the memory of the war and the Holocaust was being contested, shaped, and reshaped to fit the needs of the present. His immersive involvement in "Imperialism Unmasked" was a reflection of the complex and often painful choices that defined his life in communist Poland. It was a project that forced him to confront how memory could be manipulated and used as a tool of power, even as he sought to honour the victims and preserve their legacy. It was a reminder that the truth of history is never as simple as the narratives we construct around it, but rather, a complex tapestry of experiences, perspectives, and emotions that cannot be easily untangled or neatly categorised. [8]

The eradication of the 'un-Marxist' perspective, prominently focused on Polish heroism and sacrifice, also resulted in the dismantling of the Jewish Hall of Remembrance in Block 4. Although the Central Committee of Jews in Poland formally agreed to this, their ability to influence or oppose the directives from Warsaw's MKiS, especially after Moscow's delegation expressed dissatisfaction, was effectively non-existent. The overarching 'Marxist' narrative aimed to highlight the message that, for Jews, Poles, and all other nations, the true adversary was the fascist imperialist ideology. This ideology was seen as the driving force behind the atrocities and immense suffering commemorated at the sites where these crimes against humanity had been committed. In this light, Auschwitz-Birkenau KL was portrayed as the quintessential symbol of genocide, rooted in 'international imperialism,' purportedly orchestrated by American and British capitalists. [9]

In the years that followed, my father's role at the MKiS shifted, becoming less transparent and more shrouded in mystery. What he did during those years is lost to me. Even as his direct involvement with Auschwitz faded, new and disturbing voices began to rise from within the corridors of power in Poland. Voices that, to my father, must have sounded like a second betrayal of the dead.

Proposals began to surface, cold and calculating, suggesting that Auschwitz-Birkenau, Treblinka, and Majdanek—places soaked in the Jewish blood of millions—could be dismantled and repurposed for the economic demands of a new world. The language of these proposals was disturbingly pragmatic. The land, they said, needed to be put to economically productive use. The growing population of Oświęcim needed housing. Others, with a chilling lack of empathy, suggested that the grounds might be suitable for a large piggery, as if the echoes of the past could be silenced under the weight of concrete and industrial progress.

300

For my father, these suggestions were not merely bureaucratic oversights; they were a profound moral failure, an erasure of history that bordered on sacrilege. He had spent years steeped in the memories of Auschwitz, Treblinka, and Majdanek. He had walked the paths where so many had perished and breathed the air still thick with the silence of the dead. When he heard of these proposals, his reaction was immediate and visceral. He could not remain silent. He raised his voice in protest, a cry from the depths of his soul, addressing Kazimierz Banach, the Director of the Central Board of Museums and Monument Protection. He reminded Banach of the legislative acts passed by the Sejm, acts that had declared these sites untouchable; preserved forever as monuments to the unimaginable suffering that had taken place there. But more than that, my father appealed to something more profound, something deeper that lay beyond the dry words of legal statutes. He asked Banach to imagine the grotesque irony of future delegations walking through a piggery or the housing complex to arrive at the remnant site of Auschwitz in a landscape transformed by modern convenience and economic ambition. He painted a picture that must have chilled Banach to the bone—a picture of the world looking on in disbelief as the memory of the Holocaust was reduced to a small, sanitised corner of the land, overshadowed by the demands of progress and push for the diminishment of Holocaust as a significant event in the history of mankind.

For my father, this was about safeguarding the very soul of humanity. He understood, perhaps more than anyone, that to erase these places or diminish them in any way was to risk forgetting the lessons they held. And to forget, in his view, was to open the door to the unthinkable—allowing similar horrors to happen again. His protest was both a professional duty and a personal sacred obligation. My father, who had lost his family and his people, destroyed, could not stand by and let the memory of their suffering be dismissed by the same forces of pragmatism and indifference that once let the Holocaust occur.

In those moments, as he fought to preserve the sanctity of Auschwitz, Treblinka, Majdanek, and other death camps (e.g., Belzec; Sobibor), my father was a guardian of memory, a man determined to ensure that the past would not be rewritten or forgotten. His battle was against the slow, creeping tide of forgetfulness that threatened to wash away the lessons of history, leaving the world vulnerable to the same darkness that had once engulfed it.

Arguably, the main issue wasn't just the political manoeuvring surrounding the "Marxist" exhibition at Auschwitz State Museum but the stark disconnect between the museum's narrative and the brutal, horrific reality it was meant to portray. The museum, which should have been a solemn tribute to the atrocities committed, had instead become a tool for Stalinist propaganda, its true purpose warped by the very forces claiming to honour the victims.

For anyone who visited Auschwitz to understand the depth of the horror that had occurred there, the experience was tainted by the heavy hand of political manipulation. The actual victims—the millions of Jews and other marginalised groups who were systematically exterminated—were overshadowed by a narrative that sought to universalise suffering in a way that diluted the specific, targeted nature of the Holocaust. The reality of Auschwitz was masked behind the ideological veil of communist rhetoric against the imperialist ambitions of the West.

In that exhibition, the horror of Auschwitz was not denied. Still, it was reframed and repackaged in a way that served the needs of the Soviet regime, which was more interested in promoting its vision of history than in confronting the truth. The narrative was twisted to fit the Stalinist agenda, reducing the specific to the general and the personal to the political. The result was an exhibition that did not merely fail to convey the reality of Auschwitz but actively distorted it, turning a place of unparalleled suffering into a stage for ideological posturing.

For those who truly understood the nature of Auschwitz, this was not merely a failure of curation; it was a betrayal. The exhibition, which focused on anti-fascist struggle and internationalist solidarity, overlooked the unique suffering of the Jewish people and other targeted minority groups, instead offering a sanitised version of events that could be easily absorbed into the broader narrative of Soviet heroism. The particularity of the Jewish genocide was lost, merged into a larger, more agreeable story of oppression and resistance that fit smoothly with the communist worldview.

But Auschwitz was not just another site of suffering in a long history of human cruelty. It was a place where the very idea of humanity was systematically dismantled, where the horror was not just in the numbers or the methods of extermination but in the ideology that deemed an entire people unworthy of existence. The failure of the Auschwitz exhibition to confront this reality head-on was more than an oversight; it was a deliberate erasure, a way of avoiding the uncomfortable truths that did not fit into the narrative the State wished to promote.

The real issue was not simply that the exhibition failed to reflect the reality of the horror at Auschwitz; it was that it actively obscured that reality, replacing it with a version of events that served the interests of the State rather than the memory of the dead. In doing so, it betrayed the very people it was meant to honour, turning their suffering into a footnote in a larger political drama that had little to do with the true nature of the Holocaust. This manipulation of history, this refusal to confront the specific horror of Auschwitz, was a tragedy in its own right—a tragedy that compounded the original crime by allowing the memory of the victims to be distorted, their voices silenced once again by those who claimed to speak for them.

The deep, intrinsic grief my father carried within him—grief for his lost family and his community—might indeed have driven him to seek solace or purpose in his work at the Auschwitz State Museum.

303

Unconsciously, perhaps, he hoped that by contributing to the narrative, by ensuring that the memory of what happened was preserved, he could somehow make sense of his loss and trauma. But his more profound internal struggle stemmed from the collision between his ideological convictions and the harsh, unyielding reality of Auschwitz-Birkenau KL and other extermination camps. The "Communist Ideal," with its promise of universal equality and justice, also instilled hope in the wake of the unimaginable horrors he had witnessed. In a world shaped by this ideology, he believed that such atrocities would not and could not ever occur again. But Auschwitz was not a place that could be moulded to fit any ideology; it was a place that defied ideological explanation. Any attempt to impose a sociopolitical or religious narrative upon it would distort the terrible truth of what had happened there.

My father might have wanted to believe that the principles of Communism could somehow redeem the world, could prevent another Holocaust, and that by helping to shape the narrative of Auschwitz, he was contributing to that redemption. Yet, deep down, he must have known that no political framework, no matter how noble its intentions, could capture or encompass the true meaning of the Holocaust. The genocidal trauma inflicted on the Jewish people was beyond the reach of ideology. It was a wound that could not be healed by any doctrine, a darkness that no political light could fully dispel. To walk through the gates of Auschwitz, to stand on the grounds where millions were systematically murdered, is to confront the abyss of human cruelty in its most extreme form. It is to be stripped of all preconceptions and illusions and face the stark reality that what happened there was a betrayal of humanity. No matter the political lens through which one might try to view it, the Holocaust remains a rupture in the fabric of civilisation, a moment when the very essence of what it means to be human was violated.

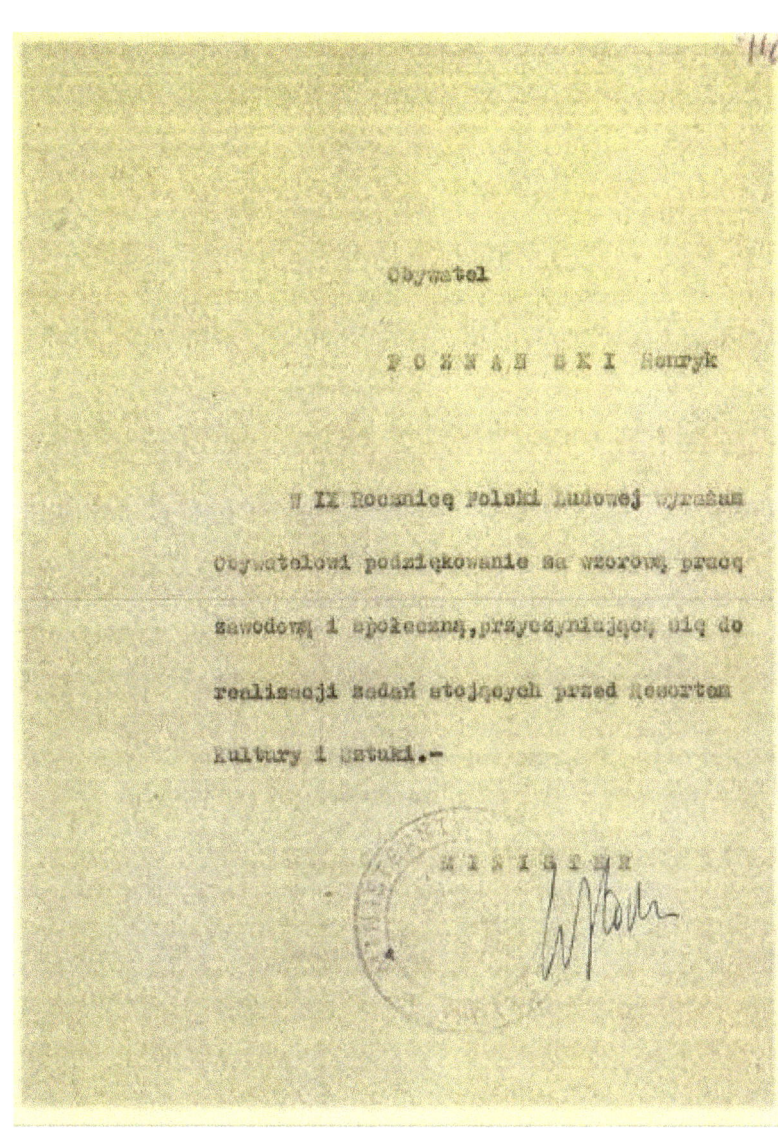

On the Ninth Anniversary of the People's Republic of Poland, Minister of the MKiS, Dr Wlodzimierz Sokorski is officially thanking my father for his exemplary work.

In that sense, my father's work at Auschwitz might have been a way for him to grapple with his grief and his sense of helplessness in the face of such overwhelming loss. Auschwitz, and places like it, demand a different kind of response—one that goes beyond political ideology, beyond any attempt to make sense of what is, in many ways, senseless. These places of horror demand a response of deep, quiet reverence, of recognition that what happened there was an unparalleled atrocity that cannot be contained within the boundaries of any one worldview.

As Huener (2003) suggests, the most we can do is to bear witness, remember, and ensure that the true horror of what occurred is never forgotten. In doing so, we honour the memory of those who perished, not by trying to fit their suffering into a narrative that makes us feel more comfortable or justified, but by acknowledging the full, devastating reality of what they endured. My father's involvement in the development of the Auschwitz Holocaust Museum was driven by his desire to find meaning and resolution to his loss and grief. Ultimately, he could not escape the profound truth that Auschwitz stands as a symbol of the depths to which humanity can sink when hatred and dehumanisation are allowed to reign unchecked. [10]

Notes

1. https://isap.sejm.gov.pl/isap.nsf/search.xsp

2. Huener, Jonathan (2003). Auschwitz, Poland, and the Politics of Commemoration, 1945-1979. Ohio University Press. Athens p. 80

3 . *Ibid.,* p. 155

4. Records of Allied Operational and Occupation Headquarters, World War II - National Archives *See*: https://www.archives.gov/research/guide-fed-records/groups/331.html

5. Huener, Jonathan (2003). Auschwitz, Poland, and the Politics of Commemoration, 1945-1979. Ohio University Press. Athens p. 53

6. *Ibid.,* p. 55

7. *Ibid.,* p. 87

8. *Ibid.,* p. 90

9. *Ibid.,* p. 101

10. *Ibid.,* p. 102

13. The Thaw

The death of Joseph Stalin on 5th March 1953 sent shockwaves through the Warsaw Pact, causing ripples that would gradually thaw the iron grip of fear that had suffocated its member states. However, the immediate aftermath in Poland seemed deceptively calm, with little visible change on the surface. But beneath that calm, the tectonic plates of political power were shifting. For the next two years, as the cold grip of Stalinism began to loosen, the public security functions of the Polish UB—once a shadowy, omnipresent force—were quietly scaled back. The once-dreaded power of the UB was reduced, a calculated move by the government to project a façade of greater transparency, showing that decisions were now being made in the light of day rather than in the shadows.

For my father, Stalin's death was a harbinger of potential chaos. The dictator's passing was not just the end of an era; it was the end of a political structure that, for better or worse, had provided a strange kind of stability. Now, with Stalin gone, that stability seemed poised to crumble. My father watched closely as Bolesław Bierut, once a loyal Stalinist, suddenly began condemning the mechanisms of control that had kept the UB so ruthlessly efficient. It was a stunning reversal in the new climate of uncertainty.

Poland was simmering with unrest—tensions that had been brewing beneath the surface were now starting to bubble over. My father understood the delicate balance that Bierut was trying to maintain. On one side, the public's growing dissatisfaction threatened to boil into outright rebellion; on the other, the UB, with its feared and hated Department X, was thrown into disarray by the defection of its top leader, Josef Światło to the United States of America. Światło's betrayal was more than a personal affront to those in power—it was a devastating blow to the secret security apparatus that had prided itself on its impenetrability. If one of their own could escape and spill the secrets of the State, then the entire foundation of the government control was vulnerable.

The system that had once kept the populace in line now seemed at risk of implosion. For my father, this period of uncertainty was fraught with danger. The political landscape was shifting beneath his feet, and the clear lines of authority he had once relied upon were now blurred. The future of Poland and his place within it was no longer certain. The death of Stalin had opened the door to possibilities both frightening and unknown, and my father, like so many others, was left to navigate a world that was rapidly changing, where the rules he had lived by no longer applied. [1]

In 1954, against the shifting political backdrop following Stalin's death, the Ministry of Culture and Art (MKiS) initiated a quiet yet significant transformation. The exhibits that once prominently featured the themes of "International Socialism" and Poland's close alliance with the Soviet Union began to be dismantled. The ideological narrative that had dominated the Auschwitz-Birkenau State Museum, framing it within the context of Marxist ideology and Soviet camaraderie, was now being reconsidered.

There was a growing recognition, perhaps driven by the thawing of Stalinist rigidity, that the representation of Auschwitz-Birkenau KL needed to return to its original narrative of 1947. This was not just a place of ideological struggle or a symbol of an international political alliance; it was, first and foremost, a site of profound human suffering, a place where the darkest depths of Nazi brutality were laid bare.

My father now witnessed a shift back to the earlier portrayal of Auschwitz-Birkenau KL as a symbol of Polish suffering and sacrifice. The narratives of Polish prisoners, their resistance, and their martyrdom, which the broader strokes of *International Socialism* had overshadowed, were being brought back to the forefront. It was a reclamation of history, a reassertion of the Polish identity within the narrative of Auschwitz, even as it acknowledged with much smaller emphasis the unique and tragic fate of the Jewish people and others who perished there.

For my father, this shift might have brought a bittersweet realisation. The ideological framework, which he had once believed could serve as a vessel to preserve the memory of the Holocaust, was now giving way to the original framework that aimed to acknowledge Polish struggle and suffering as the key element of remembrance. [2]

My father often expressed his thoughts with bitterness that seemed to cut through the air, as if he was trying to carve out a space where truth could stand unchallenged. He was particularly upset by the deliberate overemphasis on the suffering of Polish political prisoners at Auschwitz, a narrative that, in his view, overshadowed the vastly more serious plight of the Jewish prisoners, along with the much higher proportion of Jewish victims who were sent to gas chambers as soon as they arrived at the Birkenau ramp.

He would say, with a sharp edge to his voice, "They talk about the Polish political prisoners and their suffering, and yes, they suffered, but what they don't tell you—what they conveniently forget to mention—is that these Polish prisoners often had certain privileges. They had roles within the camp, positions that, though grim, offered some hope of survival. The Jewish prisoners had no such roles and no such hope."

My father was acutely aware of the grim hierarchy that existed within the camp, a hierarchy that placed Jewish prisoners at the very bottom. "If a Jewish man was separated from the larger group being sent to the gas chambers," he would explain, his voice heavy with the weight of dismay, "He wasn't given a role that might offer him a chance to survive, even temporarily. Instead, he was forced into backbreaking labour or forced to work in the crematoria as a Sonderkommando."

All Sonderkommandos were Jewish prisoners forced to dispose of the bodies of their murdered people. They lived a nightmarish existence that my father could hardly speak of without shuddering. "These men," he would say, "Lived in a world where each day was a borrowed one. They knew the clock was ticking, that their time was running out. The work was so gruelling and soul-destroying that even the strongest might only last a week or two. And those who somehow managed to survive a little longer—they were killed anyway. They were never meant to survive. They were just being used until there was nothing left to use."

In these accounts, I could hear the deep sadness in my father's voice, a sadness that came from knowing that this reality—this brutal, dehumanising truth—was often glossed over or ignored. For my father, this was a matter of justice. It was about honouring the reality of what happened, about ensuring that the voices of those who suffered the most—the Jewish prisoners who were denied even the slightest glimmer of hope—were not drowned out by the more palatable stories of survival and resistance.

In one of his handwritten statements, my father poured his thoughts onto the page with a mixture of frustration and sorrow, revealing a truth that gnawed at him. He wrote, "Many Polish political prisoners who survived the concentration camps often occupied positions of privilege within the camp's hierarchy. For example, Kazimierz Rusinek, who was a passionate anti-Semite, was a 'senior scribe' in Mauthausen KL. Rusinek then had enough leverage to help his 'mate' Cyrankiewicz transfer from Auschwitz to Mauthausen, where the possibility of survival was far greater. Similarly, Kazimierz Smoleń was a 'senior scribe' in Auschwitz KL. Most Polish Catholic functionaries were able to survive their incarceration in concentration camps."

My father's words carried the weight of a deeply unsettling reality. He was not attempting to diminish the suffering of Polish political prisoners; he knew all too well the horrors they endured. But he could not ignore the troubling fact that there existed a kind of hierarchy even within the hellish confines of the concentration camps—a hierarchy that offered some prisoners a chance at survival. In contrast, others, particularly the Jews, were condemned to death from the start.

This is not to suggest that Polish prisoners did not suffer or that they had an easy time," he clarified in his notes, acknowledging the seriousness of his words. He was not attempting to rewrite history or imply that Polish political prisoners did not experience pain and hardship. However, what troubled him deeply was the reclaimed narrative that claimed suffering was universal—that the German Nazis did not discriminate between Poles, Jews, or other nationalities. He saw this as whitewashing the brutal reality of the camps; primarily, the camps were tools of genocide against the Jews. The notion that everyone suffered equally, that the horrors of the camps were experienced impartially, was, in my father's view, a misrepresentation of the facts that diminished or even ignored the true nature of the Holocaust—the systematic, industrial-scale extermination of the Jewish people.

In his writings, there was a clear sense of unease, a discomfort with how the post-war Polish narrative was shaping the memory of the Holocaust. He knew the truth was more complex, painful, and far less convenient than what was often portrayed. His reflections were not just a critique of how history was being remembered but also a deeply personal grappling with his own role in that process, a struggle to ensure that the voices of those who suffered most were not lost in the broader story of the war.

Despite his deep concerns about how the memory of Auschwitz-Birkenau KL was being shaped by the narratives that were emerging, he found a measure of encouragement in the tangible efforts being made to preserve the site. In 1954, a substantial budget was allocated to restore the deteriorating buildings and structures within Auschwitz-Birkenau KL. This financial commitment was a glimmer of hope for him, a sign that, perhaps, the true significance of this place would not be entirely lost to political instrumentalisation.

Many elements of the original 1947 exhibition, which had been stripped away during the years of ideological manipulation, were returned to the Auschwitz State Museum. This restoration was organised with the help of former political prisoners, men who had survived the camps and who were now determined to preserve the truth of what they had endured. One of these men was Kazimierz Smoleń, a former prisoner who had become the newly appointed Director of the Auschwitz State Museum. For my father, Smoleń's appointment was a reassuring sign that those who truly understood the horrors of Auschwitz were taking the reins of its memory.

The preparations for the 10th Anniversary of Auschwitz-Birkenau's liberation were particularly significant. Set for 17 April 1955, this commemoration was a moment of reckoning, a time to reflect on the horrors that had taken place and to ensure that the memory of those atrocities would endure. The MKiS and ZBoWiD worked tirelessly to prepare the site for a potential wave of international delegates and visitors. My father watched as the plans unfolded, hopeful that the world would see Auschwitz-Birkenau KL for what it truly was—a place of unimaginable suffering and loss, but also a place that stood as a stark reminder of the dangers of unchecked hatred and bigotry.

On 17 April 1955, the small city of Oświęcim became the focal point for 150,000 pilgrims from Poland and Europe. They converged on Auschwitz to commemorate the 10th Anniversary of its liberation by the Soviet Red Army. The sheer number of attendees and the reverence with which they approached the site gave my father a sense that the world had not forgotten after all. There was a bittersweet comfort in seeing so many people gather to remember, mourn, and honour those who had perished.

For my father, this was a moment of vindication, a reassurance that despite the political forces at play, the memory of Auschwitz would not be entirely co-opted or erased. The stories of those who suffered, including his own family, would continue to be told, their voices echoing through the preserved halls and barracks of Auschwitz-Birkenau KL, reminding future generations of the depths of human cruelty and the necessity of remembering. [3]

As the crowds gathered at Auschwitz for the 10th anniversary of its liberation, the exhibition unveiled that day still bore the unmistakable marks of the ideological currents shaping the narrative of post-war Poland. Unlike previous exhibitions, this one attempted to encompass a broader narrative, ostensibly to reflect the diversity of the victims. Slogans, prominently displayed, guided visitors through the Auschwitz State Museum, each one proclaiming the horrors that had taken place on the very ground where they now stood: "Here gathered for extermination, children, youths, frail, women and men of various faiths, political views, and social backgrounds"; "Here the program of total annihilation of Jews was taking place"; "Here mass murder of Soviet prisoners of war took place"; "Here Gypsies were murdered"; "Here clergy and other religious people were murdered."

These words, while grounded in the reality of the atrocities, once again subtly twisted the story. The slogans were designed to emphasise the broad scope of Nazi brutality, suggesting that the German Nazis did not discriminate in their crimes and that their hatred and violence were unleashed equally upon all who were not of the "pure" Aryan race. But this broad-brush approach, though accurate in some respects, was also a gross distortion of the Nazis' true intent.

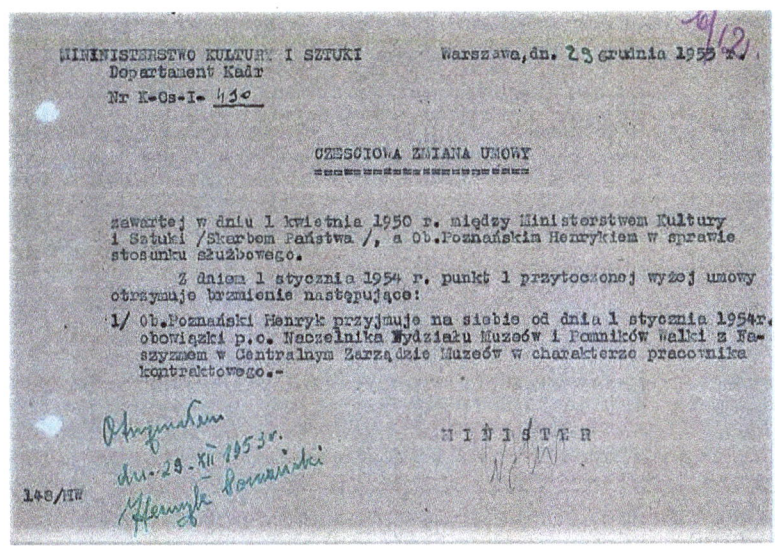

Minister Sokorski appointed my father on a contractual basis as the Chief of the Department of Museums and Monuments of Struggle and Suffering within the Central Office of Museums MKiS (23 December 1953)

The Holocaust was a meticulously planned genocide, targeting Jews for complete extermination, a reality that the exhibition, with its more generalised focus, seemed to downplay.

For the uneducated or naive visitor, the exhibition's messaging could easily obscure the specific horrors of the Holocaust. By lumping together all the victims of Nazi terror under a single umbrella, the exhibition diluted the unique tragedy of the Jews, who were singled out for systematic annihilation in a way that no other group was. The Nazis' genocidal intent was not simply about the mass murder of people who were different; it was about the total eradication of the Jewish people from the face of the earth. Yet, this exhibition, once again and in a different way than before, blurred those lines, presenting a narrative that implied a more generalised, less targeted form of persecution.

Oświęcim, the 17th of April 1955. The 10th Anniversary of the Red Army's Liberation of Auschwitz-Birkenau KL. My father is standing at the back (far right).

For my father knew, as many survivors did, that while other groups had indeed suffered and perished, the Holocaust was, at its core, a genocide against the Jews, not Gypsies, Russians or homosexuals. The mass extermination of millions of Jews was not just one atrocity among many; it was the central horror around which all others revolved. However, the exhibition, influenced by the political agendas of the time, sought to promote a narrative that could serve the broader goals of socialist ideology. This narrative portrayed the victims as a diverse collective equally targeted by universally oppressive fascism. [4]

My father was caught in the tangled web of historical revisionism, not as an architect of deceit, but as a man ensnared by the powerful tides of a post-war world seeking to reshape and sanitise the narrative of its darkest hours. He was part of the distortion that turned Auschwitz into a symbol less of Jewish annihilation and more of a universal struggle against fascism. Yet, I do not believe he was complicit nor a willing executioner of this skewed portrayal. The tragedy depicted by the Auschwitz State Museum was not just a historical event; to him, it was deeply connected to his own identity, the identity of his family, and the brutal reality of what they—and millions of others—endured.

He lacked the power to steer the narrative in a way that fully recognised the true nature of the Holocaust. The forces against him were far greater, especially in a society where the Party line dictated the "truth." Speaking honestly about the distortion of the Holocaust, and the blatant misrepresentation of the specific horror faced by Jewish victims, would have been seen as an act of subversion. My father knew he was the only Jewish official in the MKiS and therefore the most committed to memorialising places like Auschwitz-Birkenau, Treblinka, Majdanek, Sobibor, and Bełżec. At the same time, he grappled with his deep-seated identity, but not with his convictions. Those convictions, rooted in Communism, had become the foundation of his life after the Holocaust's devastation. He understood he had abandoned Judaism, not out of hostility or resentment, but because he believed Communism would prevent racial victimisation from striking his people again. Yet, in the shattered world after the Holocaust, little remained to defend or protect. The rise of Communism, or any other "noble" vision of humanity, felt pointless as it was too late, given that hate had already claimed millions of Jewish lives. Thus, in this state of ambivalence, he understood that extermination camps were not just a symbol of universal suffering but a testament to a calculated genocide aimed primarily at Jews—Jews who came from different countries with different political beliefs, religious practices, worldviews, and socioeconomic backgrounds. The enormity of that truth must have weighed heavily on him as he participated in shaping a narrative that, while not false, was removed from the wholeness of the truth—the truth he desired to be known most.

In the silence of his own heart, he grappled with the contradiction between his ideological beliefs and the reality he knew all too well. He had decided to abandon his Jewish cultural identity for the promise of something greater, something that could shield him from the horrors of the past. He must have realised that the communist regime's depiction of Auschwitz was a compromise, a distortion crafted to serve a broader political goal. Yet, he was not someone who could easily abandon his convictions, even in the face of such a compromise. The ideals of Communism had become his refuge, his way of coping with the loss, grief, and trauma left by the Holocaust. To challenge those ideals, to admit they might not fully reflect the truth of what happened at Auschwitz-Birkenau or Treblinka, would have been to challenge the very foundation on which he had rebuilt his life.

The new post-Stalinist exhibition at Auschwitz-Birkenau, while intended to honour the immense suffering of Polish political prisoners and iconic religious figures like Father Maximilian Kolbe, ultimately fell short in capturing the true essence of what had transpired on those cursed grounds. The narrative was broad, speaking to the "mass extermination of human beings" without delving too much into the specificity of the Jewish tragedy—the Shoah—that lay at the very heart of Auschwitz's existence. This generalisation, though perhaps well-intentioned in its attempt to show the vast and far-reaching impact of Nazi brutality, ultimately diluted the unique and horrific specificity of the Holocaust. The murder of Jews was not merely a segment of a broader campaign of terror; it was the centrepiece of a genocidal plan meticulously crafted and brutally executed. The narrative, as presented, failed to fully validate the Shoah—the Jewish catastrophe that was unparalleled in its scope and intent.

The omission was glaring. The exhibition's broad strokes concealed the chilling truth that while other groups—Roma, Slavs, clergy—were indeed persecuted and slaughtered by the Nazis, the

Jewish people were targeted for total annihilation. The Final Solution was not a campaign against "various human beings" but against a single race, the Jews, whose extermination was regarded as a necessary step toward the Nazi vision of a purified world.

For those like my father, who knew the depths of this truth intimately, the exhibition must have been a bitter reminder of the world's reluctance to fully confront and acknowledge the Holocaust for what it was. The emphasis on broader victimhood, though inclusive, skirted around the core of the Shoah, reducing the Jewish tragedy to just another chapter in the history of human suffering. My father's involvement in this exhibition, although likely driven by a sense of duty or perhaps a need to participate in memorialising what had happened, must have stirred deep conflicts within him. The narrative being shaped was not his own, nor did it fully honour the memory of his lost family and the countless other Jewish families who shared the same fate. It was a compromise, a diluted truth, that in its attempt to be all-encompassing, ended up being less than honest. The Holocaust was not about "*various human beings*"; it was about Jews, specifically targeted and systematically erased from the face of the earth. To obscure this was to obscure the truth itself. [5]

Not long after the 10th Anniversary commemoration of the liberation of Auschwitz-Birkenau KL, the nationalistic undercurrents became increasingly visible. Poland, which had been closely tied to Moscow since 1945, began to distance itself from Soviet control. The socialist rhetoric that had once dominated was gradually being replaced by a renewed emphasis on Polish identity and sovereignty—an emphasis that, while still couched in the language of socialism, bore the unmistakable marks of nationalism.

This political shift was not without its consequences. The diminishment of the Jewish Shoah in public memory was part of a broader trend that sought to reassert Polish nationalism within the framework of a supposedly socialist State. The memory of the

Holocaust, which should have served as a stark reminder of the dangers of unchecked nationalism, was instead manipulated to serve the very forces it should have warned against.

For my father, this must have been a brutal reality to face. The Shoah, which had decimated his people, was being pushed aside in favour of a narrative that supported the new Polish nationalist ethos— a narrative that, while outwardly about unity and resistance, was really about reasserting Polish identity at the expense of honest reflection on the past. It was a painful realisation; one he struggled with deeply. He had believed that Communism could be a force for good, that it could protect the Jewish people and prevent another Holocaust. But the reality was far different. The very government he trusted was now complicit in erasing Jewish suffering and promoting a narrative that served nationalist political goals rather than revealing the truth.

And yet, despite everything, my father kept working. He stayed at his post, overseeing exhibitions and commemorations, even though he knew the real story was not being told. Maybe he hoped that, in some small way, his efforts could still make a difference, that by preserving the memory of Auschwitz, he could keep alive the truth of what had happened there. But it was a lonely struggle that often left him feeling isolated and disillusioned.

The tension between his beliefs and the reality he faced was a constant source of anguish for my father. He had renounced his Jewish identity, not out of shame, but because he believed that Communism could offer a better future, one where such horrors would never happen again. But now, he was forced to face the possibility that he had been mistaken, that the system he trusted was itself complicit in suppressing his people's suffering.

Ultimately, my father's struggle was not just against the external forces trying to rewrite history, but also with his own inner turmoil.

He was a man torn between his ideals and the harsh reality he faced, someone who had devoted his life to a cause now seemingly slipping away. Yet, despite everything, he remained loyal to his work, driven by a strong sense of duty and a desire to honour the memory of those who had been lost. This was the tragedy of his life—a man who survived the war only to become entangled in political schemes that aimed to distort and diminish the very truth he had fought to protect. Still, he never gave up. He kept fighting, even when the odds appeared insurmountable. He was sustained by a deep love for those he had lost and a resolve to make sure their memory would endure.

∞∞∞∞∞

During the summer of 1955, Warsaw was filled with the energy and enthusiasm of young people from around the world as Poland hosted the 5th World Festival of Youth and Students. For five days, the city's streets echoed with music, lively parades, and vibrant cultural exchanges. It marked a rare moment of openness in a country usually dominated by Communist restrictions. For Polish youth, this festival was more than just a celebration — it was a glimpse into a world they had been taught to fear and reject.

As students from Spain, France, England, Belgium, and other Western and Eastern European countries mingled freely, the Polish youth first encountered the unfiltered reality of their Western European peers. They saw that these young people were not the ideological enemies they had been warned about but rather fellow students, full of life and curiosity, sharing common dreams and aspirations. The stark contrast between the propaganda they had grown up with and the reality they were now experiencing was impossible to ignore.

In the aftermath of the festival, the conversations among the students at Warsaw University took on a new tone. The excitement of meeting peers from the West gave rise to a growing awareness of the limitations and hypocrisies of their government's anti-Western stance. For many, this was a moment of awakening—a realisation that the narratives they had been fed were not as absolute as they had been led to believe.

Out of this new awareness, debates began to simmer on campus, and conversations that were once whispered in private now found their way into student gatherings and intellectual circles. The question of Poland's right to independence from the Soviet Union, a topic that had been largely taboo, began to emerge as a focal point of these discussions. The students began questioning the legitimacy of a government that seemed more beholden to Moscow than to the needs and desires of its people. They pondered the possibility of a Poland that could chart its course, free from the heavy hand of Soviet control.

These debates were not without risk. The mere act of questioning the status quo could invite suspicion if not outright persecution. Yet, the festival had planted a seed of dissent, a yearning for freedom that could not quickly be extinguished. Inspired by glimpses of openness among their Western peers, the Polish youth began to dream of a future in which Poland could stand as a truly independent nation.

This period marked the beginning of a subtle yet significant shift in Poland's younger generation's collective consciousness. The festival exposed them to new ideas, new ways of thinking, and, most importantly, the realisation that their own country could aspire to something more than being a satellite state in the Soviet orbit. The summer of 1955 would be remembered not just for the celebration it brought to Warsaw but for the quiet revolution it sparked in the hearts and minds of Poland's youth—a revolution that would grow and intensify in the years to come. [6]

In February 1956, an even more significant event occurred in Moscow: the 20th Congress of the Communist Party of the Soviet Union. Under the weight of this important event, the political landscape of the Soviet bloc began to tremble. This 20th Congress marked a turning point in the history of Soviet Communism, one that sent ripples throughout Poland and the entire Eastern Bloc. The event that symbolised this shift was Soviet Premier Nikita Khrushchev's now-infamous secret speech titled *"On the Cult of Personality and Its Consequences."*

Delivered behind closed doors, this speech was meant to be an internal reckoning with the past. Khrushchev condemned the excesses of Stalin's rule, the cult of personality that had surrounded him, and the brutal purges that had claimed millions of lives. The speech was not intended for public consumption, but its contents could not be kept secret for long. The Central Committee of the ruling Polish United Workers' Party (PZPR) soon gained access to it, and its contents were quietly disseminated among key political leaders within the upper echelons of the Polish government.

For many in Poland, this speech was like a sudden, blinding light cast upon the darkest corners of their recent past. It confirmed what many had feared but dared not speak aloud—that the man who had been revered, almost worshipped, as a saviour of the working class was responsible for some of the most heinous acts of repression in history. The revelation was shocking and disillusioning, especially for those who had dedicated their lives to the Communist cause.

Nevertheless, the shockwaves from Khrushchev's speech were not the only tremors felt in Poland during this period. In the first week of March 1956, Bolesław Bierut, the First Secretary of the PZPR, was urgently called to Moscow for a meeting with Nikita Khrushchev. Bierut was a staunch Stalinist whose loyalty to Soviet ideals had shaped much of post-war Poland's political landscape. His sudden trip to Moscow was shrouded in mystery, but what happened there would only intensify the crisis. During his visit, Bierut suffered a severe attack of "pneumonia". Whether it was the harsh Moscow winter, the stress of the political situation, or something more sinister remains a matter of speculation. He died in Moscow, and his body was flown back to Warsaw roughly two weeks later, draped in the heavy symbolism of a leader whose time had passed.

Bierut's death, coming so soon after Khrushchev's denunciation of Stalin, added fuel to the growing fire of uncertainty and unrest in Poland. The political vacuum left by his passing created a sense of instability, a sense that the old order was beginning to crumble. The once-unshakeable foundation of Polish Communism was now riddled with cracks, and no one could predict how long it would hold.

These events were both disorienting and liberating for the Polish people, especially those within the government apparatus. The unspoken rules that had governed their lives for so long were suddenly being questioned. The iron grip of Stalinism was loosening, but the fear of what might follow came with it. Would Poland move toward greater independence, or would it exchange one form of repression for another?

These unresolved questions lingered as Poland entered a new and uncertain chapter in its history. Bierut's death and Moscow's revelations had set the stage for a period of intense political and social upheaval—a time when the old certainties were overturned and the future was anything but clear. [7]

In late March and early April 1956, Poland found itself at the cusp of a transformative moment. The air was thick with possibility as thousands of Party meetings were held nationwide, gathering PZPR members in what would become a remarkable outpouring of long-suppressed thoughts and emotions. For years, the iron grip of Stalinism had silenced dissent and stifled any deviation from the Soviet line. But now, in the wake of Khrushchev's revelations and Bierut's death, the atmosphere had shifted. The once-unquestionable authority of the Party was now open to challenge, and the people were seizing this unexpected freedom with zeal.

324

As Party members gathered in their respective branches, a palpable sense of change was in the air. The meetings, which had once been little more than formalities, took on a new, more dynamic character. The fear that had long silenced dissent was beginning to dissipate, giving way to a burgeoning courage to speak out. It was like a dam had broken, releasing a flood of pent-up grievances and unspoken truths.

For the first time, Party members felt encouraged to openly criticise Stalin's actions during the Great Purge, a dark chapter in history that had seen the execution of many of Poland's older Communists—men and women who had dedicated their lives to the cause, only to be betrayed by the very ideology they had served. The memories of these purges, long buried under layers of fear and propaganda, now surfaced in passionate speeches and emotional debates. The pain of those losses was still raw, and the newly found freedom to discuss them openly brought both catharsis and a renewed sense of purpose.

Jozef Cyrankiewicz, Alexander Zawadzki, and Edward Ochab, among other dignitaries, honouring the passing of their leader, Bolesław Bierut (16th of March 1956) [8]

However, the conversations did not stop with criticism of the past. There was also a growing call for a distinctly Polish future that would not be dictated by Moscow but shaped by Poland's history, culture, and aspirations. Many Party members began to advocate for National Socialism, a concept that Władysław Gomułka had championed in his book *Polish Road to Socialism*. Gomułka's vision was one of Socialism that respected Poland's sovereignty and allowed for a more independent path rather than simply following the Soviet model.

These discussions, once unthinkable, now resonated deeply with many Poles who had long felt the tension between their national identity and the demands of the Soviet Union. There was a sense of reclaiming something that had been lost—a belief that Poland could forge its own way, guided by its unique circumstances and needs, rather than being a mere satellite in the Soviet orbit.

The debates of those early spring days, in 1956, were far deeper than politics, they were more about identity, self-determination and justice. Could Poland truly find its own way within the framework of Socialism, or was it destined to remain under the Moscow regime's shadow? Could the Party reconcile its ideals with the need for truth and transparency, or would it fall back into the old patterns of repression and control?

These were the questions that hung over the Party meetings, questions that would shape the course of Poland's future. The answers were not yet clear, for my father and many others like him. But what was clear was that the old rules were gone, and in their place was a new, unpredictable landscape where anything seemed possible, but nothing was guaranteed. [9]

The air was thick with anticipation and unease during the PZPR party branch meeting in Warsaw. Members had been speaking their minds with a boldness that would have been unthinkable just months earlier, each voice adding to the growing chorus of demands for change. In this charged atmosphere, my father, who had sat quietly for much of the meeting, suddenly rose to his feet. The room fell silent as all eyes turned to him. With a calm but firm voice, he addressed the recent enthusiasm surrounding Władysław Gomułka's book, *Polish Road to Socialism.* Many in the room had found in Gomułka's words, a true new vision of Socialism that could be truly Polish, independent of Soviet dictates. But my father saw something far more dangerous in this line of thinking. He chose his words carefully, but there was an undercurrent of passion in his tone that betrayed the depth of his conviction. "Comrades," he began, his voice steady yet filled with urgency, "I have listened to the discussions here today, and I have heard many of you express admiration for Gomułka's vision. But I must speak plainly: Gomułka's book, *Polish Road to Socialism,* is not a path to true Socialism. It is a distortion—a dangerous distortion—of what Socialism is meant to be."

He paused, letting his words sink in. He watched the faces around him, gauging their reactions. Some nodded, while others shifted uncomfortably in their seats, unsure of where he was leading.

"Comrades," he continued, his voice rising with the strength of his belief, "We must not allow this so-called 'Polish Socialism' to take root. Nationalistic Polish Socialism is a dangerous road—one that could easily lead us to the very evils we fought against during the war. Nazism, my friends, was born out of the same nationalistic collective fervour, the same desire to place one's nation above all others. We must not forget the lessons of history. We must not let Poland fall into the same trap."

His words struck a chord, evoking the bitter memories of the war and the horrors of Nazism. There was a ripple of unease in the room along with a recognition of the truth in what he was saying. He was not just speaking to the ideals of Socialism; he was invoking the past, the sacrifices, and the bloodshed that had come from allowing the 'far-right' Socialism to go unchecked.

"There is only one true road to socialism," my father declared, his voice now filled with the unshakable certainty of a man who had seen too much to be swayed by ideological fads. "And that road is the one laid out by Marx, Lenin, and Engels. It is a road that transcends borders and does not bow to the whims of Nationalism or the desire for power. It is a road that leads to true equality, true brotherhood among all workers, regardless of their creed."

He could see the tension in the room, the internal struggles of those who had dared to hope for a different path but who now faced the harsh reminder of the dangers that path could bring. My father did not offer them comfort or easy answers. Instead, he offered them a challenge—a challenge to remain faithful to the ideals of Socialism, resist the seductive call of Nationalism, and remember the lessons of history.

As he sat down, the room remained silent for a moment longer, the weight of his words hanging in the air. He had spoken as a member of the Party, and as a man who had lived through the darkest chapters of Europe's recent history. His warning was clear: Poland's future could not be secured by turning inward, by retreating into the false security of Nationalism. The actual road to Socialism was complex and fraught with challenges, but it was the only road that could lead to a just and equitable society.

The meeting continued, but the tone had shifted. My father's words had left an indelible mark on the discussion, a reminder that the choices they made in that room would shape the future of their country—and that the stakes were far higher than any of them could afford to forget.

In June 1956, the political landscape of Poland began to crack open, revealing the simmering tensions that had long been buried beneath the Communist regime's surface. It was as if a dam had burst, releasing a torrent of questions and doubts that had been supressed for too long. Within the ranks of the PZPR, the only political party allowed to operate, various factions emerged, each carrying its own set of grievances and demands for change.

During that summer in 1956, Poland stood at a crossroads, with the undercurrents of unrest bubbling to the surface in ways that could no longer be ignored. My father, deeply entrenched in the ideological battles of his time, could sense the shifting winds, although perhaps he did not fully grasp the magnitude of what was to come. For him, the cracks in the façade of Polish Communism were unsettling. They stirred memories of past struggles, of the promises made and the dreams of a better future that seemed to be slithering further away with each passing day.

My father attended meeting after meeting, where party members dared to speak truths that had long been buried. They spoke of the atrocities committed under Stalin, of the suffering that had been silenced, and of the deep scars that remained. As he listened, he felt a mix of anger, betrayal, and fear. He had always believed that the path laid out by Marx, Engels and Lenin, was the proper way forward—a path that would lead to a world free of hate and prejudice, which historically subverted humanity in ghastly ways. But now, as the party began to splinter and as nationalist sentiments grew louder, he realised that the ideals he held dear, were being corrupted, twisted into something unrecognisable.

Despite his growing disillusionment, my father remained committed to his work, clinging to the hope that the ideals of Communism could still be realised and that the sacrifices made would not be in vain. But the demands for a new Party Congress grew louder, with the voices of dissent becoming more insistent. Poland was changing in ways, neither he nor the PZPR party could control.

He often spoke to me about these times with bitterness and disappointment. He was a man caught between two worlds—the world of his ideals and the world of harsh realities. He had seen the best and worst of humanity, and yet, he could not shake off the feeling that the very forces he had trusted to build a better world were now betraying him. The dreams of a Communist utopia were fading, replaced by the stark reality of political infighting and a resurgence of Nationalism that he had feared the most.

In his quieter moments, when the weight of the world seemed too much to bear, he would retreat into his memories, into the dreams of what might have been. He would speak of the lost potential, the roads not taken, and the hope that once burned in his heart. But even as he spoke, I could see in his eyes, the growing recognition that the world he had envisioned, was simply not going to materialise. In the end, my father's journey was not just about the political battles of his time but about the more profound, more personal struggle to reconcile his ideals with the world as it was. It was a struggle that would shape the rest of his life and one that he would carry with him until his final days. [10]

In June of 1956, the streets of Poznań became a battleground between the people and the State. What began as a protest over food shortages, inadequate housing, and the failing economy quickly escalated into something far more profound—a collective outcry that shook the foundations of the Polish socialist government. The people, emboldened by the winds of change sweeping across the Eastern Bloc, took to the streets, their voices rising in defiance of the oppressive conditions they were enduring for so long. The air was thick with tension, and the protests turned violent as the day wore on. More than 60 people lost their lives, and hundreds more were wounded—their blood staining the cobblestones of the city, that voiced its desperation for change.

Initially, the government, led by First Secretary Edward Ochab, responded with the familiar rhetoric of control, labelling the protesters as reactionary provocateurs and revisionists. But this time, the words sounded hollow. The truth was clear—the protests were not caused by a few disgruntled malcontents but were a sign of much deeper unrest. The spirit of Nationalism, long suppressed, was awakening with a force that could no longer be held back. Within the corridors of power, large sections of the PZPR membership began to see the reality of the situation. This was not just a disturbance; it was a substantial movement that reflected the people's desire for a Poland that truly belonged to them, free from the oppressive influence of Soviet power.

Faced with this rising tide of discontent, the government realised that brute force would only worsen the situation. Instead, they chose a gentler approach, promising higher wages and implementing economic reforms. It was an effort to calm the unrest, buy time, and restore some order. But the people were not so easily appeased. The protests spread rapidly, sparking public meetings and street demonstrations in cities across Poland. The demands grew louder and more urgent as the people found their voice. They called for the release of the imprisoned Archbishop Wyszyński, a symbol of religious resistance against the State's atheism. They demanded the abolition of the feared public security system, the return of the white eagle to the national flag, and the removal of the Russian language from the school curriculum—a rejection of the cultural imperialism imposed on them.

By October 1956, the tension reached a fever pitch. In cities and towns across the country, monuments and symbols dedicated to the Soviet Union were defaced as the people expressed their anger and frustration. This symbolic act sent a clear message that the Polish people were no longer willing to accept their subjugation to Moscow's dictates. Polish crowds saw the defacement of these monuments as a reclaiming of their national identity, a declaration that Poland's future would be decided by Poles, not foreign powers.

For my father, these events were both inspiring and terrifying. On the one hand, he saw a powerful expression of the people's will in these protests—a sign that the spirit of resistance had not been extinguished. But on the other hand, the events of October 1956, stirred his memories of the past, of the upheaval and suffering that had shaped his life. He understood the anger that drove the people into the streets, but he also knew that the fires of Nationalism could just as easily turn into something much darker and uncontrollable.

Amidst this turmoil, my father stayed firm in his belief that genuine Socialism, as described by Marx, Lenin, and Engels, was the only way forward. However, he couldn't ignore that the Polish version of Socialism strayed from those principles. The Nationalism he observed growing within the PZPR was a dangerous undercurrent that risked undermining everything he had stood for. Still, even as he expressed his concerns, he recognised that the forces of change were too strong to halt.

In the years that followed, the events of 1956 would be remembered as a turning point in Poland's history, a moment when the people dared to challenge the status quo and demand something better. During the pivotal days of October 19-21, 1956, the VIII Plenum of the Central Committee of the PZPR took place, marking a significant turning point in Poland's post-war history. The atmosphere was tense as the Party's leadership faced the daunting task of navigating the country through the political upheavals sweeping across Eastern Europe. Edward Ochab, the First Secretary and Prime Minister of Poland at the time, stepped forward with a proposal that would shape the nation's future: he nominated Władysław Gomułka for election as the Party's First Secretary. [11]

Gomułka's election within the PZPR was far from straightforward. He was a figure who had been sidelined and imprisoned under Stalin's regime, accused of "right-wing nationalist deviation." His views were known to diverge from the orthodox

Marxist-Leninist doctrines that had been the bedrock of the PZPR's ideology. Yet, despite this, or perhaps because of it, Gomułka was seen by many as the leader Poland needed in this time of crisis. His vision of Socialism was pragmatic and deeply rooted in the belief that any ideology, to be truly effective, must resonate with the specific social and cultural needs of the people it serves.

For Gomułka, Socialism was not a one-size-fits-all doctrine to be imposed uniformly across the Warsaw Pact nations. He believed that Poland's unique history, culture, and social fabric required a version of socialism tailored to its specific circumstances. This view put him at odds with Khrushchev and the Soviet leadership, who sought to maintain a uniform socialist model throughout the Eastern Bloc. Gomułka's return to power signalled a shift towards a more independent, nationally oriented Socialism, which resonated with the Polish people's growing desire for autonomy from Moscow's control.

The Plenum's decision to elect Gomułka was a response to the growing tide of nationalist sentiment and the call for change that was spreading across Poland. It acknowledged that the old Stalinist strategies could no longer hold the country together and that a new approach was necessary to meet the aspirations and concerns of the Polish people. Gomułka's election marked a redefinition of what Socialism in Poland would mean moving forward — a Socialism that was distinctly Polish, aiming to balance the Party's demands with the realities of the Polish experience.

For my father, the election of Gomułka was a moment of deep uncertainty. He had always been a strong supporter of Marxist-Leninist principles, believing in the universal nature of Socialism as a way to achieve equality and justice. Still, here was Gomułka, a man whose views challenged the very foundations of that belief. My father understood the need to adapt Socialism to the needs of the people, but he feared that Gomułka's brand of socialist Nationalism could steer

Poland down a dangerous path, one that might stray from the true essence of socialist ideology.

The VIII Plenum reflected the deep ideological struggles in Poland and across the Eastern Bloc. Gomułka's rise to power marked the beginning of a new chapter that would see Poland gaining greater independence from Soviet control. For those like my father, it was a time of soul-searching as they sought to reconcile their ideals with the changing realities of the world around them. [12]

The relationship between Władysław Gomułka and Nikita Khrushchev, though fraught with ideological differences, found common ground in a darker, more insidious objective: the purge of Jewish leaders from the upper echelons of the PZPR. This shared goal was rooted not in a genuine concern for the well-being of the Polish people, but in the murky waters of political expediency and latent anti-Semitism.

Gomułka, though a nationalist at heart, understood the importance of aligning with Khrushchev on certain issues to solidify his power and navigate the turbulent political landscape of post-Stalinist Poland. Khrushchev, on the other hand, was driven by a deep-seated animosity towards Jews, an animosity that had been part of the Soviet leadership's undercurrent for years. Since assuming power, Khrushchev had been at odds with Bolesław Bierut, the staunch Stalinist who resisted the winds of de-Stalinization and opposed any move that might undermine the Marxist-Leninist foundations of the PZPR. Bierut, a man of Jewish heritage himself, understood that these foundations were not merely political constructs but essential bulwarks against the age-old plagues of poverty, greed, and anti-Semitism that had ravaged Poland for centuries. To Bierut and to men like my father, Marxism-Leninism offered a path toward a more just and equitable society. But Khrushchev's vision was tainted by his own prejudices. He saw the Jewish leaders within the Polish government not as comrades in the struggle for Socialism but as convenient scapegoats. In his eyes, the presence of Jews in positions of power was a liability, a target for the discontent of the Nationalistic masses who had long harboured anti-Semitic sentiments. Khrushchev believed he could pacify the restless Polish populace by purging these leaders, deflecting their anger away from the Soviet Union and its policies.

The sudden death of Bierut in early March 1956, during his urgent meeting with Khrushchev in the Kremlin, raised troubling questions. Was Bierut's death truly the result of a natural illness, or was it, as some have speculated, a convenient removal of a formidable opponent? Bierut had been a barrier to Khrushchev's plans, a leader who refused to bend to the Soviet Premier's demands for de-Stalinization and the purging of Jews from the government. His death, whether by fate or design, cleared the way for Khrushchev's vision to take root in Poland.

For my father, this period was a time of profound disillusionment. He had devoted his life to the ideals of Marxism-Leninism, believing that they held the key to a future free from the hatred and bigotry that had haunted his people for centuries. But now, he saw those same ideals being twisted and corrupted by the very leaders who were supposed to uphold them. The purge of Jewish leaders from the PZPR, carried out under the guise of political necessity, was a stark reminder that the forces of anti-Semitism, far from being vanquished, were still very much alive, even within the ranks of the Communist Party.

As Gomułka rose to power, backed by Khrushchev's tacit approval, my father was witnessing the re-emergence of old prejudices, dressed up in the language of political pragmatism. The struggle for Socialism had always been, for my father, a battle for humanity itself. But now, as the tide turned in favour of Nationalism and anti-Semitism, that struggle seemed more precarious than ever.

The political manoeuvring of Władysław Gomułka in the wake of Bolesław Bierut's death reveals a complex and calculated strategy, one that sought to balance the demands of Nationalist sentiment within Poland with the overarching influence of the Soviet Union. The elimination of Bierut—a staunch Communist and a man of Jewish heritage—enabled Gomułka and Khrushchev to implement a hidden anti-Semitic strategy as a fallback tactic in times of unrest.

Gomułka's rise to power in 1956 was marked by his ability to present himself as a champion of Polish independence while maintaining the essential ties to Moscow that were necessary for Poland's survival within the Warsaw Pact. By positioning himself as a reformer who sought to liberalise Poland and reintroduce elements of the once-banned Polish Socialist Party, Gomułka appealed to the emerging Nationalist sentiments that had been suppressed under Bierut's rule. At the same time, Gomułka was acutely aware of the need to manage potential social unrest, especially in a nation still reeling from the effects of war and occupation. The 'fallback tactic', while never overtly stated, was an anti-Semitic tool used to appease the disgruntled masses when economic or political problems would arise. In this way, Gomułka could maintain a semblance of autonomy from Moscow while ensuring that Poland remained a loyal partner within the Soviet sphere of influence.

Khrushchev, for his part, had little to lose from this arrangement. By allowing Poland to pursue a path of de-Stalinization and limited autonomy, he could present the Soviet Union as a more flexible and progressive leader in the Communist bloc, all the while knowing that the ideological and political constraints of the Warsaw Pact would still bind Poland to Moscow. The anti-Semitic undercurrents, which both leaders tacitly endorsed, would serve as a convenient means of deflecting blame and maintaining control, should the need arise.

Gomułka's imprisonment in 1951, under accusations of right-wing Nationalist deviation, further complicates his legacy. His later ascent to power can be seen as a vindication of his earlier views, yet it also highlights the precariousness of his position. He had to navigate a delicate balance between asserting Poland's independence and appeasing the Soviet leadership while managing the internal pressures of a society increasingly disillusioned with the Communist regime. Once in power, Gomułka made it clear that Poland had no intention of abandoning the Warsaw Pact or the Soviet Union. Instead, he argued that 'de-Stalinization' and 'greater autonomy' were essential steps toward a form of National Socialism that would be more in tune with Poland's unique cultural and social needs. While seemingly progressive, this vision was underpinned by the same pragmatic considerations that had driven Khrushchev's policies. Both leaders understood that in the volatile landscape of Cold War Europe, maintaining control often required a willingness to compromise on ideals and to employ whatever tactics were necessary to keep the peace.

In this shifting political landscape, my father's commitment to the Communist cause must have been tested like never before. He would have understood the need for pragmatism in politics, but the realisation that his ideals were being sacrificed for expediency would have weighed heavily on him. The harsh reality of power politics and the enduring legacy of prejudice were swiftly replacing my father's hope for lasting Communism in Poland. His dream of a united, socialist future, free from the scourges of anti-Semitism and Nationalism, was fading, leaving behind a world that was all too familiar—a world where old vestiges of hatred could be resurrected whenever it suited those in power. [13]

In the quiet, book-lined office at the MKiS, the framed portrait of Bolesław Bierut remained resolutely in place, a silent testament to my father's unwavering loyalty. While the political winds howled outside, tearing at the very fabric of Poland's Communist Party, within these four walls, the ideological foundation upon which my father had built his life stood firm and unshaken. For him, Bierut was a leader who symbolised the struggle against the forces that had once threatened to annihilate his people. He was a beacon of the future, a reminder of the battles fought, the sacrifices made, and the enduring hope that the world would finally align with the ideals he held so dear—the same ideals my father steadfastly adhered to. In the tumultuous months that followed Stalin's death, while others in the ministry whispered about change, reform, and the uncertain future, my father continued his work with the same quiet determination. Yet, behind his unflinching exterior was a deep well of reflection. He had lived through enough to understand that history was not a straight line but a series of spirals, each bringing with it a mix of progress and regression, hope and despair. He had seen how easily ideals could be co-opted or corrupted by those in power. But his commitment was not to any one man, not even to Bierut, but to the dream of a just and equal world.

In those moments of quiet contemplation, perhaps he wondered whether the struggles of the present were a necessary trial, a test of faith that would ultimately strengthen the movement he had devoted his life to. Or perhaps he simply found solace in the familiar routines of his work, where the grand narratives of history felt less immediate and where he could, for a time, forget the tumult outside.

As Gomułka rose to power in late 1956, my father noticed a quiet yet deeply personal change happening among his friends. These were people who had endured the unimaginable, their lives irreversibly shaped by the atrocities they had seen and survived. Now, they were leaving Poland one after another, seeking refuge and a fresh start in the newly established State of Israel.

In the years following World War II, Poland's Jewish population had been reduced to a mere fraction of what it once was (3,500,000), with approximately 240,000 Jews remaining in the country. The wounds of the Holocaust were still fresh, and the scars it left on the Jewish community were deep and enduring. The Kielce Pogrom in

1946 had already driven 70,000 Polish Jews to emigrate to Israel, as fear and insecurity pushed them to seek safety in their ancestral homeland.

Władysław Gomułka was appointed as the First Secretary of the PZPR on 21 October 1956

But the exodus didn't stop there. In 1949, a new wave of emigration began when Poland reached an agreement with Israel to repay its $2.5 million trade debt by allowing Polish Jews to make their Aliyah—their return to the Promised Land. This was a bittersweet arrangement, one that offered a way out for those who no longer felt they could call Poland home but also signalled the beginning of a more calculated push to diminish the Jewish presence in Poland. By 1950, however, the political winds had shifted. The Soviet Union, with its growing anti-Israeli and anti-Zionist stance, had made it clear that Poland could no longer support the Zionist state, effectively halting the Jewish Aliyah from Poland. For years, the Jewish community in Poland lived in a state of uneasy limbo, caught between a past they could not forget and a future that seemed increasingly uncertain.

When Gomułka came to power, he reopened the door, allowing those who wished to emigrate to Israel to do so with relative ease. This move, known as the "Gomułka Aliyah," was lauded by many in Israel, who viewed it as a humanitarian gesture that offered Polish Jews the opportunity to reclaim their identity and find a place to live without fear of persecution.

But beneath the surface, another motive was at play—one far more insidious. Gomułka, in his bid to consolidate power and cleanse the government of those he considered undesirable, was effectively encouraging the emigration of Polish Jews. By granting travel permits and making it easier for them to leave, he was slowly but steadily removing assimilated Polish Jews from government posts and public life, a form of ethnic cleansing disguised as a benevolent policy.

My father watched as friends and colleagues, with whom he had shared both the horrors of the past and the hope for a better future, began to disappear from his life. Each departure was a reminder of the precariousness of Jewish existence in Poland, a painful acknowledgement that the country they had fought for and believed in was, once again, pushing them out to the margins. Their exodus brought the reality to my father that the fabric of his world was unravelling, thread by thread, as those who had survived the Holocaust sought safety and belonging elsewhere. And yet, despite the growing sense of isolation and the changing world around him, my father remained.

The "Gomułka Aliyah" was not just a chapter in the history of Polish Jewry; it was a reflection of the complex and often painful reality that my father, and many others like him, had to navigate. It was a time of deep uncertainty, difficult choices, and harsh truths, marking a turning point in the lives of both those who chose to remain in Poland and those who decided to leave and settle in the new State of Israel. [14]

The following year brought a profound and almost unbearable sadness to my father's life. It was a grief that would etch itself into his soul, leaving a scar that would never fully heal. My mother, Barbara, fell ill with a mysterious and progressively paralysing condition, an illness that no doctor could definitively diagnose or cure. The doctors diagnosed Heine-Medina (Polio), but much later, my maternal family history revealed the cross-generational impact of a deadly Porphyria (Latin: Porfini). My mother's condition grew increasingly dire as days passed, with tenuous hope diminishing—like a flickering candle in a storm.

It was April 30, 1957, an overcast day that seemed to mirror the heaviness in my father's heart. He made his way to the Hospital of Infectious Diseases; his steps quickened by a growing sense of dread. The streets seemed quiet, as if the world around him had already sensed the tragedy that was about to unfold.

As he neared the hospital, he suddenly saw a familiar figure emerging from the building's main entrance. It was my aunt Wiesia, her posture heavy, face pale and drawn, with a deep concern. As she caught sight of my father, she called out to him, "Henio," her voice breaking through the stillness of the morning.

My father hurried towards her, a part of him desperate to hold onto the possibility that the news she bore was not what he feared. But as he reached her, the look in her eyes, the sorrow etched into her features, told him everything before she even spoke a word. "Heniu," she began, her voice trembling with emotion, "Basia has passed away… this morning."

The world seemed to stop at that moment. The weight of her words pressed down on him, crushing his breath. He stood there, motionless, as if time itself had ceased to exist and everything that had come before was now distant and unreachable. The overcast sky, the silent streets, the cold hospital walls—all of it faded into insignificance as the reality of his loss overwhelmed him.

Barbara, the woman he had shared his life with, the mother of his son, was gone. The illness that had gripped her with such merciless intensity had taken her away at the age of 25 years. In that instant, my father felt as if a part of himself died along with her. As he stood there, the realisation that he would never see her again washed over him with a devastating finality.

Aunt Wiesia reached out, placing a comforting hand on his arm, but there was little comfort to be found. The pain was too raw, too overwhelming. My father knew his world would be irrevocably changed from this day forward. The grief, like a shadow, would follow him constantly, a reminder of the love he had lost.

This moment, this heart-wrenching encounter outside the hospital, marked the beginning of a new chapter in my father's life—one defined by the quiet ache of loss that words could never fully capture.

At the time of my mother's passing, I was staying with my grandmother, Lucyna, in her Mokotów apartment. The walls of that familiar space had always provided a sense of warmth and safety. But after the 30th of April, they seemed to close in, the heaviness mirroring the grief settling into every corner. Lucyna, shattered by the loss of Barbara, found herself grappling with the reality of her daughter's absence. This reality felt like a cruel and surreal nightmare, after losing her two children before the end of WWII.

The MKiS extended formal condolences, offering him bereavement leave and financial assistance to purchase a gravesite at the Brudno Cemetery. On the day of the funeral, a sombre atmosphere hung over the gathering like a dark cloud, as the family and friends came together to say their final goodbyes to Barbara. The procession at the Brudno Cemetery was marked by a silence filled with the weight of unspoken grief and the shared pain of those who loved her.

Lucyna, my grandmother, stood beside my father, her face etched with the lines of age and sorrow. My aunt Wiesia was there too, her presence a small comfort amid overwhelming grief. Together, they formed a fragile circle of mutual support, each of them drawing strength from one another in this time of loss. It was also on this day, during this heart-wrenching ceremony, that my father met my mother's father for the first—and only—time. The encounter was brief, overshadowed by the circumstances that had brought them together. There were no words exchanged that could bridge the chasm between them, no shared memories to reminisce over. Instead, there was only the shared silent acknowledgment of their mutual loss, a nod to the connection that had been severed far too soon.

As my father stood at the gravesite, he felt the finality of it all—the earth beneath his feet, the cold air around him, the faces of those who had come to mourn. This was the last chapter of a life that had once been filled with hope and love, now closed forever. The reality of Barbara's passing settled in with the lowering of the casket, a physical representation of the loss that had already consumed his heart.

The year 1957 was a challenging year for my father. I believe he became depressed and was overcome with renewed grief and disappointment. After the trauma of the Holocaust and the trauma of war, the young woman he loved and wished to create a new life with had died. His best friends had departed for Israel (*Polish:* 'Palestyna'). He was left alone with his three-year-old son, unable to speak about the pain he felt, unable to tell his son what happened to his mother. Another loss that could never be fully explained, talked about, or openly shared.

My Mother (age 25, approximately six months before her death)

Notes

1. Huener, Jonathan (2003). Auschwitz, Poland, and the Politics of Commemoration, 1945-1979. Ohio University Press. Athens p. 111

2. *Ibid.,* p. 109

3. *Ibid.,* p. 114

4. *Ibid.,* p. 126

5. *Ibid.,* p. 128

6. 5th World Festival of Youth and Students, Warsaw, 1955. ttps://en.wikipedia.org/wiki/5th_World_Festival_of_Youth_and_Students

7. https://en.wikipedia.org/wiki/Polish_October

8. https://en.wikipedia.org/wiki/Bolesław_Bierut

9. https://en.wikipedia.org/wiki/Polish_October

10. *Ibid.,*

11. *Ibid.,*

12. *Ibid.,*

13. *Ibid.,*

14. Dariusz Stola (2017). Jewish emigration from the communist Poland: The decline of Polish Jewry in the aftermath of the Holocaust. East European Jewish Affairs, 2017, VOL. 47, NOS.2–3, 169–188. Institute of Political Studies (ISP) and Polin Museum, Warsaw, Poland. pp. 175-179

14. The Price of Conscience

"Most times, the world does not change in ways humanity hopes it will, and the 'good' we seek may not always prevail over the 'evil' that threatens to engulf it." - Janusz

In 1958, a pivotal shift began to take root in my father's life—a shift that marked the beginning of his plans to leave Poland. This intention did not come lightly, nor was it consolidated in haste. It was the culmination of years of disillusionment and grief, punctuated by the profound loss of my mother, Barbara. Her death, a devastating blow, seemed to strip away the last vestiges of purpose he had once found in Poland, the country he had loved fiercely and fought for with unwavering conviction.

The loss of my mother cast a shadow over the life he had built in post-war Poland, a place that had once been filled with meaning and hope. The ground on which he stood now felt barren and unforgiving, a land that had once promised so much but had delivered little in the way of fulfilment. His close friend, Leon Szer, had already made the journey to Israel a year earlier, signalling his intention to settle in Australia eventually. This connection, a lifeline to a different future, began to tug at my father's thoughts, pulling him toward the possibility of a new beginning in a distant land.

Auschwitz State Museum, where he had invested so much of himself, had once represented a beacon of hope. In this place, the suffering of Polish Jewry could be validated and recognised on a scale that matched the enormity of their tragedy. Yet, deep within his soul, he knew that the Museum's exhibition was a compromised reflection of the truth—the truth that was buried beneath layers of political manoeuvring and cultural resistance. The presentation of the Holocaust at Auschwitz was not as it should have been, at least during his time at MKiS, and he was painfully aware that there was nothing he could do to change that. The weight of this realisation bore down on him, a constant reminder of his limitations, actively operating in the work that once had given him purpose.

As time passed, so too did his hope that Poland could ever become a genuine 'Communist State.' The ideals that had driven him for so long began to erode, slowly but inexorably, as he faced the stark reality that Poland's cultural mindset was deeply entrenched in Roman Catholicism, with its powerful grip on the nationalist ideology that glorified Poland's history of Christ-like sacrifice and heroism. These beliefs, which had shaped Polish identity for centuries, left little room for the kind of transformation he had hoped to see.

In his heart, he grappled with a sense of hopelessness and a looming need to accept the reality that the change he desired for Poland would never eventuate. The realisation that Poland, with its proud history, deeply embedded Catholicism and Nationalism, might never fully embrace the values he held dear left him feeling adrift, like a man untethered from the ideals that had once anchored his life. The thought of leaving Poland, a land that had been his home, was a complex contemplation. Yet, in seeking a visa for Australia, he was not merely fleeing a place that had disappointed him; he was reaching out for a new beginning—a chance to rebuild his life in a land that held the promise of something different, if not better. Australia, with its distant shores and unfamiliar culture, represented a blank slate, a place where he could perhaps find a measure of peace that had eluded him in his homeland. This decision, fraught with emotion and uncertainty, would mark the end of one chapter in his life and the beginning of another—a journey that would take him far from the streets of Warsaw and the haunting memories of his past life in Kalish.

At the bottom of my father's descent into the dark void of despair was a profound and tragic unravelling of the hopes and dreams he had long held dear. The quicksand of Poland's shifting socio-political landscape, where Nationalism was re-emerging with renewed vigour, seemed to swallow the very foundations upon which he had built his life. The ideals that sustained him through the darkest hours of World War II and the immediate post-war years were now severely challenged.

In his heart, there may have been an unconscious clinging to a deeply rooted Jewish belief that, from immense suffering, some form of good eventually emerges. This belief, intrinsic to Jewish tradition, holds that struggle and suffering are not ends in themselves, but pathways towards redemption. For many Jews around the world, the ultimate 'good' that emerged from the ashes of the Holocaust was the rebirth of the State of Israel, a homeland where they could rebuild their lives and ensure their survival. But for my father, the 'good' was envisioned differently—not in the distant land of Israel, but in the creation of a communist utopia within Poland—a place where the horrors of the past could be redeemed through the establishment of a just and equitable society.

Yet, as the nationalist political forces rose again, this vision became increasingly fragile, like a distant mirage that receded further with each step towards it. The quicksand of Poland's shifting political tides has pulled my father deeper into a murky despair from which there seemed no escape. His hope that the 'good' could still emerge from the 'evil' and that the suffering endured could be redeemed by building a better world, the Poland he had envisioned, was essentially gone. In the end, my father's struggle was not only against the rising nationalist political change, but also against the internal demons of his grief, loss, and disillusionment. His journey was one of profound resilience and psychological depth; a journey marked by the painful reality that the world does not change as we hope it will and that the 'good' we seek may not always prevail over the 'evil' that threatens to engulf it.

In Poland, my father knew that he could not safely exist as a Polish Jew. The only identity that seemed to offer him some semblance of emotional safety was that of a Polish communist. But even this identity was now becoming fraught with danger, as the notion of communist ideology was becoming increasingly synonymous with Jewish domination of Polish politics. The pernicious idea of 'Poland for Poles' was not just a whisper in the shadows; it was growing louder, seeping into public discourse and reawakening fears and prejudices that had never entirely disappeared.

The emotional toll of this realisation must have been immense. He felt as if he had lost his solid footing, no place to stand where he could indeed be himself, both a Polish patriot and a Jewish survivor of the Holocaust. Up to this point, he navigated a world with his identity as a Polish communist at the cost of denying or suppressing his Jewish heritage—a heritage that, despite his embrace of communist ideals, was inextricably linked to the very core of who he was. The resurgence of Nationalism and anti-Semitism in Poland forced him into a painful compromise, one that required him to hide a part of himself to survive in a society that was becoming increasingly hostile to the very ideals he had once believed would transform it.

Before the war, Jews were often caricatured as embodying greed—money-driven, disloyal, and always on the periphery of Polish national consciousness. But in the aftermath of the Holocaust and the rise of communist rule, this small, decimated group of survivors, a mere 30,000 (after 1958), among 30 million Poles, became something else entirely in the eyes of many. They were now seen not just as outsiders but as the insidious drivers of Communism, pushing it into the heart of what many Poles believed was their sacred, God-fearing nation—Poland, the 'Christ of Nations.'

In the minds of working-class Catholic Poles, the notion of *Żydo-Komuna*—the Jewish-Communist conspiracy—had taken root, nourished by the same right-wing Catholic nationalism that had once justified betraying Jewish neighbours during the war. This time, however, the threat was seen as more profound and more existential, not just about the Jews but about the soul of Poland itself. This tiny, beleaguered group was now viewed as the embodiment of everything that threatened the Polish way of life and thus had to be eradicated, not just from power but from memory.

The new nationalist forces, which included former Home Army combatants (*Akowcy*), partisans, and members of the Polish Socialist Party (PPS), took up this cause with a fervour that left no room for the complex realities of wartime collaboration and complicity. Among them were those who, during the war, had handed Jews over to the Nazis, believing it was their duty to protect 'pure Poles' (Rdzenni Polacy) and cleanse the nation of those they deemed alien. The same people who had once viewed the Jewish presence as a stain on the Polish landscape now saw the survivors as a stain on the Polish soul.

In this climate, there was no place for my father's hopes, ideals, and visions of a just Polish society. The Poland of the late 1950s was free of its Jews, not just physically, but spiritually—there was not one Jewish community left, no voices to express gratitude for the sacrifices Poles made during the war. Among the emerging nationalist forces, there was a deep-seated resentment towards this tiny remnant surviving minority—now seen as 'ungrateful,' 'disloyal,' and propagating 'anti-Polonism' in the West. The narrative that emerged was one of selective memory, where the sacrifices Poles made to alleviate Jewish suffering during the occupation were highlighted, while burying the darker truths of collaboration, complicity, and betrayal. It was a narrative that left no room for the reality of what had happened, and it was a narrative that my father, despite all his faith in the ideals of Communism, found impossible to reconcile with.

In this Poland, free of its Jews, the echoes of the past lingered like a ghost, a presence felt but never fully acknowledged. And in this silence, my father's grief deepened, not just for the family he had lost, but for his ideals that were vanishing into the smoke of history.

In 1958, as the shadows of Poland's past and the uncertain light of its future converged, my father found himself at a crossroads. The decision to leave Poland—a land he had fought for, suffered for, and believed in—was difficult to contemplate. Yet, the pull of a new life, perhaps one free from the oppressive memories and the lingering ghosts of a nation still grappling with its demons, was strong. In this state of uncertainty and anxious contemplation, two gentlemen sought him out, bringing with them the weight of their own fears and hopes.

The men who sat before him in his MKiS office were not strangers to the struggle for Jewish survival and memory. Salo Fiszgrund, the Presiding General Secretary of the Jewish Worker's Union "Bund," and Bernard Mark, the Acting Director of the Jewish Historical Institute of Warsaw. Both had dedicated their lives to ensuring that the Jewish voice, the voice of a people nearly extinguished, would not be silenced in Poland. They came to him with a plea, a burden that they now sought to share with him.

"Heniek," Fiszgrund began, his voice heavy with the weight of history, "if you leave Poland, if you leave the MKiS, the Jewish martyrology will be erased." Fiszgrund's statement echoed my father's deepest concerns and despair. The resurgence of the right-wing elements within the Polish Socialist Party was not merely a political shift; it was a tide that threatened to wash away the memory of the millions who had perished. The names that Fiszgrund mentioned were names my father knew well—Mieczyslaw Moczar, Kazimierz Rusinek, Grzegorz Korczyński, and Kazimierz Sidor. These were men who harboured a deep-seated animosity toward Jews, men who saw the Jewish narrative as a thorn in the side of Poland's nationalistic pride.

351

Fiszgrund and Mark spoke of ZBoWiD, the Society of Fighters for Freedom and Democracy, and the growing influence of those within it who had once been members of ONR, the National Radical Camp—a movement that had long advocated 'Catholic totalitarianism' in Poland, steeped in virulent anti-Semitism. They warned him of the likes of Dr. Czeslaw Pilichowski, a man who, before the war, had been one of the "Razor Slashers" (Polish: "Żyletkarze"), who had terrorised Polish Jewish students on university campuses. Pilichowski, who now held a position of influence within the PZPR, was, in their view, distorting the history of the Shoah, reshaping it to fit a narrative that would exclude or diminish the Jewish experience.

"Look at the situation, Heniek," Fiszgrund continued, leaning forward as if to drive the point home, "Before the war, Pilichowski was a passionate right-wing anti-Semitic Nationalist. Today, Pilichowski is distorting the history of the Shoah" (In May 1965, Pilichowski was appointed to the position of the Director, Main Commission for the Study of Nazi Crimes in Poland, within the Ministry of Justice).

The conversation that evening centred on politics, memory, identity, and the responsibility of bearing witness to the past. As the evening stretched into the night, the gravity of their words settled in my father's heart. They were asking him to stay, to continue fighting, not only for the memory of the Jewish victims of the Holocaust but also for the truth of what had happened and for the preservation of a history already being rewritten by those who sought to erase its most painful chapters. It was a moment of tough decision. To leave would be to pursue a life free of the burdens that had weighed so heavily on him for many years. But to stay would be to honour the memory of those who could no longer speak, and to do his best towards ensuring that the rising tide of nationalism and anti-Semitism would not silence their stories.

In the end, my father chose to stay. He knew that by staying, he would continue to walk a path fraught with the constant reminder of what had been lost and the ongoing struggle to keep that loss from being erased. He felt compelled to take this path for his family, his people, and for the truth. In that choice, he reaffirmed his commitment to the ideals he had fought for all his life. Even as the world around him shifted and changed, even as the forces of history seemed to conspire against him, he held on to the belief that some things— memory, truth, and justice—were worth fighting for.

∞∞∞∞

In 1959, when my father embarked on a journey to Moscow as part of a three-man delegation from the MKiS. The delegation, composed of my father, Janusz Gumkowski, then Director of the Main Commission for the Investigation of Nazi Crimes in Poland, and Professor Ludwik Rajewski, President of the Main Commission for the Protection of Places of Struggle and Suffering in Poland, carried with them the weighty task of seeking access to documents collected by the Soviet Red Army from places that had become synonymous with human suffering—Wilno (Vilnius) Ghetto, Majdanek, and Auschwitz-Birkenau. These were not just any documents; they were fragments of history, shards of truth that could offer insight into the atrocities committed on Polish soil, evidence that could help preserve the memory of the millions who had perished. For my father, the trip to Moscow was both a diplomatic mission and a personal pilgrimage. Each document, each piece of paper, represented a voice that had been silenced, a story that had yet to be fully told.

A mixture of anticipation and anxiety marked my father's journey to Moscow. The Soviet Union under Khrushchev was different from what it had been under Stalin, yet it remained a formidable power, one that clung tightly to its secrets. The delegation's hopes were high, but so were the stakes. Access to these documents could bolster Poland's historical record, help solidify the truth about the atrocities committed by the Nazis, and serve as a bulwark against the rising tide of revisionism and ambiguity.

Upon arriving in Moscow, the delegation encountered the cold, bureaucratic face of Soviet authority. The meetings were formal, and the atmosphere was tense. My father, Gumkowski, and Rajewski pressed their case with determination. They emphasised the documents' historical significance and their importance to both Poland and the broader human understanding of the horrors of the Holocaust. Yet their words fell on deaf ears.

The Soviet authorities, cloaked in the shadow of Stalin's legacy, refused to grant access to the documents. They did not budge or offer even a glimmer of hope that these records would be made available any time soon. Instead, they pointed to a protocol established during Stalin's administration. The protocol stipulated in specific terms that the declassification of these documents would not occur until 1985— a year that seemed impossibly far away, a year that might as well have been a century away from where my father and his two companions stood at that moment.

The refusal was a blow, not just to the delegation but to my father personally. He had long believed that the truth, no matter how painful, must be brought to light, and that the memories of those who had suffered and died must be preserved and honoured. Yet here he was, faced with the stark reality that the past was still being controlled, manipulated, and withheld by those in power. The frustration was palpable, the disappointment heavy.

As the delegation left Moscow, my father carried with him a deep sense of betrayal, not only by the Soviet authorities but by the very system he had once believed in. The trip to Moscow had shown him that the road to truth was long and fraught with obstacles posed by those who feared what it might reveal.

And yet, even in this moment of despair, there was a flicker of resolve. My father returned to Poland with renewed determination to continue his work, to fight for the preservation of memory, and to ensure that the stories of those who had perished would not be forgotten, even if the documents that could tell their stories were locked away in some distant archive, hidden behind the iron curtain of a regime that still held too much power over the past.

Ultimately, the journey to Moscow became a symbol of my father's larger struggle—a struggle to reconcile his ideals with the harsh realities of a world that was often more interested in burying the truth than confronting it. This struggle would continue to define his life, one he would never abandon, even as the world around him changed in ways he could never have imagined.

During his visit to Moscow, amid the bureaucratic labyrinth and the heavy atmosphere of a nation still deeply entwined in Stalin's shadow, my father harboured a personal mission that weighed heavily on his heart. Beyond the official duties that had brought him to the Soviet capital, he needed to resolve a deeply private and urgent matter. His brother, Leon, who had supposedly been imprisoned in the Chelyabinsk Gulag in Siberia between 1941 and 1945, was the missing piece in a puzzle of loss that had haunted my father for years.

The search for Leon was fraught with obstacles, as my father quickly discovered. His first step was to seek help from the Moscow Polish Embassy, hoping the Consul could assist. But the response was not what he had hoped for. The Consul, with a tone of cautious diplomacy, informed him that this was a "delicate matter." In the Soviet Union at the time, inquiries into the whereabouts of Gulag prisoners were ventures into murky and often perilous territory, where layers of official secrecy and political caution obscured the truth.

Undeterred, my father was directed to the General Procurator's office. There, he encountered a similar mix of evasion and formality.

The Procurator suggested he contact the Chief Commissioner of the Prison Camps in the USSR. He was told this was the person who might hold the key to the information he so desperately sought. The meeting with the Chief Commissioner was arranged, and for a moment there was a glimmer of hope. The Soviet official, in a display of what might have been genuine concern or simply a gesture of bureaucratic politeness, assured my father that he would facilitate a meeting with the Minister of Internal Affairs.

But hope was fragile in the corridors of Soviet power. After days of waiting and following up, my father was finally given a set of documents—a collection of names, each representing a life, a story, a fate. The list included eight Soviet Gulag prisoners who bore the surname 'Poznański.' My father pored over the names, each a potential lead, a possible connection to his lost brother. But as he read through them, his heart sank. None of the names matched. There was no Leon or Leib Poznański among them.

It was a crushing moment. My father had come so close to the possibility of finding a trace of his brother, only to be met with silence, with the cold reality that the information he sought might never be found, that Leon might forever remain a ghost in the annals of Soviet prisons. The weight of this unfavourable outcome added another layer of grief to the already heavy burden my father carried.

Yet, even in this moment of profound disappointment, there was a resilience in my father—a determination that defined much of his life. Perhaps better than most, he understood that some battles were not meant to be won and that some truths were destined to remain elusive. But this did not diminish the importance of the search nor the love that drove him to seek answers in the first place.

∞∞∞∞

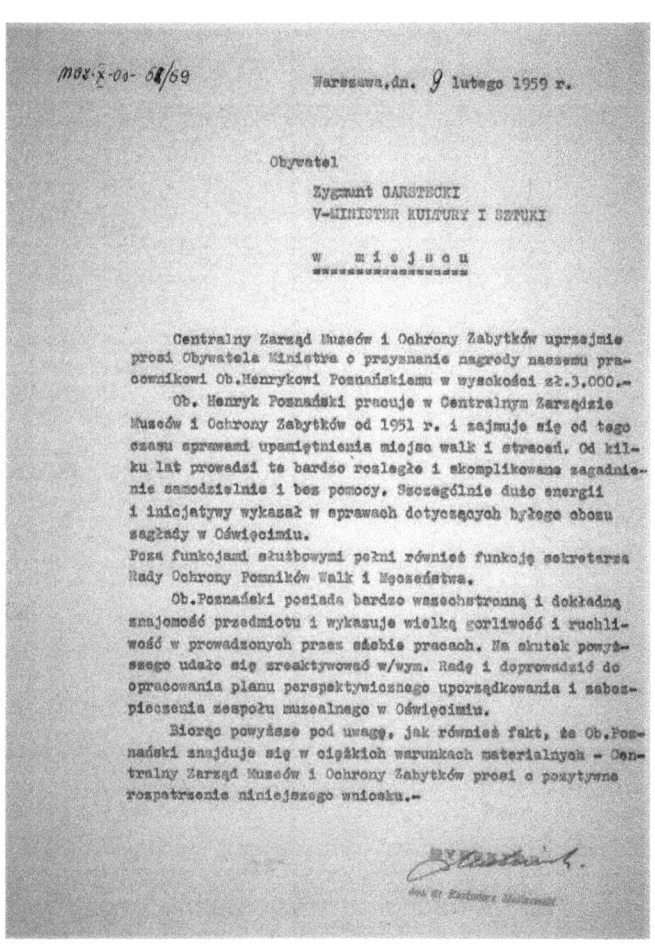

Letter from the Director Malinowski to the Vice-Minister of MKiS, dated 9 February 1959, seeking promotion for my father on the grounds of his expert knowledge.

The content of the letter is as follows:

> The Central Department of Muzeums and Protection of National Heritage kindly asks the honourable Minister to award Mr Henryk Poznański a bonus of $3,000.00 PLN. Mr Poznański has been working within the Central Department of Muzeums and Protection of National Heritage since 1951, and his role is to deal with matters concerning commemoration, protection, and preservation of sites of struggle and suffering. Over the last several years, he has been leading this critical and complex work virtually on his own without

357

any assistance. Especially he had invested much energy and initiative in relation to the preservation of the extermination camp of Oswiecim (Aushwitz-Birkenau KL). Apart from his usual administrative functions within the MKiS, he fulfills the role of Secretary to the Presidium of Protection of Monuments of Struggle and Suffering. Mr. Poznański possesses comprehensive and detailed knowledge of the subject and expresses much passion and persuasive action in the implementation of his specific projects. Because of his unique commitment, he had been instrumental in reactivating the functions of the Presidium of Protection of Monuments of Struggle and Suffering to bring about proper planning and organisation of tasks necessary to maintain an effective team of management at the Auschwitz State Museum. It is also pertinent to note that Mr. Poznański is experiencing financial difficulties, hence, the Central Department of Museums and Protection of National Heritage asks for a positive resolution of this submission. Director, Kazimierz Malinowski.

Upon his return to Warsaw, my father was met with an unsettling surprise at his MKiS office. The weight of disappointment from his fruitless search for Leon still clung to him, and now he was confronted with yet another blow—a cold, bureaucratic document, referred to as the Protocol, was resting ominously upon his desk, awaiting his attention. The Protocol was signed by none other than Kazimierz Rusinek, the Vice-Minister and Director of the MKiS, a man who had often been at odds with my father's vision of preserving the true history of the Holocaust. Alongside Rusinek's signature were the names of three other influential figures: the Minister for Trade and Municipal Economy, the First Secretary of the Central Committee PZPR in Lublin, and the President of Lublin's Voivodeship National Council. Together, these men endorsed a decision that struck at the heart of what my father believed in.

The protocol outlined a plan to replace the proposed museum at Majdanek, one of the most notorious concentration camps where countless lives had been extinguished, with a Communal Catholic Cemetery. The justification given was the documented population growth and the expansion of the City of Lublin, which, according to these officials, necessitated transforming the former Majdanek KL grounds into a burial site for the Catholic community.

For my father, this decision was not just a matter of urban planning or municipal development. It was a profound desecration of the memory of the victims, a deliberate act of erasure that seemed to trivialise the horrors that had taken place on that very soil. The creation of a cemetery on the grounds of Majdanek, a place soaked in the blood and ashes of so many innocents, felt like a final, cruel insult to the dead—a way of burying the truth along with the victims; an act of further reshaping the narrative of Poland's past.

The planned museum at Majdanek was meant to stand as a testament to the suffering of the Jewish people and others, who had been murdered there. It was supposed to be a place of remembrance where the world could come to learn, mourn, and vow never to let such atrocities happen again. But now, with the stroke of a pen, that vision was being dismantled.

Though wearied by Moscow's recent disappointment, my father did not hesitate when faced with this new challenge. With its cold and calculated dismissal of Majdanek's significance, the protocol he found on his desk ignited a familiar fire within him. He knew that this was not merely a bureaucratic decision—it was a battle for memory, for history, and for the dignity of those who had perished in the darkest chapter of human history.

Without wasting a moment, he drafted his objections, his words infused with the weight of his convictions and the urgency of his mission. He did not simply see this as an administrative oversight; he saw it as a moral failing, a betrayal of the promise that the horrors of the Holocaust would never be forgotten. He framed his objections not just as a matter of historical accuracy but as a duty to the dead, a duty

359

to ensure that their suffering would be recognised and remembered in the way it deserved.

He brought his objections directly to two powerful allies: General Janusz Zarzycki, the President of ZBoWiD, and Kazimierz Banach, the President of the Council for Protection of Monuments of Struggle and Suffering. These were men who understood the stakes, had seen the horrors of war and shared, to some extent, the burden of memory that my father carried so profoundly. They listened, they understood, and they stood by him.

With their support, the matter was not allowed to linger in the lower echelons of bureaucracy. It quickly escalated and pushed up through the layers of government until it reached Poland's highest levels of power. The issue was brought before Polish Premier Józef Cyrankiewicz himself—a man who, despite the shifting political winds, still carried the weight of the nation's suffering on his shoulders, having been a prisoner of Auschwitz himself.

Cyrankiewicz, no stranger to the horrors that Majdanek represented, recognised the gravity of the situation. Perhaps it was the collective voice of those who had witnessed the atrocities, or maybe it was the undeniable force of my father's arguments, but the decision was swift. The protocol that had sought to erase Majdanek's memory, to replace it with a cemetery that would quietly bury the past, was annulled. The grounds of Majdanek would remain a site of memory, a place where the echoes of the past could still be heard, where the noise of the living would not drown out the silence of the dead.

For my father, this was a victory, but not a triumph. It was a reminder of the fragility of memory, of how easily the truth can be buried under layers of political expediency aimed to serve society's pressing needs of the present. It reinforced his resolve to continue the fight, to ensure that the history of the Holocaust would not be distorted or forgotten. But it also deepened his awareness of the forces arrayed against him—forces that saw the past not as a lesson to be learned but as an obstacle to be overcome, a narrative to be rewritten.

In this battle, my father stood firm, driven by the ghosts of those who could no longer speak for themselves, by the memory of a family lost, and by the conviction that some truths are too important to be forgotten. His victory in overturning the protocol was small in the grand scheme of things. Still, it was a crucial one, a reminder that even in the face of overwhelming odds, the fight for memory, history, and justice must continue.

∞∞∞∞

In 1960, as the weight of the past continued to press upon him, my father was deeply immersed in a project that resonated profoundly with his sense of duty and personal history. He was heavily involved in the initial establishment of the Mausoleum of Struggle and Suffering at Aleja Szucha—a place that had borne witness to some of the most unspeakable horrors during the Nazi occupation of Warsaw. The building at 25 Aleja Szucha (*English:* 25 Szucha's Alley), once an ordinary structure, had been transformed by the German occupants into a Gestapo Detention Centre and the Office of the Commander of the Gestapo Security Police and Secret Service. Between 1939 and 1945, its walls had absorbed the cries of thousands of Poles and Jews who were detained, tortured, and ultimately executed in its cold, dark basement. It was a place where hope had been systematically extinguished, where the brutal machinery of terror had stripped away humanity.

For my father, this project, like all the previous projects (e.g. Auschwitz-Birkenau KL; Majdanek KL), represented a sacred responsibility. The history of Aleja Szucha was intertwined with the fate of his people, and the creation of the Mausoleum was a way to ensure that this history would not be lost to time or diminished by the changing tides of political rhetoric. He approached the work with a professional and deeply personal determination, understanding that the preservation of this site was crucial for the memory of those who had suffered and died there. As he walked through the building's haunted corridors, he felt the silent echoes of those who had perished there filling the air. The establishment of the Mausoleum was his way of giving voice to those echoes and ensuring that the story of Aleja Szucha would be told in its whole, horrific truth. It was a story of struggle, suffering and courage in the face of unimaginable terror—a story of the enduring spirit of those who had resisted, even in their darkest moments of life.

As it began to take shape, the Mausoleum was a testament to the resilience of the human spirit. My father knew that it was not enough to remember the past; it was necessary to confront it, grapple with its complexities, and honour the memory of those who had been consumed by it. This project was his way of doing just that—of creating a space where future generations could come to understand the enormity of what had happened at Aleja Szucha and, by extension, throughout Nazi-occupied Poland. The work was painstaking and emotionally draining, but my father was driven by a purpose that outweighed the personal toll. He was acutely aware of the significance of this site, not just for Poland but for the world. The Mausoleum was to be a place of reflection, where the magnitude of the atrocities committed could be contemplated and where the lessons of the past could be learned.

In many ways, the creation of the Mausoleum of Struggle and Suffering was a continuation of the work he had begun at Auschwitz and other sites of mass extermination. It was a reaffirmation of his commitment to preserving the truth, to ensuring that the narrative of the Holocaust and the broader horrors of the war would not be co-opted or forgotten. It was also, perhaps, a way for him to channel his grief and find some measure of peace, in the act of preserving the memory of those who could no longer speak for themselves. Through his involvement in establishing the Mausoleum, my father once again stood as a guardian of memory, a keeper of the flame that burned in honour of those who had been lost. He took on a role with the total weight of his convictions, knowing that this work was essential so that history lessons would not be lost to the passage of time.

In 1961, as the shadows of the past continued to loom over him, my father was presented with a rare and significant opportunity—an invitation from the Soviet Chief Archivist, Mr. Petrov, to revisit Moscow. This invitation held the promise of access to vital documents that could have been crucial in deepening the historical understanding and preservation efforts at the Auschwitz State Museum. For my father, this was a chance to uncover truths that had been buried, to bring to light pieces of history that were essential to the narrative of the Holocaust—a narrative that had shaped his life and haunted his every step.

Yet, as this opportunity arose, so too did new obstacles. Around this time, my father found himself in the crosshairs of Kazimierz Rusinek, a Vice-Minister with deeply ingrained anti-Semitic views that made him a bitter opponent of my father's work and ideas. Rusinek, with his unwavering hostility, saw in my father's proposals not just a challenge to his authority but a threat to the nationalistic framework that he sought to promote within the Ministry. For Rusinek, the meticulous work of preserving Jewish history and ensuring that the Holocaust was remembered as it truly happened was an insult to the narrative he wished to sustain—a narrative that minimised Jewish suffering in favour of a broader, more palatable story of Polish heroism and martyrdom.

Rusinek's opposition was not just a matter of professional disagreement; it was deeply personal, rooted in a prejudice that was all too common in post-war Poland, where remnants of anti-Semitism continued to fester beneath the surface of public life. He became an immovable obstacle, using his power to block my father's every move. When the invitation from Moscow arrived, Rusinek saw it as an opportunity to assert his dominance and derail my father's efforts.

Despite the significance of the invitation, and despite the potential it held for advancing the work at Auschwitz and for uncovering truths that had long been hidden, Rusinek refused to allow my father to formally accept it. The much-anticipated trip to the USSR, a trip that could have been a turning point in the preservation of Holocaust history, was rejected outright. For my father, denying this opportunity symbolised his broader struggle—a struggle against a system that was increasingly hostile towards the work he was doing—a system that sought to erase the very history he was fighting to preserve. In the face of this rejection, my father felt a profound frustration and helplessness. It was a bitter reminder that the fight for memory, for truth, was not just against the passage of time but also against those who would seek to distort or erase the past for their own purposes.

Like on many other occasions, this incident weighed heavily on my father's spirit. It was another instance where his convictions were tested, where the ideals he held so dear were met with resistance from those who did not share his vision or his understanding of the importance of remembering the past as it indeed was. Yet, even in the face of such opposition, he remained steadfast in his beliefs, knowing that his work was essential for the memory of all those who had suffered and perished.

Not long after the crushing disappointment of being blocked from his work, my father's health took a severe turn. The stress gnawing at him for years finally manifested in a way that could not be ignored. He was admitted to hospital, where doctors initially feared the worst, suspecting a heart attack. The man who had endured so much and carried the weight of history and the burden of his ideals now seemed to be on the brink of a collapse from which he might not recover.

In those uncertain hours, his condition was grave enough that the doctors, fearing he wouldn't pull through, moved his bed out into the corridor, a stark reminder of the fragility of life. In this bleak setting, where the sterile lights of the hospital cast long shadows, his then-partner, Genia, became his vigilant guardian. She visited him daily, her presence a lifeline as she sat by his bed, watching over him during the long, uncertain nights. She would sit in the quiet of the night, listening to the faint, uneven rhythm of his breathing, a sound that seemed to echo the turmoil inside him.

There were moments when his breath would falter, moments when it seemed as though he might slip away into the sedated darkness. But Genia, determined and unwavering, would grab his limp hand and shake it as if she was pulling him out of the depths of death, refusing to let him go. She became his anchor in those small, desperate gestures, removing him from the edge of abys, each time he drifted too close. My father later told me that she had saved his life, and there was a profound sense of gratitude in his words, a deep acknowledgment of the debt he owed her, for those days in the hospital and for her care and love that had kept him tethered to life.

Yet, there was a mystery that lingered around that time—despite the severity of his condition and the fear that he might not survive, the doctors later concluded that his heart was strong, with no signs of a cardiac infarction. It was as if the physical symptoms of a heart attack were present, but the underlying cause remained elusive, perhaps hidden deep within the layers of stress, grief, and emotional turmoil that had been building for years.

This episode was more than a health scare; it was a manifestation of the internal emotional struggles that had slowly eroded his strength. The relentless pressures of his work, the personal losses he had endured, and the constant clash between his ideals and the harsh realities of the world around him—all had taken a toll no doctor could fully diagnose. The heart, after all, is not just a muscle; it is the seat of our deepest emotions, and in my father's case, it had borne too much for too long.

It became increasingly clear that my father's struggles went beyond the physical. The doctors who treated him focused on the visible signs—his racing heart, his shortness of breath—and concluded that he was suffering from what they termed "Cardiac Neurosis" (Polish: "Nerwica Serca"). But, on reflection, I believe the real cause was much deeper, hidden in the recesses of his mind and soul. What he was experiencing was not merely a bodily condition but a resurgence of a more profound and insidious affliction: the reactivation of his Chronic Post-Traumatic Stress Disorder. The trauma of his past, the loss of his family, the horrors he had witnessed during the war—these were wounds that had never fully healed. They lay dormant, buried beneath the surface, only to be awakened by the pressures and injustices he faced in the present. The re-traumatisation he experienced was not a return to those old memories but a reliving of the emotional pain, as accurate and as raw as it had been when it first occurred in response to the actual traumatic event.

Several significant issues likely led to this reactivation. The first was the way he was treated at work, particularly by Kazimierz Rusinek. Rusinek targeted my father with cruel, calculated bullying, excluding him and obstructing his projects. For a man like my father, whose sense of purpose and identity was so deeply tied to his work, this was more than professional frustration—it was a profound disenfranchisement, a stripping away of his sense of worth. Each time Rusinek undermined him, it felt as if he were being pushed further into the shadows, making him feel that his contributions, sacrifices, and even his presence were unwanted.

But something even more devastating was unfolding around the same time: the ideological shift under Gomułka's leadership. Gomułka's newly introduced policies, which reflected Poland's acceptance of the "Polish Path to Socialism," were thinly veiled attempts to gradually remove Polish Jews from government posts. For my father, who had always believed in the ideals of Communism, this was a bitter betrayal. This dual assault—being targeted and marginalised at work, and seeing his government adopt policies that echoed the prejudices of the past—must have felt like the ground shaking beneath his feet. The security and stability he had clung to were now truly crumbling around him. It is no wonder that his body reacted as it did, and that the symptoms of his Chronic Post-Traumatic Stress came roaring back with a vengeance.

In those moments, my father was not just fighting a battle within his mind—he was fighting against the resurgence of all the demons he had tried to leave behind. The pain of feeling excluded, the fear of being targeted for who he was, the deep sense of loss and betrayal—all of these came together in a perfect storm that has overwhelmed him.

This period reminded him that the past is never truly past and that present events can reopen old wounds. For my father, this re-traumatisation was a cruel twist of fate, a reminder that the struggles of his past could not simply be left behind but would continue to shape and haunt him for as long as he lived.

Despite the intense pressures and challenges that weighed on my father during those years, he found ways to cope and keep going. What kept him moving forward was a complex blend of personal resilience, deeply held convictions and a sense of duty to the memory of those who had perished.

First and foremost, my father's dedication to his work was a critical anchor during these turbulent times. He believed passionately in preserving the truth about the atrocities committed during the Holocaust, not only for historical accuracy but also as a means to honour the memory of his lost family and the countless others who had perished. This sense of purpose was a driving force that enabled him to push through the barriers placed before him by those who sought to distort or diminish the truth.

His work was a mission. Every project he undertook and every battle he fought within the MKiS kept the memory of his loved ones alive. The idea that he could contribute to something greater than himself—something that would stand as a testament to the horrors of the past and a warning for the future—gave him a reason to endure the daily struggles he faced.

Moreover, my father's sense of responsibility to the Jewish community in Poland was central to his perseverance. He honoured the pleas of Fiszgrund and Mark, who implored him to stay in Poland to safeguard the memory of Jewish martyrdom. He knew that leaving would not only mean abandoning his work but also leave a void in the fight against the erasure of Jewish history in Poland. This sense of duty, together with the awareness that he was one of the few remaining voices for this cause, kept him anchored even when the weight of his burdens seemed unbearable.

Emotionally, my father was sustained by the support of those closest to him. Though he was not one to openly share his deepest fears and traumas, the presence of people like Genia, who stood by him through his painful moments, gave him hope and resilience. Her vigilance during his hospitalisation, quiet strength, and unwavering presence reminded him that he was not entirely alone in his struggles. The gratitude he felt toward her was not only for her care during his illness but also for the emotional solace she provided in a world that often felt cold and hostile.

Inwardly, my father's resilience was also strengthened by his ability to compartmentalise his traumatic memories. The reactivation of his chronic post-traumatic stress might have been overwhelming, but he had, over the years, learned to navigate the storms of his psyche with stoic endurance. While the trauma would never entirely leave him, he found ways to manage it—through quiet moments of reflection and meaningful connections with those who understood him.

In the autumn of 1961, unexpected windstorms swept across Birkenau KL, tearing through the camp with a force that seemed almost symbolic of the turbulence in my father's life. The roofs of many barracks were severely damaged, leaving them vulnerable to the elements, just as my father felt exposed to the shifting political winds around him. Upon returning to work, he promptly submitted a proposal to allocate a significant budget to repair the storm-damaged buildings. For him, this was a matter of respect, of ensuring that the physical remnants of the past were maintained as witnesses to the horrors that had unfolded there. But as he had come to expect, Vice-Minister Rusinek did not favourably regard his budget proposal. The proposal was dismissed not on its merits but for reasons that ran deeper, more insidiously, into the undercurrents of the political landscape. My father had long sensed Rusinek's animosity, but it was during this time that he fully grasped the reality: he was being targeted simply because he was a Polish Jew.

This realisation struck him at the very heart of his identity, a stark reminder of the suppressed reality he had tried to reconcile with his communist ideals. Yet here he was, in communist Poland, facing the same ancient hatred that had plagued his people for centuries. With Gomułka's Thaw in full swing, it became increasingly clear that anti-Semitism, though often hidden, was not only surviving but also thriving once again. The storm that had damaged the barracks at Birkenau KL was nothing compared to the storm brewing within him—a storm of disillusionment, grief, and painful awakening to the reality that even in communist Poland, the old prejudices had never truly died.

Yet, even in the face of this harsh truth, my father did not abandon his work. He knew that preserving Birkenau KL and remembering

369

what had happened there was more important than ever. It was not just about repairing buildings; it was about restoring the narrative and ensuring that the truth of the Holocaust was not lost amid political machinations and the resurgence of old, ingrained attitudes. This work, this commitment to memory, became both his burden and his solace, a way to cope with the overwhelming challenges that threatened to consume him.

In those moments, as he fought against the tide of anti-Semitism and the indifference of those in power, my father's resilience shone through. He understood that his struggle was not just personal—it was part of a broader battle for truth, justice, and the preservation of a history too many wished to forget or distort. In that struggle, he found the strength to continue, even as the world around him seemed determined to undo everything he believed in.

Kazimierz Rusinek, Vice-Minister of the MKiS; former Kapo in Mauthausen Concentration Camp. Activist within the Polish Socialist Party and a passionate supporter of a Polish reactionary Nationalist, Mieczysław Moczar, who organised anti-Semitic political action against the so-called 'Zionists', which took place in Poland in March 1968 [1] and continued throughout 1969. [2]

The worst was yet to come. In April 1962, my father received another protocol, this time outlining plans that filled him with a sense of impending dread. The document proposed a new roadway that would cut through the grounds of Auschwitz-Birkenau KL, a place sacred to the memory of those who perished there. The decision was endorsed at a Regional Committee meeting in Cracow and approved by the Presidium of the Regional National Council. The roadway was to extend across the protected area, perilously close to Auschwitz's Block 11, where the infamous 'Wall of Death' stood—a site where countless prisoners had met their end. Nearby stood the Theatergebaude building, once a repository for the personal possessions of the murdered victims, carefully sorted and sent to Germany, a grim reminder of the systematic cruelty that had taken place there. The proposal to pave over this piece of ground was signed by none other than Lucjan Motyka, the first Secretary of the Regional Commission of the PZPR, a name that sent a chill down my father's spine.

Motyka's signature on the protocol was not merely a bureaucratic formality but a personal vendetta, a way to brandish his teeth once again. My father knew this was no mere coincidence. Motyka had not forgotten my father's complaint letter to Edward Ochab in 1950. That letter, which had once caused a rift between them, now seemed to haunt my father like a spectre from the past. But this time, the stakes were higher, and the political landscape more treacherous. The covertly anti-Semitic climate seeping into every corner of Polish society left my father little room to manoeuvre. He knew that any misstep could have dire consequences.

Yet my father could not, in good conscience, accept the protocol. With a determined heart, he refused to support it. He responded to Motyka's proposal by citing the 1949 Act, which protected such sites from desecration. It was a stand that took courage and left him in a precarious position.

Two weeks later, he was summoned to the Minister's Office within the MKiS. Minister Galinski, who had always treated my father with a semblance of respect, greeted him with a friendly demeanour, but the words that followed were fraught with much more profound meaning. "Henryk," Galinski said gently, "it is easy to disagree and to reject, but it is more difficult to agree and to accept." There was no mistaking the underlying message. Galinski advised caution, urging my father to tread carefully in these uncertain times. He assured my father that he had placed Motyka's proposal on hold and would await further instructions. But the unspoken advice was clear: it would be wise not to take any further action on the matter.

My father left the office that day with a profound sense of frustration and helplessness. The struggle he had been engaged in for so many years—the fight to preserve the memory of those who perished and to ensure that places like Auschwitz-Birkenau were treated with the reverence they deserved—was now under threat from forces far more insidious than he had anticipated. Even so, my father remained resolute. He knew he could not allow the memory of the Holocaust to be paved over, either literally or metaphorically. The road ahead was uncertain, but he would continue to walk it, guided by the conviction that some things were too important to be compromised, no matter the cost.

My father, 1961

Notes

1. Stola, Dariusz (2017). Anti-Zionism as a Multipurpose Policy Instrument: The Anti-Zionist Campaign in Poland, 1967–1968. The Journal of Israeli History, Vol. 25, No. 1, March 2006, p. 178.
2. https://pl.wikipedia.org/wiki/Kazimierz_Rusinek_(polityk)

15. Poland's 1968 Anti-Zionist Chimera

When my father entered an exceptionally early retirement at 43, his life became a complex tapestry of emotions. It must have felt like bitter irony: to have fought for a new Poland, only to be cast aside not for lack of merit but because of his innate identity—his Jewish heritage. His life's work, preserving the memory of the millions who perished in the Holocaust, was marred by the quiet resurgence of anti-Semitism within the very ranks of those who were supposed to be his comrades. In the silence of his early "special pension," he was left to grapple with the ghosts of his past. The faces of his parents, brothers, and the family he could not save continued to haunt him. He had aspired to keep their memory alive in a nation that, despite all its sacrifices, was still unwilling to fully acknowledge the Jewish tragedy. The monuments and museums he helped establish and strived to protect had become symbols of his own struggle, one he could not resolve within himself. And yet, through it all, something kept him going—perhaps the stubbornness that had always defined him, the will to endure despite every obstacle thrown in his path. He had lost much, yet he was not broken. While his ideals had not withered with age or disappointment, he came to a cold realisation that, in his homeland, the promises of Communism had not materialised as he had envisioned.

My father's later years reflected a man wrestling with both his past and his future. His mind was a battleground where memories of loss and betrayal clashed with a yearning for hope. He must have found solace in small things—the quiet moments with those who loved him, the knowledge that his work, even if thwarted by politics, had left a mark on history. The battle for memory and truth was one he never truly abandoned. In the end, what kept him going was perhaps the most human of impulses: love. Love for his family, his unshaken ideals, and love for his homeland, Poland. His life, like that of so many who survived the horrors of war and oppression, was defined by resilience. Even in the face of betrayal, even as the world around him shifted in ways he could not accept, he remained true to his sense of justice and dignity. He carried the weight of history on his shoulders, yet he did not succumb to it. In many ways, he was a living testament to the idea that even in a world filled with suffering and injustice, the human spirit could endure, resist, and still find purpose and meaning.

The tide of hatred and deceit had finally engulfed my father in 1968—a year of profound moral distress, despair, and, hardest of all, the choice to leave Poland for good.

After Israel's stunning victory in the Six-Day War of 1967, the Polish Government, closely aligned with Soviet interests, unleashed a flood of anti-Israeli rhetoric. The propaganda machine roared to life, spewing vitriol that cast Israel not as a nation defending its very existence but as an imperialist aggressor backed by the United States. Every newspaper, radio broadcast, and television segment painted a portrait of tiny Israel as the villain, mercilessly attacking its four Arab neighbours—Egypt, Syria, Iraq, and Jordan. What was omitted from these messages and carefully concealed from the Polish people was the reality that those Arab states, armed to their teeth with Soviet-supplied jets and tanks, had attacked Israel with the singular, chilling goal of erasing it from the map. Their leaders openly called for the annihilation of the Jewish state and the extermination of the Jewish people once again. The rhetoric in the Arab capitals was eerily reminiscent of Europe's darkest days. Yet the Polish media twisted the narrative, portraying Israel as the powerful aggressor against peaceful, innocent Islamic nations.

For my father, this blatant distortion of the truth was unbearable. He had lived through the horrors of anti-Semitic persecution; he had seen firsthand how propaganda could be wielded as a weapon to justify unimaginable atrocities. Now, he was witnessing the resurgence of that same poisonous ideology—this time, not under the banner of Nazism, but cloaked in the language of Socialism, anti-Zionism, and anti-Imperialism.

He felt the walls closing in around him, not just politically but personally. The anti-Israel stance of the government was not merely a matter of international policy; it quickly morphed into an all-out attack on Polish Jews themselves. Jews, once again, were branded as outsiders, as disloyal citizens whose allegiance lay not with Poland but with the distant Jewish land. The old ghost of the "Żydo-Komuna" (i.e. Jewish Communist Conspiracy) resurfaced—Jews as the architects of Communism, now recast as enemies of the State because of their suspected ties to Israel and the USA.

In these bleak days, my father's heart must have ached with a painful recognition. This was not the Poland he had fought for. This was not the socialist dream he had believed in with every fibre of his being. Instead, it was the bitter realisation that the Jew hatred was never extinguished. It had merely gone underground, only to resurface again, uglier and more insidious than ever.

I can still see him sitting at the table in the loungeroom, gazing through the window, the shadows lengthening as dusk fell, feeling the weight of Gomulka's anti-Zionist propaganda pressing down on him. His struggle and his sacrifices—it seemed as though it all had been for nothing. Poland, the land he had loved and served, once again was betraying its tiny remnant population of citizens with Jewish heritage. This wave of propaganda, this vicious campaign against Israel and Jews, was like rubbing salt into unhealed old wounds for my father. The lies, the twisted narrative, and the vilification of the Zionists seemed all too familiar. And yet, what could he do? He might have fought back, written letters, and spoken out in his younger days. But in 1968, there was no room for resistance. The walls had closed in too tightly, and my father resigned himself to this bleak reality. He watched as more friends and colleagues left Poland, the only home they had ever known. He watched as the fabric of the remnant Polish Jewish community, already so fragile after the Holocaust, began to unravel completely.

And yet, even in his resignation, I believe my father carried a quiet defiance. As a 48 year old pensioner, he may not have had the strength to fight the propaganda machine, but he did not give in to its lies. In his heart, he knew the truth. He knew what Israel stood for and what his immediate surroundings had become.

The year 1968 brought my father a level of distress I had never witnessed before. At the same time, despite the challenges he faced, particularly after being forced into early retirement in 1962 at the age of 43, he had always found ways to stay engaged, motivated, and optimistic. My father was never one to sit idle; he filled his life with projects and activities that kept his mind sharp and his spirit active.

In 1964, he co-authored a book with Janusz Rawicz, *A Guide to Places of Struggle and Suffering in Poland Between 1939 and 1945*. The book was written under the auspices of the Ministry of Culture and Art (MKiS), a project that must have given him a sense of purpose. In 1965, he enrolled at Warsaw University to study German Philology. In 1966, he spent almost six months visiting his cousin in Paris—a rare and cherished opportunity to experience life beyond Poland's tight political and social confines. In 1967, he decided to remodel the kitchen, a seemingly small project in which I vividly remember being personally involved. In these ordinary activities, he found solace and, perhaps, a way to keep himself anchored amid the unsettling events unfolding around him.

Another aspect of his life was also new and vibrant. In 1961, my father remarried. Theresa (Wiesia) and my half-brother, Roman, brought new hope and energy during these challenging years, when

377

the shadows of geopolitical tensions were ever-present, lurking just behind the veneer of normalcy.

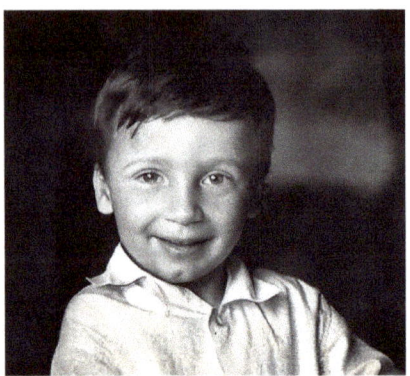

Romek

Wiesia

I recall one particular outing towards the end of May 1967, when my father and I went to the local cinema. In those days, every film screening began with a short preview—a 15-minute black-and-white film presenting a collage of current affairs and political events from the past two weeks. This "newsreel" was State-controlled, of course, but it was still a window into the broader world, albeit heavily curated. On that occasion, I remember watching Nasser's fiery speeches in Egypt. The film depicted Poland, alongside the brotherly Soviet Union, as firmly aligned with the Arab states. These states were portrayed as on the right side of history, receiving ample military support from the Eastern Bloc to fend off what was framed as Israel's "expansionist aggression." Even as a child, I sensed the gravity of the situation—this wasn't just distant foreign politics. This was a conflict that touched something deep within my father, and, by extension, something personal within me. As we sat in the dimly lit theatre, the tension in the air felt palpable. I remember turning to my father and asking, in a whisper, "Tata, what will happen to the Jewish people in

Israel?" He leaned towards me closer, and with a calm and measured voice, he replied softly, "Don't worry, son. Israel is not going to sit and wait to be destroyed."

I remember his response to me felt both reassuring and defiant. Despite the overwhelming odds—four Arab states, backed by the full force of the Soviet Union and its allies, including Poland—my father remained composed. Deep down, it was as if he knew history had not yet written its final chapter. He seemed to believe that Israel, small though it was, would not fall without a fight. It struck me then that my father's calm was not born of naiveté but of hard-won wisdom. He had seen enough in his lifetime to know that those who had survived past horrors would not be so easily erased.

Yet, as calm as he appeared on the surface, I wondered what thoughts must have been racing through his mind. How much of his composure was, for my sake, to shield me from the fear and uncertainty he may have felt within? The propaganda machine in Poland was in full force, twisting the narrative to suit its purposes, while the more profound truth—the survival of a people—remained unspoken.

That brief exchange in the cinema was just the beginning. What followed in 1968 would shatter whatever fragile calm remained in my father's life. The evenings became a sanctuary for him when he would sit by the radio, tuning into the crackling, forbidden voice of the West: 'Radio Free Europe.' It was an act of quiet defiance against the oppressive weight of the Polish government's propaganda machine. Each night, he would strain to hear the world beyond Poland's borders, a world where truth had not yet been drowned in the murky waters of State-controlled narratives. I can still picture him leaning forward, focused, adjusting the dial with precision, his ear catching the faint, interrupted signals that cut through the noise, offering him a lifeline to another reality.

The news that flowed from that battered old-fashioned radio was unlike anything Polish media would dare to report. To the State-run broadcasters, Israel was painted as the imperialist aggressor, backed by the West, a tiny Goliath threatening the helpless Arab nations. But my father knew better. He knew the truth lay in those muffled reports sneaking across the airwaves. I imagine there was a flicker of pride, perhaps even a quiet joy, when he learned that tiny Israel had done the impossible—crushed the armies of its much larger adversaries in a mere six days.

For my father, that victory meant more than just a military triumph. It was a beacon of resilience, of survival against overwhelming odds. As a man who had lived through unimaginable horrors, who had lost everything, this triumph must have stirred something in his soul—a vindication of sorts, a reminder that even the smallest of nations, the most persecuted of peoples, could stand tall in the face of annihilation. Like his own, Israel's survival in those six days symbolised hope. Yet, amidst this fleeting joy, I sensed a quiet sorrow, for in communist Poland, to feel such joy for Israel's victory was to live in silent rebellion against the rising tide of anti-Semitism, a force that had never truly disappeared.

The early promise of Gomułka's '*Polish Path Towards Socialism*' had, by the mid-1960s, devolved into a growing sense of disappointment among the Polish masses. When Gomułka first rose to power in 1956, many believed that he might guide Poland toward a more independent future, free from the iron grip of Soviet control. There was hope that Poland could carve out a new path that allowed for national sovereignty while still maintaining its place within the Warsaw Pact. For a time, Gomułka seemed to strike a delicate balance, navigating between the demands of Moscow and the growing yearning for change at home. But as the years passed, it became clear that this hope was fragile, and the reality of daily life remained bleak. People were tired of the State-run media's relentless portrayal of progress and prosperity while their lives remained marred by food shortages, low wages, and a lack of opportunities. The shops, with their drab displays and bare shelves, mirrored the state of the country—stagnant, colourless, and weighed down by an economy that couldn't deliver the future Gomułka had once promised. A future of prosperity seemed ever more distant, while the allure of Western products, with their vibrant colours and superior quality, mocked the dreariness of Polish life. Anything from the West that managed to slip through the cracks—a bar of chocolate, a piece of clothing—felt like a glimpse into a world that was unattainable but tantalisingly close.

Gomułka was caught in a paradox. His *"Polish Path"* required loyalty to the USSR but also demanded that he address the increasingly vocal discontent in his nation. He was forced to walk a tightrope to keep the Soviet Union's confidence while managing the rising frustrations of the Polish people, who were growing weary of empty promises. It was a delicate dance that grew harder to maintain as the years went by.

The situation worsened when Alexander Dubček rose to power in neighbouring Czechoslovakia in 1968. Dubček's bold reforms, which sought to introduce liberalisation and democratisation, sent shockwaves across the Eastern Bloc. It was a vision of Socialism unlike anything the Warsaw Pact countries had seen—Socialism with a human face. To the Polish people, struggling under the weight of Gomułka's rigid rule, it was a glimpse of what could be. But to Gomułka and the Soviet leadership, it was a threat. The idea that such reforms could occur in the Eastern Bloc was unthinkable, further exposing the cracks in Poland's political landscape.

For my father, these developments confirmed the internal conflicts he had been grappling with for years. He had placed his faith in the communist vision, believing it could bring equality and justice. But the reality of what has unfolded was far from the ideal he had hoped for. The new Poland—one that could rise from the ashes of war and stand on its own as an inclusive society—was now a mere delusion. The whole nation seemed to be sinking back into the shadows of control, stagnation, and disillusionment.

It was becoming clear that even in this new "Socialist" Poland, the old prejudices remained, simmering beneath the surface, ready to emerge when the political winds would shift or when Poland's foreign policy proved to be a lost cause, driven by the 'Big Brother'—the Soviet Union.

The unravelling of Poland's political landscape reached a critical moment in early 1968, when Adam Mickiewicz's play Dziady (The Wretched) unexpectedly became the catalyst for a dramatic cultural and political confrontation. The play, a beloved masterpiece of Polish literature, had long held a special place in the hearts of Polish intellectuals, artists, and everyday citizens. For nearly two centuries, it had been celebrated for its themes of resistance and national pride, and for its implicit critique of Russian imperialism, written during the period of Tsarist rule from 1815 to 1918.

But in February 1968, this iconic work was at the centre of a storm that no one could have anticipated. A Soviet delegate visiting Warsaw attended a performance of *Dziady* and left the theatre both shocked and offended. What had been a long-standing symbol of Poland's cultural defiance against Russian Tsarist oppression was now interpreted as a thinly veiled critique of the Soviet Union itself. The delegate reported back to Moscow, and soon enough, the message came directly from the top: Brezhnev's voice echoed in Warsaw with a sharp command—*"Vieslav! You've got to shut down that play!"*

The demand from Moscow put Gomułka in an impossible position. On the one hand, he had to maintain the façade of Poland's cultural autonomy, part of his delicate balancing act with the Polish people. On the other, there was no room to defy Moscow's will, especially on something as deeply symbolic as anti-Russian sentiment. Gomułka knew that yielding to Brezhnev's command risked igniting even more discontent among the Polish intelligentsia and youth, already frustrated by the oppressive political atmosphere.

For my father, this incident marked a turning point—a stark reminder of how fragile Poland's sovereignty was. The play itself, a timeless expression of Polish defiance against foreign domination, now became a symbol of the country's continued subjugation under Soviet rule. To see a play like *Dziady* censored at Moscow's whim was a profound insult to Polish pride and heritage. The idea that even art, a medium through which Poles had historically expressed their longing for freedom, could be so quickly stifled underscored the harsh reality of life under Gomułka's regime.

The censorship of *Dziady* was not just an act of political obedience to the Soviet Union; it was a silencing of the Polish soul. Mickiewicz's words, which had given voice to generations of Poles in their fight for self-determination, were smothered by the ideology that was supposed to champion the people's cause. With that bold move to suppress *Dziady*, a powerful ripple of defiance surged through Warsaw's intellectual circles, and soon, it was the students of Warsaw University who took up the banner of protest. For them, *Dziady* symbolised Poland's struggle for autonomy and dignity, embodying its resistance against foreign domination. The decision to silence Mickiewicz's words ignited a fire that had long been smouldering beneath the surface—a fire fuelled by frustration with the Soviet-imposed regime and the continuous erosion of Poland's economy and sovereignty. [1]

As the students marched down Krakowskie Przedmieście, their chants echoed through the streets, a rallying cry for freedom of speech and the right to openly discuss Poland's relationship with the Soviet Union. What had begun as a protest against the censorship of a play quickly transformed into something much larger—an outcry against the Soviet oppression that had gripped the country for decades. It was a pivotal moment, crystallising the growing dissatisfaction with Gomułka's government and its subservience to Moscow.

My father watched these events unfold with a mixture of hope and despair. On the one hand, the youth—bright, passionate, and unafraid—dared to voice the very frustrations that had weighed on his heart as a young man. On the other hand, he knew all too well the dangers that came with defying the system. The protests of March 1968 were not just a student rebellion; they were a confrontation with a deeply entrenched power structure that had little tolerance for dissent.

As the protests intensified, the streets of Warsaw descended into chaos. The PZPR party machine struggled to contain the rising tide of social discontent. Students clashed with riot police, their voices drowned out by the sound of truncheons and boots. Intellectuals, writers, and artists—many of whom had once supported Gomułka's vision of a "*Polish Path To Socialism*"—now stood in solidarity with the students, demanding an end to censorship and repression.

For my father, this has been a painful paradox. Here was a generation, free from the traumas of war, daring to challenge the very system he had believed could deliver equality and justice. And yet their cries for freedom echoed the same desire for autonomy and dignity that had driven him through the darkest days of the Nazi occupation. He found himself torn once again, between his deep convictions in the ideals of Marxism and his growing realisation that the system in place was failing to deliver on its promises. It was not based on Marxist ideology but rather on nationalist socialist revisionism.

The student protests reflected a nation yearning for something more. They expressed a deep-rooted desire for liberation, not only from Soviet control but also from the moral compromises that had come to define life in post-war Poland. For those like my father, the protests stirred something profound—a recognition that the path ahead was more complex and uncertain than he had ever imagined.

Gomułka, fearing the demonstrations could spark broader dissent, unleashed something far darker. With the guidance of Mieczysław Moczar, the notorious Minister for Internal Affairs, Gomułka set in motion the 'fall-back' tactic he had prepared with Khrushchev years earlier—the age-old strategy of scapegoating the Jews. The sudden pivot to an anti-Zionist campaign was a chilling reminder of how deep the roots of anti-Semitism ran, even in a communist state that claimed to fight inequality and prejudice.

For my father, this was a moment of bitter disillusionment. How could it be that a nation so ravaged by war could so easily be manipulated into believing that a tiny remnant population of Jewish Holocaust survivours—was somehow to blame for the country's woes? It was absurd to think that 30,000 middle-aged Polish Jews, along with their children and the elderly, could wield such influence in a nation of 32 million Poles.

The ground had already been prepared the previous year. The anti-Israeli bias that swept through Poland following Israel's victory in the Six-Day War had morphed into a fully-fledged anti-Zionist campaign in March 1968. It was an easy leap for the government to equate Zionism with treason and to portray the Jews as a subversive element within the Polish state. Gomułka, ever the opportunist, seized this moment to solidify his position, using the tiny remnant Jewish community as scapegoats to deflect attention from the real issues— Poland's failing economy and the growing discontent with communist rule.

When Gomułka addressed the Polish United Workers' Party (PZPR) on 19 March 1968, the scene was a spectacle of orchestrated fervour. As he stepped into the Congress Hall of the Sejm, the gathered members began chanting in unison, urging him to be bold and speak his mind about the supposed Jewish conspiracy that had thrown Poland into chaos. "Wiesław, śmielej!" (English: "Vieslav, be bold") they chanted, urging him to unleash his accusations against the Zionists. After several minutes of this mantra-like chant, Gomułka finally began his speech. His words were carefully chosen, yet the message was clear. He spoke of Zionism, disloyalty, and subversion—but everyone in that hall knew who he was talking about. The Jews, they were "the problem".

For my father, this speech was a cruel betrayal delivered in a cold, condescending tone, a final nail in the coffin of the communist ideal and its core principles of equality and solidarity. Gomułka, clearly and boldly, invoked those very principles to justify intolerance and hate. The anti-Zionist campaign that followed was relentless. Jews were purged from government posts, universities, and public institutions. [2]

March 19th, 1968 - Wladyslaw Gomulka at the Congress Hall of the Polish Parliament – the Sejm

The media's message to the masses became an unwavering echo of Gomułka's passionate rhetoric. Day after day, newspapers, radio broadcasts, and television programs hammered home the urgent call: it was time to "wake up and realise that the Zionists are ruling Poland under our noses, and as long as we allow this, there will be no positive change for the Polish nation." These words seeped into the collective consciousness of the Polish people, absorbed eagerly like parched earth soaking up the rain. Rumours ignited and spread with alarming speed, whispered in markets, echoed in factories, and discussed in hushed tones over family dinners. The notion that Jews were overrepresented in government branches, infiltrating every department, took on a life of its own. These unfounded yet potent whispers fanned the flames of suspicion and dissatisfaction that had been smouldering beneath the surface. The idea of an unseen enemy manipulating the nation's fate offered a simple explanation for their complex hardships.

Masses poured into the streets, not in protest but in support of Gomułka. They carried banners, chanted slogans, and united their voices into a single cry in support of the government's stance. Radio and television broadcasts amplified these demonstrations, showcasing Gomułka's passionate speeches and portraying a nation united against a familiar foe. Suddenly, there was an answer to the question: Why had life in Poland become so stagnant and unfulfilling? It's because of the Zionist Jews.

For my father, this was a time of profound despair and isolation. He watched as his fellow countrymen, people he had stood shoulder to shoulder with during the war, now turned against a small, vulnerable remnant Jewish community. The irony was bitter: the very people who had suffered immeasurable losses were now being blamed for the nation's woes. The anti-Semitic undercurrents that had once lurked in the shadows were now boldly coursing through the mainstream, sanctioned and propagated by those in power.

He understood only too well how the government's manipulative tactics preyed on the populace's frustrations. The promise of prosperity under Socialism had not materialised for many Poles. The economy was stagnant, opportunities were scarce, and the monotony of daily life weighed heavily on their spirits. It was all too easy for them to accept the narrative that an internal enemy was to blame and that expelling this "hidden" adversary would pave the way for national rejuvenation. The mass rallies, the fervent support for Gomułka, and the unquestioning acceptance of propaganda—all harkened back to darker times. There was no doubt in my father's mind that such blind allegiance could only lead a nation torn between its ideals and the seduction of scapegoating and prejudice.

He confided in a few trusted friends, sharing his fears in whispered conversations behind closed doors. "They are chasing shadows," he would say, his voice tinged with sorrow. "Blaming the innocent will not fill empty shelves or warm cold homes in winter." Yet, he knew his words were like pebbles thrown into a vast ocean, creating ripples that would quickly fade away.

As the campaign intensified, so did his sense of urgency. He contemplated his family's future, but the thought of leaving his homeland filled him with a profound ache. Yet the encroaching darkness left him with few illusions. Staying might mean enduring a resurgence of the very hatred he had fought his entire life. The betrayal cut deep into his soul, leaving wounds time alone could not heal. [3]

In simple terms, the media spread a narrative that prominent Jewish intellectuals and politicians, including Kuron, Michnik, Staszewski, Modzelewski, Berman, and Zambrowski, were secretly Zionists. It was implied that these individuals, despite their roles in the Polish political system, cared more about Israel than Poland. The message was clear: they were part of a revisionist force working against Poland's interests and undermining the socialist future that Gomułka's government was striving to build.

Party members and much of Polish society believed this message. The belief took root that Zionists had infiltrated the government and were conspiring to destabilise the country's security from within. This conspiracy theory portrayed the "Zionists," as a hidden enemy, an anti-Polonist force that had to be eradicated.

The media played a central role in spreading these views. The front pages of Trybuna Ludu (the People's Tribune, the PZPR's leading newspaper) featured images of street demonstrations, with banners denouncing Zionism. Anti-Zionist rhetoric filled the papers, often using caricatures of Jews with exaggerated features and huge noses. These satirical depictions reinforced old stereotypes, dehumanising Jews, and promoting anti-Semitism in public discourse. The orchestrated government message was that Zionists, operating under the guise of Polish intellectuals, were inciting the student protests at Warsaw University. This propaganda framed the Jewish intellectuals not as critics of Gomułka's government but as enemies of the State, leading an assault on Poland's national interests from within. [4]

In those days, it was difficult to point fingers and accuse Gomułka of harbouring anti-Semitic sentiments. After all, his wife was Jewish, and that fact alone seemed to provide a convenient shield against such allegations. Moreover, within the ideological framework of Communism, any form of racism—anti-Semitism included—was officially condemned and strictly forbidden. Communism, with its principles of equality, was seen by many as a sanctuary for Jews who had faced centuries of persecution. It promised a world free of racial hatred, where nationalist tendencies and the prejudices they bred would be eradicated. For my father and countless others, Communism was supposed to be the ideological fortress that would finally protect the Jewish people from the age-old menace of anti-Semitism.

But, the reality was far more complex. Behind Gomułka's communist veneer lay a more insidious truth. Despite his outward appearance, he shared the tacit nationalist values of his fellow members of the Central Committee of the PZPR. These men, many of whom had quietly slipped into the party's ranks in the mid-1950s after Stalin had banned the PPS, clung to their nationalist and anti-Semitic beliefs. They had been loyal to leaders such as Piasecki, Rusinek, Moczar, and Motyka, and now they rallied around Gomułka as he carried the mantle of leadership.

Polish workers and members of the PZPR Party demonstrating.
against the Zionists in their midst

It was this loyalty to Gomułka and his vision of a "National Socialism" that allowed these hidden currents of anti-Semitism to resurface in post-war Poland. What was meant to be a haven of equality under Communism became instead a place where Polish Jews found themselves targeted. However, this time, it was couched in political anti-Zionist rhetoric rather than overt racial hatred. [5]

Moczar understood the sentiments of the Polish people and the deep-seated currents of nationalism that lay beneath the surface of the political landscape. He recognised that most Poles were indifferent to Poland's support of Arab states against Israel in the war. For many, this was a distant conflict with little personal relevance. However, Moczar saw an opportunity to harness this indifference into something more powerful—a resurgence of nationalist sentiment that he could exploit to his advantage.

In a cunning move, he convinced Gomułka that the so-called "Zionists" within the government were nothing less than a "fifth column," a hidden and subversive group working to destabilise the Polish state from within. For Gomułka, who was already facing growing pressure and unrest, this perspective provided a clear and convenient enemy to target.

By embracing Moczar's vision, Gomułka empowered him to incite nationalist and anti-Semitic elements within the government and broader society. Moczar played his cards skilfully, reviving the sentiments of right-wing nationalist factions and Home Army loyalists, who had long harboured grievances against Jews. He found fertile ground in a society where anti-Semitic values, though suppressed under the veneer of communist equality, had never entirely disappeared. For Moczar, this was the perfect moment to consolidate his power within Gomułka's administration by stirring up these dangerous sentiments.

Moczar's strategy was insidious, as it allowed Poles to express their anti-Semitic beliefs openly, no longer constrained by the ideals of communist unity and solidarity. He cast Jews, or "hidden Zionists," as enemies within—individuals loyal not to Poland but to their self-serving interests and the State of Israel. These so-called Zionists were portrayed as saboteurs, spreading hatred towards the actual "Indigenous Poles"—the Polish Catholic faithful. Moczar's rhetoric legitimised prejudices that had long simmered beneath the surface. He presented Jews not merely as outsiders but as an existential threat to the very fabric of Polish identity.

Moczar, with his keen understanding of Polish society's undercurrents, knew his anti-Semitic campaign would resonate deeply with Home Army loyalists. These individuals held a long-standing grudge against the Soviets and, even more so, against the Polish Jews who had returned with the Soviet forces in 1945 and swiftly assumed positions of power in the newly established government. To the Home Army (AK), these Jews were not only communist collaborators but also the very obstacle that had prevented AK from taking its rightful place in Poland's leadership. Moczar exploited this deep-seated resentment with precision, orchestrating a campaign of anti-Semitic persecution that would sweep through the Polish government and society like a tidal wave. [6]

Moczar's tactic was simple yet devastatingly effective. He ordered the Ministry of Internal Affairs (MSW) to investigate the backgrounds of public servants, university professors, journalists, and factory workers alike. Anyone with Jewish heritage, however distant, became a target. These individuals, regardless of their contributions to society, were systematically bullied, marginalised, and dismissed from their posts. It was a purge reminiscent of Europe's darkest times, with Moczar defining Jewish people, particularly those in the communist PZPR Party, as enemies of the State. The "Zionists," as they were labelled, were made to carry the burden of Poland's political and economic woes, scapegoated for everything that had gone wrong in the years since the war.

In a chillingly Goebbels-like fashion, Moczar crafted an image of the Zionist as a sinister figure lurking behind every misfortune. In his propaganda, a Zionist was not just a political opponent; they were the embodiment of evil itself. He portrayed them as scheming, manipulative political imposters who had wormed their way into positions of power only to betray the working class. They were provocateurs, saboteurs, and elitists who cared nothing for the common Polish people. Moczar's Zionist was a figure devoid of morals, a corrupt politician with no allegiance to Poland or to Communism, but rather a cosmopolitan puppet of American imperialism. A Zionist was not just a Jewish nationalist but an enemy of the working masses, an anti-egalitarian influencer seeking to undermine everything the communist state stood for. Moczar's rhetoric, dripping with venom, painted Zionists as exclusivists—people who separated themselves from the struggles of ordinary Poles, caring only for their own narrow interests and not for the collective good. This portrayal fit neatly into the growing nationalist fervour, feeding the belief that Poland had been infiltrated by foreign Jewish agents seeking to manipulate and exploit the country for their own gain. Moczar's rhetoric tapped into the darkest corners of Polish society, unleashing a wave of anti-Semitic sentiment that once again made Jews the target of blame and hatred. For my father, it was a painful reminder that even in a society built on the promise of equality, old prejudices could still rise to the surface, weaponised by those in power for their own ends. [7]

Moczar was a master at exploiting long-standing anti-Semitic sentiments and latent paranoia that had festered in Polish society for centuries. He wielded the Ministry of Internal Affairs (MSW) like a blunt instrument, fuelling suspicion and hatred. Through carefully curated intelligence reports, Moczar's MSW became the conduit for a flood of propaganda that infiltrated both the upper echelons of the Politburo and the everyday lives of Polish citizens. His narrative was clear and insidious: Zionists—an all-encompassing term for Jews—were not just enemies of the State but cunning conspirators with secret ties to the West, aiming for nothing less than world domination.

393

Mieczysław Moczar and Władysław Gomułka [8]

Moczar's strategy was brilliantly calculated. He preyed on the vulnerabilities of a population already struggling with the hardships of post-war Poland, where economic instability and scarcity drove people to look for someone to blame. His MSW fed the public a steady diet of "evidence" that Zionists were not only hoarding power but also looking down on the hard-working, devoutly Catholic Polish masses with arrogance and disdain. They were depicted as a foreign elite, fundamentally un-Polish, occupying government positions that rightly belonged to the "pure" Poles—the "real" citizens who had suffered and sacrificed for their nation. In this portrayal, the Zionists were nothing but opportunists, parasites feeding off the efforts of others.

This wasn't just political posturing. It tapped into Poland's Judeophobic psyche, a fear and hatred stretching back centuries and entwined with the country's Catholic identity. Moczar's propaganda played on the familiar trope of Jewish superiority, suggesting that Jews had always seen themselves as "chosen" and, therefore, inherently superior to their Polish counterparts. For many Poles, the message resonated. The Zionists became the embodiment of all their

394

grievances, a convenient scapegoat for economic hardship and political stagnation. It didn't matter that many of these Jews had survived the Holocaust or that they numbered only 30,000 in a nation of 32 million (0.01%). What mattered was that their presence could be blamed for Poland's problems and that their existence could be portrayed as a direct threat to the very fabric of Polish society. And Gomulka, in their eyes, was complicit in allowing this "threat" to persist. His reluctance to act decisively against the Zionists, a "horrible racial minority," only fuelled their anger.

Gomułka's careful handling of the Polish Jewish minority was not merely a personal strategy but a crucial part of the broader anti-Semitic campaign orchestrated by his government. This approach became a key element of the regime's so-called anti-Semitic chimera—a fabricated narrative that cast Jews as an omnipresent threat to Polish society. Moczar skilfully manipulated this narrative, turning Gomułka's restraint into supposed proof of Jewish dominance within the government. To the Polish Catholic majority, Gomułka's caution was recast as a weakness, suggesting that the nation's leader was under the influence of a mysterious and malign minority.

For many Polish Catholics, who saw their country as the "Christ of Nations" and prided themselves on its moral superiority, this perception evoked a profound sense of betrayal. The idea that their leader—charged with safeguarding Polish sovereignty and identity— might be submitting to a group they had been conditioned to distrust and fear was intolerable. This belief, deeply rooted in long-standing cultural and religious narratives, reinforced the sense that Poland's very essence was under threat from within. Gomułka's actions were thus interpreted not as political prudence but as a capitulation to forces that undermined the nation's integrity.

For my father, this unfolding nightmare felt like a profound betrayal of his faith in Communism. Moczar's campaign must have struck a profound blow. The system that had promised to eradicate hate was now being used to foster it.

After the devastation of the Holocaust and World War II, Bolesław Bierut's communist regime tightly controlled and suppressed public expressions of anti-Semitism. In the newly established communist Poland, overt racism had no place, as the regime sought to rebuild the nation and create a united front, at least in appearance, in the wake of unimaginable loss and trauma.

However, after 1956, when Gomulka took power, the regime's anti-Israeli stance provided fertile ground for the re-emergence of anti-Semitism. Anti-Israeli propaganda became a convenient façade, a politically acceptable way for old prejudices to seep back into public discourse. In truth, the "anti-Zionist" rhetoric was merely a modern mask for centuries-old hatred, rebranded to pass for ideological opposition rather than ethnic discrimination.

For the Polish masses, already conditioned by centuries of Catholic teaching to harbour resentment towards Polish Jews, the word "Zionist" carried an elusive, foreign quality. It was not a term that resonated with their historical understanding of Jews, nor did it have the visceral impact of the old slurs. There was confusion about what Zionism meant—was it a political movement? A religious entity? An enemy of the Polish State?

The absurdity of this confusion was captured in a bizarre yet revealing moment during one of the government-sponsored anti-Zionist demonstrations. Polish demonstrators, unfamiliar with the concept of Zionism, confused the term with "Syjam," the Polish name for Thailand. They carried placards with slogans like "Syjoniści Do Syjamu" (Zionists go to Thailand), a testament to how disconnected many Poles were from the very ideology they were being encouraged to condemn. This misunderstanding revealed a deeper truth about how abstract and poorly understood the term "Zionism" was to the average citizen, whose anti-Jewish prejudices were far more visceral and longstanding than any abstract political ideology.

For my father, this moment must have been particularly disheartening. It revealed not only the depth of ignorance and confusion among the general populace but also how easily the State could weaponise ignorance to justify persecution. The anti-Semitism he thought had been eradicated or at least suppressed by the communist regime was now thriving under a new guise, and its resurgence was bolstered by the very system that was supposed to have liberated Poland from such backwardness.

The use of the term "Zionist" as a stand-in for "Jew" in Gomulka's Poland was a deliberate attempt to cloak old prejudices in new political rhetoric. It gave the regime plausible deniability while allowing those old hatreds to flourish again. This rebirth of anti-Semitism, thinly veiled as anti-Zionism, was perhaps more dangerous than the overt racism of previous eras because it pretended to be something else. It pretended to be a legitimate political stance, a defence of national sovereignty against foreign influence. In reality, it was the same age-old scapegoating dressed in new clothes.

The anti-Zionist chimera didn't stop at painting Zionists as foreign agents of subversion—it also cast them as scapegoats for every failure and flaw within the communist system itself. In a twisted narrative, Zionists were held responsible not only for Marxist revisionism but also for the most violent and repressive aspects of Stalinism. The crimes of Stalin's regime, the purges, the betrayals, the mass incarcerations—suddenly, these were no longer the actions of Soviet Communism but of "Zionist Communism," a shadowy and malevolent force that had corrupted the pure intentions of the Socialist State. [9]

This narrative of "Zionist treachery" served as a convenient tool for Gomulka and Moczar, who sought to distance themselves from

Stalin's dark legacy while shifting blame onto a marginalised group that could be easily demonised and persecuted. In this distorted worldview, Zionist Jews were no longer merely enemies of the State but ideological saboteurs who had poisoned the communist dream from within.

The message was clear: Poland's struggles—economic, political, and ideological—were not the result of systemic failings or poor governance but the direct result of a Zionist conspiracy that had betrayed the Polish people. "Zionist Communists had taken everything they could from us," it was claimed. "They had never truly been loyal to Poland." Their allegiance lay elsewhere—rooted in a global network of financial manipulation, political control, and ties to the West, particularly the United States. [10]

The accusation that Zionist Jews were beholden to the American dollar carried a deeply rooted anti-Semitic undertone. It wasn't just that they were untrustworthy; their loyalty, it was alleged, had always been to money, usury, and the pursuit of power through control of financial systems. This age-old stereotype, used for centuries to vilify Jewish communities across Europe, was repackaged and deployed once again to stoke fear and resentment.

The notion that Zionists disrespected the Cold War—because they had families and connections in the West—further cemented their status as enemies within. In this view, Zionist Jews were not just subverting Poland; they were traitors to the entire communist cause, using their connections to Israel and the West to undermine the Warsaw Pact and all it stood for. Their hearts, it was claimed, were not with Poland or the working masses but with Israel—and, by extension, with American imperialism.

For my father, this wave of anti-Zionist rhetoric would have been particularly painful. He had spent his life believing in the ideals of Communism, believing that it offered a path toward a more just and equal world. But now, in the very system he had dedicated himself to, he found his identity, his history, and his very existence being used against him. The regime he had served with loyalty was now positioning people like him—Jews, Zionists—as the root of all its problems. The betrayal was twofold: not only was the state betraying its promise of equality and justice, but it was using the Jewish people, the very people who had suffered the most under fascism and Nazism, as its scapegoats. The narrative being pushed by Gomulka and Moczar wasn't just a political manoeuvre; it was a revival of the same old anti-Semitic ideas that had haunted Jewish communities for centuries, now couched in the language of ideology and national loyalty.

Notes

1. Stola, Dariusz (2017). Anti-Zionism as a Multipurpose Policy Instrument: The Anti-Zionist Campaign in Poland, 1967 –1968. *The Journal of Israeli History*, Vol. 25, No. 1, March 2006, p. 178.

2. Stola, Dariusz (2017). Jewish emigration from communist Poland: the decline of Polish Jewry in the Aftermath of the Holocaust. *East European Jewish Affairs*, 2017, VOL. 47, NOS. 2–3, 169–188. Institute of Political Studies (ISP) and Polin Museum, Warsaw, Poland. pp. 175 -179

3. https://en.wikipedia.org/wiki/1968_Polish_political

4. Stola, Dariusz (2004). *Fighting against the Shadows: The Anti-Zionist Campaign of 1968"*, in Robert Blobaum (ed.), Antisemitism and Its Opponents in Modern Poland, Ithaca (Cornell University Press) 2004

5. Stasiński, Maciej & Oseka, Piotr (2017). Josef Tejchma: W Marcu 1968 Gomułka uwolnił antysemickie demony. *Ale Historia.* Wyborcza.PL *See:*

   https://wyborcza.pl/alehistoria/jozef-tejchma-w-marcu-1968-r-gomulka-uwolnil-antysemickie.htm

6. Stola, Dariusz (2004). *Anti-Zionist Campaign in Poland 1967-1968.* Institute of Political Studies at the Polish Academy of Sciences

7. Stasiński, Maciej & Oseka, Piotr (2017). Josef Tejchma: W Marcu 1968 Gomułka uwolnił antysemickie demony. *Ale Historia.* Wyborcza.PL *See:*

   https://wyborcza.pl/alehistoria/jozef-tejchma-w-marcu-1968-r-gomulka-uwolnil-antysemickie.htm

8. *Ibid.,*

9. *Ibid.,*

10. Stola, Dariusz (2004). Fighting against the Shadows: The Anti-Zionist Campaign of 1968", in Robert Blobaum (ed.) Antisemitism and Its Opponents in Modern Poland, Ithaca (Cornell University Press) 2004

16. Exile to the West

In the summer of 1968, when the anti-Zionist campaign finally came to a close, the landscape of Poland was irrevocably altered. The mass exodus of Polish Jews—many of them intellectuals, scientists, artists, and party members—was one of the most devastating aftershocks of Gomułka's political manoeuvring. What had once been a vibrant and diverse Jewish community, one that had endured centuries of persecution, including the horrors of the Holocaust, was now reduced to a trickle of memories and fading presences. [1]

Gomułka's words, spoken with cold precision, echoed through the lives of thousands: "If there are any remaining party members with Jewish backgrounds who do not like party politics, they have a choice—go to Israel or declare your loyalty to the party and Poland." It was a chilling ultimatum that left no room for debate or reflection. For those who stayed, it was a bitter choice between public silence and a lifetime of concealed identity. For those who left, it was the final severing of a centuries-old connection to the land they had called home.

The departures from Gdański Station became a haunting symbol of this forced migration. Day after day, groups of Jews, once integral to Polish society, gathered with their belongings, their hearts heavy with the knowledge that they were leaving not only their homes but also the very notion of belonging. Thirty thousand souls, descendants of families who had lived in Poland for generations, now faced an uncertain future.

For those who travelled to Israel, there was a mixture of hope and trepidation. They were heading to a land that symbolised survival and the possibility of renewal—a homeland that had risen from the ashes of genocide. But for many, Israel was not their first choice. It represented an ideal, a spiritual home, but not necessarily a practical one. The decision was far more complex than a simple choice between the two destinations.

In Rome, the American Jewish Joint Distribution Committee (JOINT) had set up temporary quarters for the emigrant families. Many refugees settled temporarily in rented apartments along Rome's Via Vittorio Emanuele. In local parks or during breaks in English classes, people actively debated their futures—the merits of starting anew in Israel versus settling in the West. For many, Israel was a distant and unfamiliar concept. They had lived through Stalinism and Gomułka's Poland; they knew what it meant to be caught between competing political ideologies. For them, the United States, Sweden, France, Denmark, Canada or Australia seemed like safer harbours— places where they could quietly rebuild their lives without the weight of ideological pressure.

The uncertainty and loss that lingered in the air must have felt unbearable at times. They had their friendships, jobs, established families, and sociocultural or recreational pursuits in Poland. But now, with Gomułka's campaign fresh in their minds, their lives had been irreversibly disrupted, and their ordinary lives unravelled.

For those like my father, who had stayed, the emigration of friends and colleagues left a gaping void. The offices, homes, and cafés where Jewish intellectuals had once gathered to discuss ideas, argue over books, and dream of a better world now stood eerily silent. There was an unmistakable hollowness—something unspoken yet deeply felt. Warsaw seemed to breathe differently, as if its pulse had slowed with the departure of so many who had once given it life and culture.

My father must have watched these departures with a mixture of sorrow and resignation. He knew that if he stayed, he would have to bury his true self and hide his Jewishness behind a facade of political conformity. And if he left, the journey would be both a liberation and a heartbreak—a new beginning carrying the weight of centuries of history, loss, and survival.

The 'exodus' from Gdański Station marked the end of an era. Yet it also marked the beginning of a new chapter—one in which Polish Jews would carry their heritage into new lands, forging new identities while never entirely leaving the old behind. [2]

One of many goodbyes at Gdanski Station in Warsaw between 1969 and 1970
[3]

The events of 1968 marked a profound and final chapter in my father's relationship with Poland, a country he had loved, fought for, and suffered alongside through its most turbulent eras. The anti-Zionist campaign, the scapegoating, and the coerced emigration of thousands of Polish Jews left my father emotionally drained, disillusioned, and disconnected from the very heart of the nation he once believed in. The promise of an ideal, the communist dream that had sustained him through so many dark years, had turned into an empty shell, crumbling under the weight of Nationalism and anti-Semitism. He must have wondered what was left of the Poland that could have been.

In the midst of it all, my father held onto his convictions as if they were the last remnants of a world that had disappeared. He was neither naive nor blind to the realities that unfolded around him. Still, he clung to a hope—however fragile—that true Socialism, as envisioned by Marx and Lenin, might still triumph over the distortions that had taken root in Gomulka's government. Yet, how bitter it must have been for him to witness how these ideals, once a source of light and promise, had been twisted into tools of division, suspicion, and hate.

By the summer of 1969, as he 'watched' the exodus of fellow Jews from Gdański Station, my father must have felt an overwhelming sense of loss—not just for those leaving but for the country that was letting them go. Many were survivors, those who had clung to life through the inferno of the Holocaust, only to be pushed out of the land that had been their home for eight centuries. These were not faceless "Zionists" or "conspirators"; they were mothers, fathers, children, and friends—Poles who had shared the same soil, the same air, and the same history.

As he stood at a distance from these events, perhaps reflecting on the irony of his own position, he must have wondered: Had all the sacrifice been for nothing? He had spent years within the machinery of the Polish government, believing he could help build a future in which the horrors of the past would never be repeated. He had dedicated his career to ensuring that the sites of suffering, places such as Auschwitz-Birkenau, Treblinka, and Majdanek, would be preserved not just as memorials but as eternal reminders of the depths of human cruelty. But now even that sacred work seemed overshadowed by hatred and ignorance that swept away all he held dear. There was nothing left to hope for—the time came for him and his family to leave Poland as well.

It was not an easy departure. Although Theresa's brother, Henryk, and his wife, Krysia, had come to say goodbye, the platform felt painfully empty. The absence of many friends and comrades, and the muted farewell in a city central to his life's work, must have been a heavy reminder of how much had already been lost.

As the train pulled away from Gdański Train Station at 6:45 pm on 27 August 1969, my father watched with quiet resignation as the familiar landscape of Warsaw faded into the distance. His face was a mixture of sadness and determination, a reflection of the difficult decision to leave the homeland he loved.

We were leaving for Australia, a place that offered hope and a new beginning, though the future was uncertain. My father, with his deeply held socialist beliefs and his dedication to the memory of those who perished in the Holocaust, was now on a journey into the unknown. The summer in Poland was waning; with it, a chapter of his life was closing. What would Australia offer him? Would it be a place of healing, or would the scars of the past continue to follow him wherever he went?

On May 29th, 1970, after a month at sea aboard the passenger liner *Marconi*, we arrived at the Station Pier in Port Melbourne. Leon Szer and his family greeted us, and though they were kind and welcoming, I wonder what my father felt at that moment. Did he feel relief, hope? Or did he feel the weight of all that had been left behind—unknown graves of his family, friends, the work he had poured his soul into for many years? Leon and his wife Maria made the transition easier for us. They embraced us, helping my father to feel that perhaps there was a future after all. Their home, filled with warmth and a sense of family, offered a brief respite from the storm that had been raging in my father's mind for years. But the ghosts of the past were not easily exorcised. How could they be? After all, this man had lived through so much—war, loss, political betrayal, and the weight of history pressing down on him at every turn.

In the years that followed, Poland continued to wrestle with its own history, a history my father had been so deeply entrenched in. In January 1987, Polish literary critic Jan Błoński, in his article "Poor Poles Look at the Ghetto", noted that Poles witnessed the mass destruction of their Jewish neighbours yet were reluctant to talk about it. [4] If some did, their responses were generally defensive, filled with justifications for their behaviour during the Holocaust. Błoński suggested that instead of trying to justify or defend themselves, Poles ought to stop blaming political systems, social or economic conditions whenever confronted about the Holocaust that took place on their soil. Whilst such common responses may constitute unconscious defences against potential accusations of being implicated in the crimes or of being indifferent, it is best to come clean and admit that they were 'guilty'. Guilty of not making sufficient effort to prevent the Holocaust from happening.

Jan Błoński's article would have resonated with my father. Błoński's message was clear: Poles had witnessed the Holocaust yet had remained silent, reluctant to fully confront what had happened in their midst. Błoński's article was a call to conscience. It was an invitation to finally face the truth, to stop running from it, and to admit the uncomfortable reality that too many had been bystanders during the darkest chapter of human history.

I believe my father would have understood this deeply. He had spent much of his life trying to preserve the memory of the Holocaust, fighting against the erasure of Jewish suffering in Poland. Ensuring that Auschwitz and places like it were remembered for what they were was central to his work. Yet for decades, successive Polish governments had framed the Holocaust within the broader narrative of Polish heroism and national sacrifice. It was not until May 1990, long after my father had left Poland, that the International Council of the Auschwitz-Birkenau State Museum formally acknowledged the overwhelming Jewish tragedy that had occurred there. The resolution was long overdue, yet even as it was reached, I wondered whether my father felt vindicated or whether the pain of knowing how long it had taken was too much to bear.

By the time my father passed away in 1996, he had lived a life filled with purpose but also with profound sorrow. His battle with cancer was the final chapter in a life that had seen so many battles and so many losses. On the 9th of March 1996, he left this world quietly, in Melbourne, far from the land he had once fought for and loved. But his final resting place was not to be in Australia. His remains were interred in the Powązki Military Cemetery in Warsaw, among the heroes and comrades of his past, a fitting place for a man who had given so much of himself to the struggle for memory and justice.

By the time my father passed away in 1996, he had lived a life filled with purpose but also with profound sorrow. His battle with cancer marked the concluding chapter of a life that had endured countless struggles and losses. On 9 March 1996, he departed this world quietly in Melbourne, a city far removed from the homeland for which he had fought and which he had cherished deeply.

Despite spending his final years in Australia, my father's wish was not to be laid to rest there. Instead, his remains were returned to Poland and interred in the Powązki Military Cemetery in Warsaw. There, he was placed among the heroes and comrades of his past—a fitting tribute to a man whose life was dedicated to the pursuit of memory and justice. In this hallowed ground, surrounded by those who shared his convictions and sacrifices, my father found his final resting place.

In the final years of his life, his thoughts often turned inward. He had weathered so many storms—wars, occupation, the Holocaust, political purges—but the storm that raged within him was perhaps the hardest to endure. He wrestled with questions that had no easy answers: What had been the point of it all? What was the value of sacrifice, loyalty, and conviction if the very ideals he had fought for could be so easily twisted, tarnished, and discarded? These were questions that could not be easily answered.

In many ways, my father's life was a testament to the complexity of history, the intertwining of personal and collective experiences, and the struggle to find meaning in a world that often seemed to be losing its way. He held on to his beliefs with admirable and tragic tenacity, never fully letting go of the hope that a better world was possible. In the end, he left behind not only a legacy of political activism and historical preservation but also a legacy of resilience, of fighting for what was right, even when the odds were overwhelmingly against him.

As I reflect on his life, I am filled with both sadness and pride. Sadness for all he endured, for the weight of history that bore down on him so heavily. And pride in the way he carried that weight, never giving in to bitterness or despair, always believing that a better future was worth fighting for.

∞∞∞∞∞∞∞∞∞∞∞

Notes:

1. Stola, Dariusz (2004). Fighting against the Shadows: The Anti-Zionist Campaign of 1968" in Robert Blobaum (ed.) Antisemitism and Its Opponents in Modern Poland, Ithaca (Cornell University Press) 2004

2. *Ibid.,*

3. *Ibid.,*

4. Błoński, J. (1987). Poor Poles looking at the Ghetto. Tygodnik Powszechny. January 1987.

www.ingramcontent.com/pod-product-compliance
Lightning Source LLC
Chambersburg PA
CBHW051130120626
46547CB00012B/739